THE CORPSE IN THE KI

The Corpse in the Kitchen

Enclosure, Extraction, and the Afterlives
of the Black Hawk War

ADAM JOHN WATERMAN

Fordham University Press

NEW YORK   2022

Fordham University Press has no responsibility for the persistence or accuracy of URLs for external or third-party Internet websites referred to in this publication and does not guarantee that any content on such websites is, or will remain, accurate or appropriate.

Fordham University Press also publishes its books in a variety of electronic formats. Some content that appears in print may not be available in electronic books.

Visit us online at www.fordhampress.com.

Library of Congress Cataloging-in-Publication Data

Names: Waterman, Adam John, author.
Title: The corpse in the kitchen : enclosure, extraction, and the
    afterlives of the Black Hawk War / Adam John Waterman.
Other titles: Enclosure, extraction, and the afterlives of the Black Hawk
    War
Description: New York : Fordham University Press, 2022. | Includes
    bibliographical references and index.
Identifiers: LCCN 2021047116 | ISBN 9780823298778 (paperback) | ISBN
    9780823298761 (hardback) | ISBN 9780823298785 (epub)
Subjects: LCSH: Black Hawk War, 1832—Historiography. | Black Hawk, Sauk
    chief, 1767–1838—Death and burial. | Sauk Indians—Historiography. |
    Indians of North America—History—Philosophy. | Settler
    colonialism—United States—Philosophy. | Middle
    West—History—Philosophy. | Collective memory—Middle West. | Critical
    discourse analysis.
Classification: LCC E83.83 .W38 2022 | DDC 973.5/6—dc23
LC record available at https://lccn.loc.gov/2021047116

Printed in the United States of America

24 23 22   5 4 3 2 1

First edition

For Erma and Millie, and Finn, Leo, and Quinn

Contents

I went away and forgot you. A while ago I remembered.
I remembered I'd forgotten you. I was dreaming.
—MAHMOUD DARWISH, *MEMORY FOR FORGETFULNESS*

Introduction

Little is known about James Turner except his name, but Sarah Welch Nossaman knew more about him than she cared to remember. "[The] burial place was near old Iowaville, on the north side of the Des Moines River, under a big sugar tree. It was there Doctor Turner severed the head from the body." Sitting up with an ailing neighbor, somewhere between nowhere and no place, alone in the dark but for the light of the hearth, in November 1838, Nossaman became an unintentional witness to a gruesome sacramental, a Grand Guignol of frontier cruelty, a subtle dance made all the more ghastly for its antiseptic dispassion, its indifference to the materiality of flesh and the blood, to the reality of the body, to the body as the unbearably real. Nossaman never forgot the night they came to clean the bones. "[He] thought if he could only steal [the head] he could make a fortune out of it by taking it east and putting it on exhibition." Whatever reveries she might have indulged at the hearth, whatever presentiments of home and comfort that space might have conveyed— associations between fire, warmth, and light, making and crafting—are overwhelmed by fire as a purely chemical wickedness. "We knew the evening he went to steal the head and sat up to await his coming. He got in with it at four o'clock in the morning and hid it till the afternoon of the same day, when he cooked the flesh off the skull."[1] Almost nothing is known about James Turner, but this is the beginning of the story, and these are the things that we do know: On a cold night in November 1838, somewhere near the edge of the world, James Turner walks away from his home, from his family and friends, from the fire and the circle of light and warmth and food, a voyageur now among the lonely places, among the quickness of shadows. Following the riverbank, he disappears into the night, inky and black, into an obsidian glare, ancient and obscure. This is a place saturated by writing, yet forever out of its reach, a place that will not make sense, that refuses sense, but begs much of sensation. When he returns from this place, this point of inflection between the world and the word, we do not know where he has been. But we know that he has come back with a body. We know that he comes back with its parts.

Here are some other things that we know: Under cover of night, one evening in November 1838, Doctor James Turner went to steal a corpse. This was nothing particularly unusual. Among his intimates, Turner was known as a medical doctor, and as part of their training, nineteenth-century medical students routinely violated fresh graves so they might obtain the tissue necessary for their explorations in human anatomy. Within the profession, grave robbery was an entirely respectable exercise, one of the many mechanisms by which authority over the otherwise in-accessible realm of human interiority was vested in the figure of the doc-tor. For these students, grave robbery was a means to an end as well as a highly social ritual, a bonding among colleagues united in their contempt for the genealogical alignments, social entanglements, and physical vulnerabilities that constitute the immanence of human community, its conventions, and superstitions. While the graves most routinely violated belonged generally to people who were poor or indigent, racialized as non-white or otherwise marked as disposable, when supply was low, students were not particularly discriminating, lifting fresh corpses wherever they could find them. Indeed, the first urban insurrection in the postrevolu-tionary United States occurred in New York City in 1788, after it was dis-covered that students at New York Hospital had exhausted the supply of human tissue from the "Negros Burial Ground" before moving on to corpses interred at Trinity Church cemetery, which was reserved for whites. Even though the Doctors' Riot, as the incident came to be known, inaugurated a period of legislative change that would come to redefine the relationship between medical professionals and the public, as well as the disposition of human remains and the study of anatomy, the practice of body-snatching continued well into the nineteenth century, when it was finally—and reluctantly—abandoned as new regulations designed to af-ford medical schools with a ready supply of human remains came into effect.[2]

Little is known about James Turner except his name; however, we do know that he was no medical student, nor is it certain that he was much of a doctor. Like a student, he had designs on the flesh, but it was less for study than for display, the occasion for an entertainment, the exploitation of skin and sinew as the repository for bone, a calcium scaffold groaning under the weight of darkly effulgent fantasies of wealth and fame as well as war and blood. Resident of a tiny frontier community in what would soon become Iowa Territory, the body he planned to steal belonged to someone who was familiar to Turner and the community to which he belonged, as well as to an incipient association of consumers, a national public of people reading, looking, listening, gossiping, grasping. This body had borne the respirant vitality of one who had been, less than a month before, a neighbor, if not a friend, a figure of both local and national regard, a person afforded some measure of dignity and respect. It was the body that had borne the Sauk Indian warrior commonly known to his intimates as Makataimeshekiakiak, or Black Hawk, the body that had borne certain dreams. Seven years earlier, in 1832, Makataimeshekiakiak had obtained notoriety among white settlers as the leader of a campaign to reclaim Sauk lands just east of the Mississippi River, near Rock Island, the site of the principal Sauk village, Saukenuk. Over the course of the previous decade, as settlers trespassed ever more egregiously on Sauk lands, defended by an increasingly routinized military force, Makataimeshekiakiak had asserted Sauk rights over their historically held lands along the east bank of the Mississippi, and by 1831—as the trickle of settlers became a veritable flood—he had begun to assemble a coalition of Indigenous nations whose confederation, he hoped, might curb US expansion into the Upper Mississippi lead region.

Although unsuccessful in stemming the tide of white settlement, over the course of an abortive, three-month-long conflict between Native peoples and settlers, settler militias, and the military arm of the federal state, Makataimeshekiakiak would become fodder for a rapidly expanding national press; his name and deeds were made over by apocryphal news reportage, amplifying his person and augmenting its meaning. In the months and years following his surrender to then Lieutenant Zachary Taylor at Fort Crawford in Prairie du Chien, Makataimeshekiakiak would be made over as a celebrity eminence: a mysterious, inscrutable, glamorous figure through which to imagine—though not to realize—the myriad possibilities inherent to emergent notions of personhood, liberalism, and consumption as well as labor and property as frameworks for the realization of human freedom.[3] Among Americans, Makataimeshekiakiak would come to be known as Black Hawk, and the war he fought as the Black Hawk War. He would become one of the most widely celebrated Native leaders of the nineteenth century, a man honored by his displaced people as a counselor and a sage, a friend and a companion; yet among settlers, his person would be all but effaced by fantasies of the Noble

Savage and the Disappearing Indian. Like these familiar tropes, "Black Hawk" was a figment, though not necessarily a fiction. Black Hawk was less a person than an effect of the circulation and citation of narratives that, in their accumulation, contributed to the elaboration of an effectively literary contrivance, a sedimentary figure composed from the detritus of print. Steeped in a culture of sentimentality in which mournfulness at the ostensible demise of individual Native people served to obfuscate the material violence by which Indigenous nations had been made subjects of state-sanctioned and enforced debility, he was a conveniently sympathetic figure among settlers—"a noble but doomed primitive railing against [the inevitability of] progress" that served to assuage the aggrieved conscience of a nation routinely engaged in the process of constituting itself through contrived spectacles of grief and rituals of mourning, that is, socially sanctioned expressions of public affect that gave form to an otherwise insensible national feeling.[4] As a person, Makataimeshekiakiak was substantive, enfleshed. His life was constituted in relation to other lives, sutured through historically dynamic networks of affiliation and kinship that transformed the bare fact of life into the possibility of living. As a media confabulation, Black Hawk was a sacrificial totem through which to conjure the false intimacy of the nation. He belonged to the physically embodied, historically dynamic, and sensually registered conditions of kinship that constituted the substance of Sauk nationality and sovereignty, even under conditions of imminent deprivation occasioned by their sudden violent dispossession.

We know James Turner's name but we do not know Black Hawk. This is not for any lack of knowledge but rather a consequence of its miasmatic abundance, for the gauze of words that hangs about the man which is both transparent and misleading, enveloping and obscuring. As a literary figment, Black Hawk belonged to the market, to the culture of display and exchange, to kitsch, to the commodity emptied of all purposeful use. Makataimeshekiakiak, for his part, belonged to a broader frontier community, one composed of Native peoples—some displaced, others not; some friends, others not—as well as settlers, squatters, trappers, and traders; a motley group of people bound together through chance, necessity, and force. These were people who, for all their differences and long histories of conflict and distrust, were nonetheless continually working to negotiate the terms of their coexistence, to find ways to exist with each other as dependents of the land, mutually beholden to its ecological and geophysical benevolence, its magnanimous vitality. Among this community, Makataimeshekiakiak may have been Black Hawk, but Black Hawk was not a celebrity. For his friends and relations, Makataimeshekiakiak was, among other things, a customer, a fisherman, a friend, an enemy, a rival, a general, a revered leader, a son, a husband, a father, and a feeble old man. When James Turner approached Makataimeshekiakiak's burial that evening in November 1838, he was not interested in the conditions of the flesh or the histories of the communities to which it was heir, nor was he interested in the study of the body as a contribution to medical science. Turner was interested in Black Hawk the totem, the media confabulation, the commodity fetish. He was concerned neither with the intimate entanglements that drew Makataimeshekiakiak into communion with his fellows nor with the forms of community those entanglements nurtured and sustained or the ethics of kinship by which Native peoples had long negotiated their multiplicity.[5] No mere carnivalesque of social conventions in service of medical science, Turner's act perpetrated a direct assault upon the material practices through which the Rock Island Sauks, in a moment of desperation and displacement, had come to organize their sense of themselves as a people through the expression of their relationship with place; to make themselves at home by making kin and by observing the ethics of kinship through which overlapping Native sovereignties were negotiated and maintained. Moreover, his act constituted a brutal refusal of settlers' obligations to the ethics of kinship as a means of manifesting cohabitation among Native peoples and settlers, a pointed rejoinder to the materiality of Native sovereignty as a framework for negotiating social and political relations.

I begin from this place—from the seemingly incongruous pairing of body-snatching and celebrity, from the ignominious history of medicine and the often elusive filaments of public notoriety—as a means to approach the entanglement of settler communities and Indigenous nations, the mutual obligations of settlers and Native peoples under the terms that were generally common among Indigenous national sovereignties as well as the material forms through which both peoples expressed their relationship to place, peoplehood, and belonging. I do not idealize any of these relationships—among Native peoples, among settlers, or among Native peoples and settlers—but rather hope to capture some aspect of what Mohawk scholar Taiaiake Alfred has described as "the actual history of our plural existence" at a moment and place in which settlers had become increasingly indisposed to that plurality; a moment when that plurality had become a significant impediment to the realization of capital and material histories of plural existence gave way to a fiction of history as a family romance, to a story about the family as a figure through which to subvert the substantive materiality of Indigenous kinship and the forms of social and political affiliation they expressed.[6]

Like most contrasts that I invoke throughout the book, the distinction I draw between these two moments should not be taken too literally. These are rhetorical conveniences, modes of figuration. Effective, if flawed, such analytic contrivances allow one to approach processes that move incrementally as well as cataclysmically. Wielding the knife along the bone in search of the joint, categorical distinctions allow for the critic to digest the meal, to expose and dissect the elements of a process at a wholly arbitrary moment of their interruption, thereby laying bare the space of the dialectic—and the dialectical subversion of the categorical—that mildewed carapace of bourgeois thought. Categorical distinctions impose themselves as a matter of course under the dumb cacophony of settler colonialism. A viciously efficient means of carving up the world, these distinctions preserve the mythology of the family romance, of difference as well as of love and hate, of the hideous fact of dependency and all the ways it militates against difference as absolute. As Manu Karuka has indicated, within the framework of the United States as a settler colonial state, the sovereignty of the settler as a subject of liberal self-fashioning could only be realized through the acknowledgment of a prior Indigenous sovereignty that is later effaced—from memory and from custom, if not from law.[7] Against a Lockean fantasy of self-fashioning realized in the act of taking possession, the settler emerges only through a disavowed relationship to Indigenous sovereignty that perpetually haunts any sense of security he might hope to attain through his fidelity to a social contract and the state. Indigenous sovereignty thus remains powerfully present, not only as it inheres in the self-determination and self-expression of Native peoples but also as a conceptual and material phantom that stalks the horizon of settler experience. For the settler, Indigenous sovereignty is an unconscious residue that is both seen and unseen, everywhere and nowhere, in the law and on the land. It is a phantom, only to be seen through dreams, in that horrible moment between sleeping and waking when, in the monstropolous dark, every unknown object becomes hideous. While the legacy of Indigenous presence is necessary to the legal and conceptual formation of the settler state, its history and the obligations it entails must be forgotten, unremembered, or disavowed.

The book approaches the literatures of Black Hawk and the Black Hawk War as a means to trace both a partial history of these entanglements and the conditions of their disavowal. Understanding their disavowal as yet another form of entanglement, it presents an irregular and untimely history; it approaches its subject obliquely, hoping to eliminate, through a consideration of the literatures of the Black Hawk War, some aspect of the ways in which the legacies of our plural existence have been woven into the very texture of the land and the lives of the people that have shaped the land. While there is no dearth of scholarship on Black Hawk or the Black Hawk War, its history, or the literary cultures to which it gave rise, much of this scholarship has sought to capture something of the Black Hawk War by approaching its literatures directly. Although such an approach might offer certain insights into the history of the war, much of what the literatures of the Black Hawk War might teach us about Black Hawk—about the conflict that bears his name; about the actual history of our plural existence; about settler colonialism as a socioeconomic formation; about the affective consequences of the disavowal of kinship and the punishing brutality of its most capricious disseminations—remains hidden from view. Looked at straight on, the Black Hawk War appears as something antique, a dusty object resting unobtrusively to the side of the room, vaguely beckoning. A conversation piece, the Black Hawk War is where we turn when the serious matters have been exhausted, the discussion has flagged, but we do not want the evening to end. A minor collectible, looked at straight on, the Black Hawk War is a faux porcelain curio; and Black Hawk is but a decorative flourish, an accent meant to distinguish an otherwise forgettable piece. Imagine an unfinished painting: a study, a sketch, part of a meditation on an interior, the thing appears out of focus, an illegible smear on an otherwise competent reproduction of a lifeless room. Approached from the front, it appears as a distortion within the space of the frame, a stain corrupting an elegantly composed portrait of domestic absence, an irregular excrescence within an otherwise unobtrusive description of a neatly composed room. To approach it from the side, however, to adopt an anamorphic relation to the frame, is to have the image in the picture come into focus, to see things clearly for having adjusted the typical conventions of perspective and distance, for having left behind pedestrian attachments to the social conventions of signification. Standing to the side, glancing at the object, the unspeakable image that haunts the painting comes into focus, and one sees the death's head that was always there, looming, waiting, ponderous with stories, a digest of all things.

To look too closely at the Black Hawk War is to lose sight of it by trying to know it, to get lost in inoffensive but meaningless details, and to neglect the negative space in which the object sits, the negative space the object summons about itself.

This book lingers in the negative space. It is only glancingly concerned with the Black Hawk War. It looks askance at the circumstances of the war, capturing Black Hawk, his person, his portrait, out of the corner of its eye. It considers relationships between the circumstances of the Black

Hawk War, of entanglement and disavowal, and the history of extraction and primitive accumulation. It looks for the murky, often inscrutable histories of coercion, displacement, and theft by which what is common is rendered private, taken over as a resource dedicated to the valorization of capital. For Marx, this process was largely focused upon the legislative enclosure and regulation of land, the making of once common land into private property. Here, the enclosure of land is understood in relation to the practical abrogation of Indigenous sovereignties, all of the ways in which state power seeks to impose itself upon the already constituted terrain of Indigenous peoples' social and political affiliations. These processes, moreover, are understood as coextensive with other manifestations of enclosure. These are instances of primitive accumulation that might at first appear figurative but that, I maintain, are best understood as contiguous with the ostensibly literal, socioeconomic dimensions of enclosure—moments of differently expressed materialities, some physical and others more ephemeral. To this end, enclosure as conceived here touches upon the juridical and physical enclosure of land and its conversion into a resource; but it also touches upon the question of desire, of the enclosure of desire, of bodies and their needs and affects. It looks to enclosure as a prelude to extraction, exhaustion, enervation, elimination. It draws the history of primitive accumulation as a story about the originary, generative moment of capital into a conversation with settler colonialism as a means of organizing and managing populations and resources. The process of enclosure belongs to the history of capital before the beginning; it puts the lie to the melancholy reality of the eternal return, the world without end, amen. Attending to enclosure is to give space to that which enclosure forecloses. It thinks the before of capital as a sign of faith in what comes after.

The book's title, *The Corpse in the Kitchen*, may be misleading. The book is not about a corpse. There are no kitchens. The title enacts that which the book critiques; it performs an instance of enclosure by conscientious misrecognition, the attempted domestication of the colonial uncanny through an instance of linguistic misapplication. James Turner stole Black Hawk's physical remains and brought them into his brother's home so that he might clean them by boiling them in a kettle, as if he were preparing a stock; a reduction of gelatin, marrow, and scraps of flesh; a cannibal feast. This was, however, no usual domestic chore; it was neither obscured by appeals to fashion or taste nor hidden away in the scullery. James Turner did hide what he was doing. He brought Black Hawk's remains into his home, and he boiled them over the hearth.

This is where the Turner family would have prepared their food, but a hearth is not a kitchen. An effectively bourgeois contrivance, "kitchen" designates a room that is separate, a space within the home in which the ugliness of food, of flesh and its preparation, is conveniently sequestered, the nutrient demands of the body and its maintenance, its reproduction, kept out of sight. A kitchen is a fortified space within a home, one that obscures the gross materialities of social reproduction behind doors and below stairs, allowing for the domestic to come into its own as a space purified of its associations with the body, its processes and its needs, its secretions and its sex. A kitchen is both a room and a state of denial, a repression. The hearth was an invitation, a burlesque, an appeal, a gaping mouth spewing light and heat, a source of comfort, as well as danger. As Bachelard has indicated, to sit before a fire is to bind oneself to reverie, a waking dream of wandering in place. The banishment of flame, a kitchen renders the dream private, individual. Sitting before the hearth, the dreamer dreams a dream that is common and unbound; or rather, a dream that is bound to the flame as an unbound agency, a dream of home and of place, a technology of cooking and smelting, a clearing of brush, a torch to the cottage, a blazing of trails. A kitchen hides the flame, all that it creates and all that it kills. The hearth is its cousin and not nearly so discrete. All too eagerly proud of its place within the settler's home, its responsibility to the dynamics of enclosure and extraction, colonialism and capital, the hearth invites you to explore the making and the murder, the nefarious business of the nocturne. The hearth is the devilish illumination in the unfettering darkness, a barricade against the siege of the night. The hearth colonizes the gloaming. The kitchen hides that which it sees. The hearth demands that you watch.

Likewise, similar issues emerge with respect to the corpse. While the physical remains of Black Hawk's person, his body, feature prominently, they are neither dead nor undead. As Povinelli has indicated, the categorical distinction between life and death, effervescent and inert, is largely one that looks for observable signs of respiration as a presentiment of motion, of movement as a sign of life.[8] This schematization of the living and the dead turns upon an unbearably human sense of time as limited by the time of our respiration such that only the obviously respirant and mobile seem endowed with especial vitality. Approached from the time of the world, from the standpoint of the geological, respiration and mobility, the capacity for growth and for change, seem more equitably distributed, the calcified and the mineral now expressing themselves with a heretofore unknown degree of vivacity. Calcified and mineral but also organic, Black Hawk's physical remains were a vital component of Native survivance—the domain of new life, of multifarious instances of new life, of soil and its nutrients, of plants and the animals they sustained, as well as the ostensibly figurative ways of life that were routed through his body, the ways of life that found expression and refuge through death and burial.

Turner stole a corpse and in so doing, he upended these lineages, this life. Turner tried to steal these lives, but he could not uproot them. They are planted there still, somewhere at the edge of the world. There, in that place where the words cannot go, they grow lush, wild, and verdant. They prepare themselves for a banquet, as provisions for the bacchanalia before the war, the food that will sustain the people when they reclaim the fields, as they plant the seeds, as they remake the world again anew.

There is no kitchen, but there is food. This is the order of the meal.

Chapter 1 situates the theft and excarnation of Black Hawk's remains in relation to the history of lead and lead mining and the ecological impact of capital and extraction on the social and geophysical fabric of the Upper Mississippi River Valley. It approaches Indigenous sovereignty as expressed through the composition of land and participation within its inherent geophysical dynamics, aspects of which are indelibly altered by the formation of commercial infrastructures dedicated to the production and circulation of raw material in the form of minerals. The apparent banality of lead disguises its significance within the ecology of violence, of maiming and killing, that effectuates the materiality of the state, that transforms the fiction of the state and state sovereignty into a sensually meaningful aspect of social life through the assertion of a monopoly on the legitimate use of force, its potential distributed, at command, across space. Fashioned as bullets, lead is made an instrument of inscription, writing the state into the land through the application of violence upon bodies and, through bodies, upon minds.

Chapters 2 and 3 follow lead in its transformations along the commodity chain, moving away from its application as an implement of physical violence to its place within an ecology of words and images, its function within the culture of print. One element from which nineteenth-century smiths fashioned type alloy for use in printing presses, the lead uncovered in the Upper Mississippi caused a steep drop in the costs associated with the printing trade, giving rise to new arrangements in publishing, new and expanded markets, and new configurations of leisure and leisure time. It was through print that Black Hawk was first brought before an eastern reading public, and it was through Black Hawk that many of these readers came to think of themselves as bound to a collectivity, a figure united through injury and warfare. In chapter 2, I look at the ways in which the representational culture of Jacksonian America participated in the enclosure of the body and its affects; the ways in which the sensuality of the body—of captivity, of the encounter with the other—gave rise to permutations of desire that exceeded the myriad frames in which the singularity of desire was captured and stowed. The text of this analysis is implicated in this process through the replication of blocks of text, the blocks of text that composed the substance of news reports, reportage as both containment and exhibition, a desire to enclose as well as to see. I explore the ways in which the desire for the other unfolds onto the desire for the otherwise, for an indefinite other way of being that is, despite its slipperiness, infinitely compelling. Chapter 2 looks for the desire for the otherwise in reports from Black Hawk's 1833 tour of eastern cities. Chapter 3 looks to the ways in which the culture of historiography surrounding Black Hawk and the Black Hawk War participated in the foreclosure of those desires, the conversion of the desire for the otherwise into a resource harnessed to the realization of the nation and the state as baleful expressions of social collectivity. It treats the historiography of the Black Hawk War as a quasi-liturgical formation, a setting for the ritual conjuring of the nation through remembrances of bloodletting, reenactments of pain and suffering, and arduous journeys toward home, the reward for all that has been endured.

Chapter 4 approaches the enclosure of desire through attention to the affectivity of the body and its relationship to food and to agriculture. It situates the history of the primitive accumulation and the Black Hawk War in relation to the expansion of commercial agriculture in the United States and the emergence of the United States as the global hub of cereal crop production within industrial capitalism. Looking to the theft of Indigenous land, the enclosure of fields, and the creation of farms—that is, the development of infrastructures dedicated to the concentration and circulation of agricultural produce among different nodes for the distribution of labor and money—the chapter explores the ways in which the commercialization of food production intervenes upon the relationship between food and sociality, more specifically, between food as an expression of an intimate, oral relationship among people that is erotic but not explicitly sexual. I trace these relationships through a consideration of the epigenetic history of maize—through the history of maize as a companionate species of the animal and the human—both as an expression of human ingenuity and the deep time of Indigenous presence in the Americas but also as an emblem of human dependency upon its nonhuman relatives, that is, the forms of life that give life to the human, both figuratively and literally; the forms of life through which the human is given leave to express itself.

Chapter 5 turns from the question of food and consumption to the study of digestion as part of the history of medicine and the enclosure of the body. It returns to the themes present in earlier chapters, to the question of the body and its medicalization and the relationship between the medicalization of the body and its status as a vehicle for the manifestation of value, that is, for the valorization of capital through the application of labor and the expropriation of labor-time. Drawing on research conducted by Dr. William Beaumont at Fort Crawford in Wisconsin at the time of the Black Hawk War, the chapter looks at Beaumont's research on the stomach, its processes and its secretions to think the medical laboratory as a stage for the expression of sexual longing that emerges in the shadow of disgust with the body and with the self. Chapter 5 thinks the disciplines as applied to the stomach as extensions of an intensified regulation of time, a way of marking time and standardizing time, of building the body around the time of capital as the time of maximum productivity and minimum recovery. Against this, it looks to the temporalities embraced by Black Hawk in his narrative; specifically, the temporality of dreaming and blacking, mourning, as these escape not only the logics of instrumentality and economic reason but also the conventions animating the passage of time among Native peoples. The chapter looks at the dream as emblematic of an interiority that cannot be seen, discerned only through its echoes, strangely distorted sounds from the unconscious that, in darkness, move along the face of the deep.

A dream, a breath, now a story: This is not a history of the Black Hawk War. It is perhaps better understood as the history of a joke, a study of the settler history of the Black Hawk War as a joke. Not a joke in any conventional sense but rather a joke in the purely disinterested, interpretive sense by which psychoanalysis understands jokes, a joke as a description of something pressing urgently along the seams of the unconscious. When Freud wrote about jokes, he described them like dreams: an effervescence of images, compressed by language, given to puns and solecism, the unlikely, unintentional substitution of one word for another, their often arbitrary collision of pictures, of words and ideas, revealing a train of associations by which the unconscious reaches out through sleep into waking life, bending language, shaping behaviors, announcing its presence.[9] As in dreams, what Freud found in jokes was a loose thread, a place where the knitting had started to unravel, a place where the skein of the stories we are weaving begins to slacken, the warp abandoning the woof and threads twisting themselves into known but strange and unrecognizable shapes that compel an involuntary physical, bodily response: laughter. What Freud was perhaps less engaged by were the ways in which, shared among people, the telling of jokes, and the laughter they elicit, serves to cement the relations that bind the social. These jokes may be riddled with errors and inconsistencies, given to overly crass revisions and poor retellings—with aphasias, amnesias, awkward cadences, bad timing, and bowdlerization—but in these accidental upheavals, these unaccountable instances of punctuation, the joke somehow becomes all the funnier. It turns back on the teller; it invites a response; it does not make sense; nonetheless it tells a truth, even if that truth is only about the joke, or the telling. It may not get a laugh, but it fascinates. It invites a retelling of the botched retelling.

As a piece of settler lore, the history of the Black Hawk War is perhaps best understood as this kind of a joke. Nothing about it is funny; nonetheless it fascinates, it invites repetition, it reveals. It provokes some kind of physical pleasure, some small joy. The story of the Black Hawk War has been told so often that it seems unreasonable that we should respond; that we should laugh or cry or shout or fume; that we should experience the name of the conflict as an incitement. But for some reason we do. Why do we keep returning to it? What are we trying to forget through so much remembering? What is it that hides along the spine of the book, that goes scurrying from recto to verso every time we turn a page?

We do not know its name, but we know it is equal parts funny and tragic and that the tragedy is utterly hysterical. And we know also that hysteria is about the body, of the body, and in the body.[10]

This book thinks about the history of the Black Hawk War as a joke, trying to figure out just what kind of a joke it is. It looks at the joke, it takes it apart; it wants to figure out why it works, why we tell it, and what kind of work is being done when it is told. This is a story about a story that both inhabits and makes the body of the settler. It is a story about that body and the world it chooses to fashion, about the body and its comforts, if not its pleasures. It is a story about what happens to the world absent the body, when—after enclosure—that body is exhausted, eliminated, exquisitely dead, and all but forgotten.

The true history of what transpired over this slight period of months in 1832 belongs to those with the right to retell it: to the Sac and Fox Nation of Oklahoma, to the Sac and Fox Tribe of the Mississippi in Iowa, to the Sac and Fox Nation of the Missouri in Kansas and Nebraska, to the communion of Indigenous peoples. What is told in

Meskwaki, in Thakiwaki, and in the languages of those who have been forbidden to use their mother languages holds the story of the actual history of our plural existence.

What follows is, for the most part, the history of a joke, of a hysteric: a case study in the illnesses and derangements of settler colonialism.

1 /   The Indifferent Children of the Earth:
      Lead, Enclosure, and the Nocturnal
      Occupations of the Mineral Undead

The story of the Black Hawk War has long been promulgated as a tragic
romance, an opportunity for settlers to meditate on the pathos of Native
peoples as victims, while waxing on about the inevitability of westward
expansion and the propulsive drive of American capitalism. This is, in
part, a story about the hubris of those who, inspired by frenzied dreams
of imperial splendor, sought to bring about a new world by throttling the
old. It is a story about the men who sought to cut down forests, clear the
prairies, and dam the rivers, carving into the earth an infrastructure of
markets, extraction, and accumulation. These men hoped to transform
the bones of the old world into resource materialities for the new. As
written, the tragic romance of the Black Hawk War is one such resource,
the history of Indigenous struggle enclosed and expropriated for the
purposes of capital. As with much that settlers have written about Native
peoples, the story they tell about the Black Hawk War is generally repetitive and largely therapeutic. It is less about Black Hawk or the Black
Hawk War than about the act of storytelling as a vehicle of catharsis, a
means of exculpation, and an expression of penance. Even as the conflict
between settler militias, federal troops, and Black Hawk's motley collection of Native insurgents raged, settlers told themselves some version of
this story out of a need for contrition, to be freed from the wages of sin.
Through the telling and retelling of the story of the Black Hawk War,
many found some measure of contentment, some shallow reconciliation.
Expunging themselves of their complicity in the sins of their fathers, heed-
less of the violence wrought by enclosure and extraction, settlers refused to
countenance their enduring impact upon the land and how the capitalist

mode of production was transforming the lives of the people who served the land, the people who belonged to the land. Capital and colonialism were repressed, their inherent violence rendered unconscious.

Not all, of course, were contrite, but it does not matter. The story of the Black Hawk War was also, conveniently, a story about how one might hide certain inconvenient facts through insouciant display. Leave the truth out for everyone to find and no one will notice it. This is a story about the pathos of the Black Hawk War as a compulsively absorbing tragic romance, a devotional meditation upon sin and the near occasions of sin. It is also a story about the ecstatic euphoria that accompanies the grace of absolution and the forgiveness of sin that obscures a far more pertinent, far less delightfully masochistic revel. This is a story about invasion as avocation, as inheritance, and as infrastructure. It is about enclosure, extraction, and elimination, processes by which multifarious entangled forms of life—human, animal, plant, mineral, terrestrial, and atmospheric—have been represented, consumed, and made subject to exploitation as commodities, as resources, as things.[1] This is a story about settler colonialism as a vibrant aspect of racial capitalism, a project by which wildly, gratuitously entangled forms of social life as well as geological and ethereal forms of life have been violently disconnected from the ecstatic conditions of their mutuality and made disposable, that is, their utility and their vitality have been eclipsed by the latency and potentiality of value. It is a story about how the expression of Indigenous sovereignty has been undermined by processes of enclosure and extraction, how the transformation of vitalities into resources has been contiguous with the ways in which settler colonialism has objectified Native peoples and Native lives for the purpose of commanding and controlling Indigenous peoples and Indigenous resources, for attempting the degradation of sovereign nations by making them wards. This is a story about racial capitalism as a project of resource extraction and labor exploitation, about the imposition of a racial category upon myriad peoples as a means of evacuating their differences in pursuit of strategies for management and control, for the instrumentalization of populations as resources or wastes. It is about the imposition of racial categories as an aspect of the settler disavowal of Indigenous sovereignty, about the seemingly petty, bureaucratic, martial acts of violence that comprise the decidedly unspectacular slow violence of settler colonialism as a way of life, and the ongoing reproduction of dispossession as a means of capital formation, of investment, fetishization and accumulation.[2]

In this chapter, I explore one aspect of the story of the Black Hawk War as it relates to the disavowal of Indigenous sovereignty. I explore different forms of storytelling as part of the social and economic instrumentalities of racial capitalism. Rather than tell the story of the Black Hawk War as one of sublime violence or tragic romance, I look at the historical circumstances of the Black Hawk War as coextensive with a history of continuous enclosure and extraction that is part of an ecological history of capital in which the violence of settler colonialism registers as a geophysical trace. I survey the death and burial of Makataimeshekiakiak—as well as his excarnation and resurrection as the reified, totemic Black Hawk—as a means of exploring extraction through a consideration of its infrastructures. I understand infrastructure as the dynamic trace of the history of primitive accumulation, a range of material edifices that describe a legacy of social processes by which counter-sovereignty, the state, and capital have been carved into lives and into the land and given substance as a function of their physical and affective monumentality. Infrastructure abets extraction, which appears here as a means of conceptualizing social interventions upon the geophysical, the often-absentminded instances of violence by which exuberantly, gratuitously entangled forms of life are disconnected from the ecstatic conditions of their mutuality. Made disposable, their utility and their vitality eclipsed by the latency of surplus-value, extraction transforms vitalities into resources, vehicles for the realization of value which are also opportunities to catalyze the process of valorization, converting money-capital into capital, and capital into wealth through the enclosure of life and its consequent extraction.[3] Extraction, here, intervenes upon forms of social and cultural life as well as geological and ethereal life—of animal, mineral, photosynthetic, respirant, sedentary, and eldritch life—as a technique of capitalist accumulation, transforming otherwise dynamic relations among myriad forms of life into the substance of a thing, a raw material disposed primarily toward the process of production and self-fulfilling prophecy of value under capital.

Moreover, I approach the material legacies of the Black Hawk War through a social history of enclosure and extraction as well as the geophysicality of lead. A punishing banality, lead may seem an unlikely protagonist in a story about colonialism, warfare, capital, and desire. Nonetheless, the history of regional lead production—of mining, smelting, transporting, and trade—is crucial to the story of the Black Hawk War, as it was the putative lead boom of the 1820s that drew settlers into the region and into conflict with Native peoples. In addition, it was the readily acknowledged presence of vast, unexplored reserves of terrestrial lead throughout the Upper Mississippi River watershed that gave rise to federal interest in the region, as the state fought to establish its control over regional lead deposits as a means by which to establish its sovereignty. Reserving for itself ultimate rights of access to lead as a technology of violence, fashioned as bullets, Mississippian lead presented the state the ability to impose itself as the agency by which territory and life would be shaped and by which Indigenous sovereignties would be eliminated as meaningful vectors for the mediation of social life.[4] If, for Max Weber,[5] the state is that agency which exercises the only legitimate monopoly on violence within a given society, the Black Hawk War was a crucial moment for the establishment of that monopoly in the United States as well as the assuredness of its exercise as a critical aspect of the federal state. While the federal monopoly on violence is largely notional, the insistence upon that monopoly, the performance of control, gives rise to the state as a social fact, a fiction of a body, bound to the expression of state power and manifest through movement and gesture, citation and inscription.

In tracing a history of lead and lead extraction as it relates to the state, to capital, and to the politics of their representation, I look at the history of Makataimeshekiakiak's death and burial—as well as the circumstances and representation of his nefarious resurrection as the confabulation Black Hawk—to explain the material substance of Sauk sovereignty in its entanglement with the emergence of what Manu Karuka has called the prose of US counter-sovereignty.[6] If counter-sovereignty describes the reactive and thus inherently fragmentary legal patchwork through which notional claims to unimpeded national territorial sovereignty are resolved in and through the figure of the state, I take the prose of counter-sovereignty to designate the myriad forms of writing by which such legal notions are made sensate and the fissures within counter-sovereignty are concealed. The prose of counter-sovereignty, in this sense, is comprised of myriad forms of writing, some are of a more literary character, some traffic in the legal, the bureaucratic, and the ostensibly scientific. I understand the prose of counter-sovereignty in relation to the infrastructures of enclosure and extraction as forms of composition. These are techniques of state formation, capital accumulation, and settler socialization, to be sure, but they are also means of telling stories, of imposing a particular story upon the land in the hopes of eliminating other stories—in this case, the myriad stories through which Native peoples manifest and negotiated their sovereignties, presences, and histories. Through storytelling as an act of oral expression, phonetic prose, or other means of graphic expression, as well as through the deliberate composition of the land as text, Native peoples maintained a range of techniques for the expression of their sovereignties, techniques either illegible to the architectures of counter-sovereignty or of only passing, antiquarian interest.[7] Against these multitextured oral, graphic, and geological modes of expression, processes of enclosure and extraction, of capital and racial formation, present themselves as particularly visceral means by which colonial and state powers have found expression.

My argument takes cues from theorists of Native sovereignty, but also from scholars in media studies and language studies who have sought to highlight the myriad forms of writing that composed Native worlds, including those that reshaped the surface of the earth. Arguing with many commonplace assumptions about writing and orality, media and communication, Birgit Brander Rasmussen and Matt Cohen have proposed ways of looking at written languages that are nonphonetic and inscribed through technologies not necessarily devoted to formal modes of address or the conveyance of meaning.[8] These inscriptive techniques and linguistic forms constitute elements of a grammar, a prose form that serves to compose landscapes of Indigenous sovereignty and self-determination through the narration of place. In their effort at consecrating the earth for capital, extractive technologies and infrastructures physically revise the landscape narratives that orient the historically dynamic terms of Indigenous kinship, sovereignty, and self-determination. While converting dense arrangements of ecological vitalities into commodified resources available for exploitation by capital, these extractive inscriptions continually interrupt the sociohistorical and material substance of Indigenous sovereignty and thus contribute to the elaboration of necropolitical death worlds that enable the biopolitical realization of the settler as a form of life. Most obviously, these death worlds encompass not only landscapes of vigilante and martial violence directed toward the deliberative killing of Native peoples; they also encompass the forms of slow death wrought by ecological degradation and economic collapse as well as theft and toxification of otherwise common resources, including terrestrial inscriptions that allow for the elaboration and reproduction of memory, kinship, and belonging.

I approach Makataimeshekiakiak's grave as one component of an infrastructural topography that registers histories of indigenous peoples' entanglements with the geophysicality of place, matter, and memory. I am interested in thinking continuities between the enfleshed and the calcified as shaped by the struggle over the integrity of resource vitalities, as carried out by places and peoples constantly under assault by the forces of commodification and capitalization. My engagement with the substantive corporeality of this place—as well as with Makataimeshekiakiak's burial as a vibrant piece of the manifestation of Indigenous sovereignty—provides a backdrop against which to highlight the geophysical interventions carried out by later colonial and national infrastructures and their relationship to ongoing processes of enclosure, extraction, and elimination, particularly as it concerns the history of lead and lead mining as adjunct to the history of settler colonialism as a martial formation. I read the theft of Makataimeshekiakiak's physical remains and their subsequent rearticulation as the body of Black Hawk as indicative of and coextensive with a range of material impositions upon existing topographies of Indigenous sovereignty. These topographies are perhaps most viscerally signaled by the transformation of spaces of cohabitation into spaces of indiscriminate yet systematic killing, spaces of policing and securitization made possible by the transformation of terrestrial lead into projectiles.

When considered in relation to the larger geophysical dimensions of Native sovereignty and the unfolding of settler colonialism around the forms of extractive enterprise, the theft of Makataimeshekiakiak's remains should be read not as a metonym for extractive capitalism but as contiguous with the physical infrastructures of extraction as a dimension of racial capitalism and its consequences for the unfolding geophysicality of place.[9] The violation of his burial and the theft of his body thus sits in an immediate relationship to the ongoing history of extractive capitalism as it has shaped and reshaped the headwaters of the Upper Mississippi River Valley—first through the advent of the commercialized fur trade, the decimation of beaver stocks, and the attendant alteration of the carbon cycle and then in relation to the regional agricultural and lead mining economies. The development of agricultures of scale over the course of the mid-nineteenth century would knit the Upper Mississippi River Valley into the caloric networks that were marshalled to the purposes of sustaining populations of workers through the productive centers of the United States and Europe. Lead mining would come to support both killing and publication as acts of national and state formation in the United States—indeed the lead deposits of the Upper Mississippi River Valley poured into networks of institutionalized violence by which Jacksonian-era "Indian removal" was carried out, giving rise to an economy of print supported by a ready availability of lead-based type alloy. The destruction of the terrestrial narratives of Native presence and Native technologies of memory through the extraction of regional lead resources thus gave impetus to the expansion of the capacity of the settler to project his memory through print. Thereby they expanded the terrestrial domain of the prose of counter-sovereignty, demonstrating the truth of the claim of the state to sovereignty as an affectively meaningful dimension of social life; meanwhile the bullets fashioned from the same lead ensured the security of the settler project, its biopolitical forms preserved through necropolitical death worlds, through the violence—fast and slow—of occupation as a way of life.

In what follows, I explore geology as a dimension of geography, taking both as elements within the prose, the inscriptive grammar, the infrastructure of counter-sovereignty. I consider relationships between the discourse of geology and processes of extraction as contributing to the secretion of the geological as a dimension of counter-sovereignty, as a monumental instance of its prose. Taking quite literally the Weberian provocation that the state represents that agency which claims a monopoly on the exercise of legitimate violence, I read the state interest in geology and extraction in the Upper Mississippi River Valley as a means by which to establish its dominion by monopolizing lead as one of the most elemental implements of violence: that is, lead as the basis of a shot, as a projectile through which to enact the production of death and death worlds, through which to threaten death and to adjudicate the distribution of violence as a means to produce and enforce state command over space. Against the stilted prose of counter-sovereignty, of geology as a dimension of extraction, I consider the relationship between the entanglements of myriad forms of life and the expression of Indigenous sovereignty. I explore burial as a practice of Indigenous sovereignty, contiguous with Native peoples' terrestrial stewardship as well as their substantive engagements with the myriad forms of life that express themselves through the land, instances of nonhuman life that live as kin with the human and that condition the expression of Indigenous sovereignties. In thinking the relationship between Indigenous sovereignty and capitalist extraction, I look at the continuities and ruptures between settler and Indigenous practices of mourning as well as at the representation of death and formations of memory. I examine the question of the elegiac as it is routed through Black Hawk's 1834 text, *The Life of Makataimeshekiakiak, or Black Hawk*, to explore both settlers' and Indigenous peoples' approaches to mourning as well as the ways in which mourning is externalized and made monumental, a dimension of space and life as distributed across the terrestrial surface. Through Black Hawk's text, I elucidate a form of memorialization that comprises the texture of geophysical space and the ways in which the Rock River Sauks composed histories through inscriptions upon the surface of the earth and interventions upon its ecological metabolic.

Black Hawk's burial, I argue, should be understood as a text that echoes and extends the more conspicuously literary work that composes his narrative; a text that seeks to translate the work of the narrative into the life of the land through a conscientious intervention upon the geophysical. For the Sauks, Makataimeshekiakiak's burial was part of an emerging geology of social relations—one roughly continuous with earlier histories of their settlement, their sovereignty, and the corresponding conditions of self-determination—recorded through the purposeful composition of their terrestrial surface. I treat the violation of this text as coextensive with the geophysical interventions perpetrated by the incipient Upper Mississippi mining industry as it gives life to property through the death of riparian ecologies and fictions of sovereignty and security manifest through calculations of distance and projections of force. An implement of death, lead is corrosive in its own right; manufactured as shot, it is the medium of a new language, a form of writing committed to the elimination of people, the erasure of their presence. In the closing section, I return to the relationship between geology and extraction as practices of counter-sovereignty and instances of its prose through a consideration of the theft and dismemberment of Black Hawk's corpse.

Burial as Inscriptive Practice

In the story of the Black Hawk War, the violence of conflict is both spectacular and sublime. In reality, of course, it was neither; rather, it marked an intensification of the otherwise mundane abrasions that constituted some portion of the everyday life of Indigenous peoples under settler colonialism, slowly working their way along the body and into the land, rubbing, scraping, and exposing raw flesh. Within this effervescence of injury, extraction was merely one occasion; an obtrusive, if unremarkable, expression of colonial desire; a slow laceration of Indigenous bodies and Indigenous land. Likewise, James Turner's career as a body snatcher did not mark him as criminal or unique. Medical students stole bodies; so did speculators who sold corpses to medical colleges that sought to equip their students in support of their studies of human anatomy. Doctors were fascinated by necrotic tissues of all sorts, especially those that might betray some compelling physical distinctiveness or abnormality. Routed through the discourse of archaeology, the theft of Indigenous peoples' bodily remains found some measure of intellectual legitimacy; the study of those remains, however, was often indistinguishable from the jealous acquisition of bodies as trophies, as curiosities fashioned for display. While Turner may have harbored some perverse intellectual curiosity regarding the physical aspect of Black Hawk's remains—of the various ways in which his life as a warrior, or the fever that killed him, might have been recorded in and through the medium of his body—

according to Nossaman, Turner's ambitions for Black Hawk's remains were largely pecuniary; they expressed the logic of the commodity and the spectacle, the culture of consumer kitsch that contemporaries would call "Blackhawkiana." Nonetheless, for Turner and his contemporaries the violation of Indigenous burials and the theft of Indigenous remains—as a rhetorical if not a physical, material practice—was often entangled with the risibly prosaic effusiveness, the explicitly gendered and sexualized expressions of white supremacy, characteristic of Jacksonian Indian policy. Within the ambit of that policy, notions of proper burial were central to the intellectual labor by which Indian removal was justified, Native sovereignties were extinguished, and the establishment of property in land was manifest—in law if not in fact. "Doubtless it will be painful to leave the graves of their fathers; but what do they more than our ancestors did or than our children are doing now? . . . Does Humanity weep at these painful separations from everything, animate and inanimate, with which the young heart has become entwined? . . . Is it more afflicting to [the Indian] to leave the graves of his fathers than it is to our brothers and children?"[10] Speaking before Congress in 1830, Jackson denied any characteristic Indigenous relationship to death and mourning, quietly abrogating the right of the earth "to receive and shelter her children's remains," as well as the epistemological framework from which that right was derived, the recognition of land as constituting a form of life, a surface bound up with the expression of myriad forms of life.[11]

Presented as a defense of the fundamental justice of his program for what he and his supporters referred to euphemistically as Indian removal, Jackson, the genocidal Nephilim, poses as a man possessed of a great and powerful empathy, his noblesse demonstrated in his effusive affinity with the suffering of Native peoples. This was, of course, an entirely opportunistic posture. Evoking the figure of the Indian dead in his speech before Congress, Jackson effaced all but the most ephemeral, bodily, and affective meanings that might be ascribed to burial as an Indigenous cultural practice. He thus reduced the meaning of death and burial to the emotional work of mourning as a personal, psychological drama—as an unreasonable attachment to a place, expressed through the remains of persons—that comprised a measure of Indian backwardness. Employing a Socratic sleight of hand through a series of rhetorical questions, Jackson allows for grief and mourning to signal some common humanity that binds white people of European descent and Native peoples as Indians; yet, he conveys a difference in styles of mourning that is figuratively sexualized, posed between a stoically endured, properly channeled manly grief and a hysterically effusive, irrational, and irresponsible womanly desolation.[12] Europeans who became settlers gave up all that was familiar for that which was alien and hostile: their sacrifice included the renunciation of whatever attachments they might have felt respecting the graves of their ancestors, becoming manly and self-possessed—subjects of a properly acquisitive, egoistic liberalism—in the movement beyond such melancholy devotions. By contrast, Jackson suggests that Native attachments to place and to the dead are based in emotion rather than reason and are thus invalid and revocable. In being forced to move from the scenes of their ancestors' burials, Native peoples, Jackson implies, might become equally capable subjects of Christianity and of property, cured of their hysterical attachments to the physicality of death and its afterlives.

Reading differently racialized schemas of grieving as expressions of binary gender difference, Jackson's queries served to underscore legitimate and illegitimate relations to place, between those for whom place is necessarily transitory and those for whom it is an obligation, a duty, or—within the framework of his logic—an obsession. Already subject to dispossession by the federal government, here, the rhetorical moves Jackson makes with respect to Native peoples reinforce his presumption of their incapacity as subjects of "Christian community": Native peoples are properly subject to removal, he implies, because their passionate attachment to place as a function of the interment of human remains admits their fundamental errancy with respect to the norms that expressed the culture of liberalism and democracy. Moreover, the imputation of manly versus womanly, patriarchal versus queer forms of mourning conveyed a sense of difference with respect to the capacity for narrative and the denial of Indigenous burial as a socially and politically consequential act of signification. It underscored a sweeping denial of Native peoples' capacity to act as stewards of their own histories, just as much as it denied Native peoples the capacity to act as guardians of their historical patrimony. Recorded and remembered in and through the land and the multifarious forms of life that it sustains, the work of burial, of sedimentation and decomposition, constituted just one of the myriad ways in which Native peoples contributed to the shape of the land, to its contours and forms manifest through extraordinary instances of collective, transhistorical labor. Enveloping the physical remains of the dead as history, assuming the vitality of decay as part of the life of the land, burial was a conscientious act of signification, one whose radiant strands were irrevocably, irrepressibly entangled with the expressive continuities of Indigenous histories and Indigenous sovereignties. For Jackson and his co-conspirators, this manifestation of language had to be disqualified, to be hidden from view or reconceptualized—for settlers—as mindlessly decorative. Absent a legible rhetorical posture, Native burial was a curiosity, an aesthetically striking but socially meaningless amusement.

Jackson's meditations on burial and mourning asserted their significance as indices of civilizational aptitude. His compeer and intimate, Secretary of War Lewis Cass, developed this position at greater length, taking up questions of language and monumentality as elements within the charnel house of Indigenous sovereignty. Surveying the extant literature of the field, Cass insisted that Indigenous languages were wholly lacking in subtlety. They were merely declarative, he argued, incapable of expressing concepts of any sort. Absent the transitory verb forms by which passage or change might be molded into an experience of temporality, Native peoples are insensitive to historical processes, to historical memory, to the remote objectivity of the past. Mired in the eternal present of their inflexible languages, Indigenous peoples, for Cass, were incapable of thinking history, much less accounting for its contingencies or recording their various manifestations. If spoken language was "barbarous," written language was necessarily impossible. In an 1836 address before the American Historical Society, Cass drove these points home; he declared that while Native peoples may have been a monument to the antiquity of the Americas, that monumentality was purely coincidental, a function of their inescapable presence in the Americas. In themselves, Native peoples—as Indians—were unchanging and incurious, fundamentally incapable of expressing an interest in their own past, the desire to recall the past through the composition of a record, or the peculiar semiotic genius that distinguished peoples of European descent as both agents of history and architects of historical memory. Indians lacked the phonetic and the linguistic capacities necessary for the capture, preservation, and transmission of the past as a function of language, as well as the capacity to alienate the past through its capture by language as a mode of inscription. For Cass, Europeans were able to write and to build monuments; Native people were monuments, but they did not write. Moreover, the structures they built, the spaces they shaped, could not be monumental, much less linguistic, insofar as monuments were necessarily performative, deliberative, structures bearing the whole weight of a long dead culture, shaped by beliefs and norms reflected across those cultures. "The moral habits of the aboriginal inhabitants cannot deceive us. They are as unchanging as the Arabs. . . . [They] have no broken columns nor dilapidated walls to carry us back to the infancy of time, few crumbling monuments to teach us the lessons of humility, [they are] a living memorial, more solemn than these."[13] Imperiously disregarding the extraordinary achievements of

Arab architecture—to say nothing of the foundational contributions of Arab scholars to the development of historiography—Cass disappears all evidence of Indigenous monumentality, or Native peoples' sense of their own historicity, to make room for the more legibly dynamic, dynastic claims of American superiority. Delivered in his capacity as founding president of the American Historical Society, Cass's reference to "dilapidated walls" and "crumbling monuments" was meant to evoke a semiotically abundant Greco-Roman antiquity, as well as the historical continuity of those ancient aesthetic forms with then contemporary Federal architecture, its practices and styles. To the extent that these continuities were taken to represent a dynamic aesthetic conversation that was taking place between nations and across centuries, dilapidated walls and crumbling monuments *meant* something; Native monuments—Indian monuments—did not, except perhaps insofar as they were interesting attributes of the geological record or compelling anthropological data, enlivened by the whiteness of the gaze, brought to bear as a function of the scientific method.

The refusal to acknowledge the inherent and broadly social significance and sociolinguistic signification of Indigenous monuments—most especially those monuments dedicated to burial as a technique for the enclosure of calcifying, necrotic life and the elaboration of new expressions of terrestrial, plant, and animal life—for Cass and his colleagues, was a crude if effective means of resolving what was an otherwise unbearable antinomy within the intellectual tradition that informed their claims to scientific legitimacy and intellectual superiority as well as the relationship between their role as researchers and writers and the prosaic, prose infrastructures of US counter-sovereignty. Logically dependent upon the presumed emptiness of America as a waste, a land unburdened by history as a record of those dynastic political relationships—relationships born of arcane sexual intrigues—that elsewhere constrained the free circulation and accumulation of capital, the forms of Enlightenment and post-Enlightenment thought that underwrote the material forms of settler counter-sovereignty could not be reconciled with the monumentality of Indigenous burials insofar as those burials might be taken as evidence of an Indigenous capacity to shape history, to record and preserve history, to construct an archive of the past for the present and the future. Within the intellectual tradition most germane to Cass, his designs for the extirpation of Indian land and the elaboration of a liberal vocabulary of property in land, Indigenous burials could not stand as evidence of continuity between the Indigenous present and past but only as bearers of some mute, impenetrable meaning; or, as utterly meaningless earthworks that were without purpose, mere ornaments, a gauche terrestrial raiment.

While both settlers and scholars recognized the manifest abundance of Indigenous burials throughout North America, the most magnificent of these—the so-called Indian barrows of the Ohio and Mississippi River Valleys—were generally presumed to have emerged from some remote antiquity, with no meaningful connection to living Native communities, and no legible semiotic capacity for living Native peoples, much less for the settlers whose investigations were predicated upon the anxious expectation of Native peoples' death or their disappearance.[14] For settlers, gorged on the philosophical pretenses of European liberalism, the presence of these barrows was an insolvable intellectual puzzle, one that, while hardly inhibiting the theft of Indigenous land, nonetheless presented certain ethical difficulties, certain conundrums, a gnawing sense of unease with respect to the righteousness of claiming Indigenous land as property. Whereas, for the purposes of Enlightenment thought, Native peoples as "Indians" were presumed to be nomadic and indolent—lacking in meaningfully complex social organization or a language given to the preservation and exteriorization of memory—Indian barrows were evidence of histories of Native presence as well as legacies of systematic, well-ordered labor. The legacies of industry evoked by the presence of the barrows indicated a history of land use consonant with Lockean theories of property, especially since those theories emphasized the establishment of property and the possession of land through the work of "improvement" and cultivation. To take burials seriously as monuments would have risked the recognition of Native peoples as subjects of their own history, that is, authors of their own historiography and equally capable of manifesting the forms of creativity and meaning-making—of the conveyance of meaning through thoughtfully complex applications of language, of sounds and their inscription—that were asserted to be the exclusive province of Europeans. To take burials seriously as monuments, structures deliberately composed as palimpsests of Native history and Native memory, would mean the intellectual invalidation—or, at the very least, the moral and ethical complication—of European claims upon the Americas, since burials, as one of the many guises in which Indigenous monuments appeared, constituted a form of Lockean "improvement," one element of an infrastructure of place and belonging, if not possession.

Geology as Enclosure

Although Cass is readily identified as one of the villainous architects of Jacksonian-era "Indian removal," marking his proclamations before the historical societies as hopelessly partisan, the evacuation of the labor involved in the composition of barrows, mounds, and their attendant social and sociolinguistic resonance was abetted, in no small part, by the less aggressively partisan efforts of contemporary geology. Coterminous with the study of geography and the formation of a terrestrial and legal grammar of property, the first stirrings of geology were hopelessly entangled with the survey of Indigenous land and the expropriation of its vitality—that is, with the production of land as inert, dead, a readily commodified space for investment, for development, for fantasies of ownership and self-possession. Developed in the United States, in tandem with the Public Land Survey System, the early pioneers of American geology were often preoccupied, if not obsessed, by Native earthworks and mounds, as their presence often proved a hindrance to their work as surveyors as well as a genuine curiosity, evidence of some purposeful construction. The much-lauded "father" of American geology, Charles Whittlesey, conducted his earliest and most compelling research during his years as a surveyor for the Public Land Survey, his investigations into the historical character of Native peoples and their earthworks contiguous with his work as assistant to the chief surveyor in the Ohio River Valley. Measuring base and meridian, township and range, taking notes and hauling chains, Whittlesey and his peers carved Indigenous land into lots, enacting its material, physical circumscription through the bureaucratic registration of their unassuming, ungainly maps through the apparatus of the state.

Whittlesey's implication in the production of space for the state—the space of property, of counter-sovereignty, of settlement, investment, and capital accumulation—was largely inseparable from his work in archaeology and ethnology, all of which were implicated in his ongoing investigation into the presence of Native earthworks, of Native burials. "Figure A of the second sketch, represents the base of an irregular mound, forty feet high, two hundred and fifty feet on the longer axis, and one hundred fifty feet on the shorty. It appears to be composed of the light loamy soil of the vicinity . . . [an] immense number of human bones were found in comparative preservation, embedded in limestone gravel."[15] In his descriptions of Indigenous mounds, first published in 1850 in his *Description of Ancient Works in Ohio*, Whittlesey took great care to collect and preserve, to observe and to measure, the physical dimensions of those mounds; he was also particularly curious as to the relationship of their material, physical substance, to the singular geological features of the adjacent topography. These same observations were shockingly dispassionate with respect to the mounds as reliquaries, as deliberate architectural forms with distinctly social meanings. Rather than investigating those meanings or exploring the relationship between the ostensibly ancient mounds and contemporary expressions of Native life, Whittlesey imposes his peculiar surveyor's vocabulary upon those earthen architectural forms, breaking them down for parts: "Figure A," "second sketch," "forty feet," "two hundred and fifty feet," "axis," "shorty." Carving up the mounds as raw material for geology, Whittlesey disassociates the physical substance of the mounds from their material signification as bearers of Native meaning. Not just records of a historical Native presence, the ways in which the barrows are composed—the ways in which they are drafted as conveyances of memory, messages from the past to the present and the future—go unrecognized and unread. Drawing attention to "human bones" that were "embedded in [karst] limestone gravel," a singular aspect of the "light loamy soil of the vicinity," Whittlesey treats the mounds as physical expressions of the surrounding topography. Relationships between that and the sedimented, transhistorical labor of the mound builders, as well as the sociohistorical relations of construction, disappear into the verdure. While tacitly acknowledging the labor and the historicity of the mounds as architectural formations, the slow process of their elevation as a function of labor over time and the impact of that labor upon the surrounding terrain go unconsidered, as do the corresponding histories of Native peoples, the continuities between past and present forms of social and cultural life, and the overlapping, material contributions of the many nations whose presence had shaped the physical geography of the Ohio River Valley. Instead, Whittlesey presents his concerns as explicitly antiquarian, cataloging parts with no regard for living cultures, but in the hope of new constructions, new architectures, new elevations. "My object," he writes, "has been throughout merely to present additional facts for the use of the antiquarian, performing the part of a common laborer, who brings together materials wherewith some master workman may raise a perfect edifice. . . . I do not feel inclined to attribute the great works of Central and Southern Ohio to the progenitors of our Aborigines; but in regard to those of Wisconsin and Minnesota there is room for doubts and ample discussion."[16]

This explicit invalidation of contemporary Native peoples' historical relationship to the mounds—their relationship to the mounds as architectural formations—was to disregard the historicity of Native peoples as subjects of labor, to disregard the historicity of their labor as a measure of sociality, of culture, the mark of a purposeful engagement with land and its shape, an architectural form erected over time through the sedimentation of labor in land, and land through labor, and to disregard the sedimentation of that labor over time. A means of enclosure, the representations of geology effected the expropriation of Native labor as a dimension of the vitality of the land and thus contributed both to the obfuscation of Native peoples' labor as a dimension of their relationships to the larger historical, geophysical dynamics of the region and to the disentanglement of those geophysical dynamics from the deliberative narrative protocols that underwrote the expressions of Indigenous sovereignties. The discourse of geology, in this sense, contributed to the process of enclosure by offering a set of frameworks by which to figuratively enact the separation of otherwise irreducible elements of the land and its life—its metabolic—into components, pieces heralded as resources or disregarded as waste. While the mounds, from this perspective, might well have been thought of as belonging to the discourse of unproductive land as waste, drawn within the aspect of Whittlesey's geology, they endowed the national fantasy of the figurative Indian with a quasi-scientific legitimacy, establishing a point of antiquarian reality that superseded the proliferation of all ideological fabulations. A science of the earth, geology contributed to the disentanglement of the mounds from the land—or rather, by identifying the mounds as architectural formations, as constructions, geology staked a claim to the ahistoricity of the land itself, endowing the mounds with a certain grudging sense of historicity in order to posit the deep time of the surrounding terrain, separating its formation and its dynamic from the sociality of human life as well as human labor from the relationality of labor and the sociality of land as a form of life.

Geology, History, and the Substantiation of a Fiction

The disentanglement of land, along with its geophysical vitality from histories of labor and histories of use, was one of the characteristic maneuvers of geology as a claimant to scientific legitimacy, one that was reflected in contemporary historiography and its hypothesized estimation of relationships between peoples and nations, between hierarchies of race and the family of man. In its singular fixation upon the mineral as the most perfect expression of the ahistoricity of land, with respect to the history of the Black Hawk War, geology abetted the not-entirely-human drama that was the most conspicuous—as well as the most overlooked—pretext for the forms of military fortification that followed the notional enclosure of the Upper Mississippi River Valley. This was a drama that revolved around many interrelated moments in the history of primitive accumulation, instances of enclosure and extraction that absconded with the vitality of Indigenous land, the history of Indigenous people as laboring over the life of the land, transforming the land as bearer of the substance of Indigenous sovereignty into a desiccated thing, a half-life absented from the land as a record of the life of the land, and the life of the people who belong to the land. This was a drama that revolved around nothing so magisterial as lead.

Lead was not immediately a consequential measure of value, unlike silver or gold, as the substance from which projectiles were forged and type alloy pressed; nonetheless it was an incredibly significant resource, a means of killing that foretold significant asymmetries in the capacity for the distribution of force. This was, of course, of enormous consequence for the vitality and transformation of the state from a notional construct into a vehicle with the capacity to define its borders and insist upon its laws, to make itself felt, if only through the potential to deal out the potential of death. As early as 1804, the federal government had taken an explicit interest in the lead mines of the Upper Mississippi River Valley, with then Treasury Secretary Albert Gallatin seeking legal mechanisms by which he could dispossess miners whose property claims were protected by the articles of the Louisiana Purchase. The inspiration for this early proprietary interest in the lead region was economic, but the strategically instrumental use-value of lead was as a projectile. Wildly insecure in its sovereignty, the consolidation of control over the lead of the Upper Mississippi was of enormous strategic importance for the young United States as an independent republic. During the War of Independence, the relative paucity of lead resources available to the thirteen colonies had been a serious impediment to the prosecution of the war against Britain. As the conflict with Britain expanded after 1775, lead statues of George III and other British statesmen that dotted colonial cities and towns were pulled down and refashioned as bullets, while older, long-defunct mines were reopened. In Virginia, site of the largest colonial lead deposits and the greatest supplier of lead during the American Revolutionary War, Tories conspired to undermine lead production as part of a larger campaign against Patriot militias.[17] By 1779, a large portion of the Southern forces had been deployed to defend lead mining operations in Virginia. After the war, when a momentary depression occasioned the collapse of the Virginia mining industry, many of the men stationed there would chase rumors of lead riches west, eventually settling in and around the lead regions of Southwest Missouri and the Upper Mississippi River Valley. Arriving before the period of US hegemony, many American miners were swept up in schemes for filibusters and secession, including some who were drawn into the orbit of Aaron Burr's conspiracy to establish an independent nation in the west.

Federal interest in the region in the period immediately following the Louisiana Purchase was thus initially predicated upon a desire to regulate the production of lead in bullets to prevent the possibility of military challenges to its hegemony. Confronted by the insurrection in Saint-Domingue and increasing traffic between the Jacobins of Haiti and the enslaved population of the North American mainland, the security of plantation agriculture—if not the general security of the nation—rested upon the capacity to marshal and distribute force, which meant capturing and extracting lead and contributing to its manufacture as shot. The consolidation of control over lead, in both instances, was part of a vision of security as realized through force, where the capacity to effect the distribution of force over space was central to the enactment of the state as the guarantor of the nation, the authority covering over the myriad fissures within the nation itself, as well as the impossibility of realizing a coherent territorial sovereignty under conditions of settler colonialism and invasion. For Jefferson and his government, this toxic brew, with all its various, potentially explosive contradictions, was resolved through the creation of a land-lease system that would allow for settlers to locate and work mines, while preventing either the consolidation of monopolies or the unregulated commercialization of the same. In March 1805, Congress would pass an appropriations bill that paved the way for the appointment of land agents and commissioners to ascertain the "state of titles" to lead mines in the Louisiana Territory; by 1807, further legislation had declared specific tracts of land, identified as mineral-rich, as part of the public trust.[18] Taking its cues from President Thomas Jefferson and his cabinet, Congress effectively granted itself ownership over the mineral resources of territory that comprised parts of present-day Missouri, Illinois, Iowa, and Wisconsin, claiming oversight of nearly two million acres.

Their authority, they claimed, was little more than notional. The first miners to the region readily expanded their claims beyond their boundaries, leading to endless squabbles over land rights, many of which ended up in protracted court battles over property divisions. In Missouri, where miners had long operated under principles of common ownership, they chafed at even the most ineffective federal attempt at enforcing regulations over the industry, with some of the larger owners eventually abandoning their claims. Nonetheless, the land-lease system, as promulgated under federal law during the Jefferson administration, provided another means of figurative enclosure, one that presumed the more comprehensive, more systematic forms of figurative enclosure that would come with the Public Land Survey, as well as relays with more sensual, more physical forms of enclosure that would come with the expansion of an American military presence. In the absence of systematic modes of policing, or

of any significant interest in policing settlers, settlement in the lead region took off in the years following the War of 1812. The war had revealed
how unprepared the United States was to engage in a protracted conflict
with a foreign power, particularly with respect to the question of munitions. The lead deficit was a vexing problem, rendering refined, manufactured lead shot enormously dear. The immense profitability of locating
and mining lead for shot, to be sold to the US government, was enough
to inspire an ever-expanding gang of profiteers to enter the trade, despite
the various restrictions that had been set up around mining operations
little more than a decade before. Jefferson and Gallatin might have hoped
to maintain some oversight on the development of the lead trade; surely,
they would have liked to prevent the emergence of monopolies that were
both a threat to the state and to the Jeffersonian vision of a nonindustrial
West, where the revenues from land sales and leases would go to pay down
the national debt. The land-lease system, however, provided a framework
for the first settlement of the region and the exploitation of its resources,
especially its mineral resources, which were becoming ever more important to the public interest. Providing a mechanism for both the conceptual and the literal enclosure of the lead region, land-lease, in the absence
of public authority, offered a framework for the invigilation of property
as well as the imagination of property as a framework for the conceptu-
alization of extraction, commodification, and accumulation.

American settlement of the Upper Mississippi lead region began in ear-
nest in 1819, when US citizen Jesse W. Shull laid claim to a site just north
of the Fever River. Based on reports from Julien Dubuque's Mines of
Spain, US authorities had long suspected that this area was far richer in
mineral resources than anyone had yet determined. In 1810 alone, nearly
400,000 pounds of lead from Dubuque's mines had been sold at Prairie
du Chien, one of the old French market sites on the Upper Mississippi
region; there are no records to indicate just how much lead had been extracted that year, nor testimony to indicate how much might have been
shipped down river to appease Dubuque's Saint Louis creditors. Nonetheless, Shull's choice of claim was likely intended to test this intelligence, and his arrival marked a new chapter in federal regulation of the
lead industry, its territories, and their adjacent populations. When Shull
set up operations, he was under the protection of military guard, as
would be the next significant group of settlers, who arrived with Colonel
James Johnson—brother of future Vice-President Richard Mentor Johnson—in 1822. That year, mining operations in the region surrounding
the Fever River had grown large enough to employ a labor force of some
five hundred, mostly drawn from the local Winnebago communities, at a

production rate of some 170 tons.[19] While not quite as significant as the load taken from Dubuque's mines just ten years earlier, the growth potential of the region was such that, in 1827, the administration of the land-lease system under the federal Land Office was moved to the Johnson settlement on the Fever River; that year, Johnson's settlement would be renamed Galena, the Latinate term for the mineral that had made it rich.[20]

Between 1825 and 1828, the settler population in the Upper Mississippi Valley lead region would grow from two hundred to ten thousand, collectively producing some seven thousand tons of lead. Ores were smelted locally, drawn off, formed, and shipped in seventy-pound cylinders called "pigs." Pig lead formed the basic unit of trade for the industry for many years, until more sophisticated means of processing sheet lead were introduced. Most pig lead was produced using crude log furnaces, described in painstaking detail by T. A. Rickard. Rickard's description of the furnaces of the lead region suggest their resemblance to the exacting geometry of the land survey and the political geography of property relations. "The log furnace was built upon a bank or hillside so as to have a descent of forty-five degrees. . . . In the first place there was a strong wall built parallel with the bank, connected with walls at right angles, four feet apart." Here, the hearth becomes a technology of geophysical inscription, part of the infrastructure of capital and extraction which leaves itself as a trace that reshapes the land. This geophysical intervention was further abetted by the role of the furnace in harnessing fire as a technique of elimination and purification, a means of wiping away the substance of place and leaving the miner with a pure ore product. "After the walls were up, there was a hearth laid, made of one flag-stone having the proper inclination so that the lead would flow down into the basin in front of the furnace. The hearth being made, there were side walls placed upon the hearth, nine inches high, and from nine to twelve inches wide." Purifying ore, as a vehicle for the manipulation of fire, the furnace makes another set of marks upon the landscape through the consumption of timber. "As burners for the logs, stoke holes were left in the front wall, ten inches wide by twenty inches high. Logs were cut of a proper length, say three feet ten inches long, and from fourteen inches to two feet in diameter. The large logs were first rolled in upon the side walls, which raised them from the hearth to leave room for air and wood." Assembled out of elements extracted from the land that contributed to the transformation of the land and its multifarious geophysical dynamics, the furnace can be set to its vulcanian purpose. "That being set, it was ready for the mineral. Each eye would receive from three to four thousand pounds. The furnace being charged, a slow fire was kindled under the logs, and continued to burn until it arrived at a dull red heat." The smelting process released toxic elements into the air. "The fire was then drawn from below to give time for the sulphur to pass off. The sulphur, logs and barking would keep up a moderate combustion, which was left about six hours." Having released a portion of its toxic residues, the furnace was again prepared for further service, the melancholy repetitions of capital carried out as an ongoing burden upon the land and its entwined forms of life. "It was then ready to have a fire kindled again in the eye under the logs. A brisk fire being kept up, the lead would flow down into the basin, which was kept hot by a fire upon it until the lead was cast into pigs."[21] Harnessing fire, the furnace burns away all that is impure in the ore, and in so doing constitutes itself as a powerful geophysical force, one that carves capital into the sides of hills, into river bluffs, into the river, as its solid residues are washed away into the river by the rain.

Initially, the process of rendering lead from crude ore and shaping it for transport was exceedingly wasteful; even after the introduction of more sophisticated furnaces by British settlers from Yorkshire, only 65 to 70 percent of the product was retained. The residual slag was generally processed for its ore remainders, then dumped. Toxic piles of lead residue continued to dot the landscape of the Upper Mississippi until into the 1960s. The banality and invisibility of lead toxins provide an apt metaphor of the career of lead extracted from the mines of the region. The bulk of the lead produced regionally was shipped elsewhere, but there are few records that account for the extent of its distribution or its ultimate purpose. Steamboats began servicing the lead camps as early as 1822, but once loaded and shipped, the ore disappears into the commodity chain, propelled by the abstractive violence of the market into a variety of different guises. Lead ores, of course, made up part of the alloy from which printers fashioned type; the oxides derived from lead were also a hugely important component of paint. The lead boom on the Mississippi was part of a larger trend, in the United States, toward colorized facades and domestic interiors, as well as the creation of an expanded sphere for the circulation of print. Nonetheless, the greatest portion of lead drawn from the region was spent in the manufacture of bullets. Between 1820 and 1860, almost all the ammunition produced for small arms in the United States was fashioned from lead taken from the mines; and the single biggest consumer of small arms was the US military.[22] Fashioned as projectiles, Mississippi Valley lead would become the instrument by which myriad forms of violence would be distributed across the face of North America, vehicles for the culture of death dealing by which a structure of occupation would come to be realized.

While much of the lead drawn from the Upper Mississippi River Valley would find its way east into markets where it would be fashioned into type, feeding the ever-growing hunger for print, much more was fashioned into bullets that would impose their own cruel grammar upon the land. Until 1833, none of the lead was produced, locally, as shot. Work had begun on the construction of the first local shot tower in 1832; it was interrupted, ironically, by the events of the Black Hawk War. Among settlers, shot was produced in homemade soapstone molds, fitted to form a spherical cavity into which molten lead could be poured to rest until it hardened.[23] Of the ammunition produced for the use of the US Army, most was fabricated by military personnel in "laboratories" designed for the production of cartridges. While larger arms, like howitzers and mortars, generally deployed cast iron projectiles, the bullets used in small arms—like the smoothbore flintlock and half-stocked Harpers Ferry rifles employed by the corps of volunteers and regulars who served in the Black Hawk War—were composed from a core of lead, which was then fashioned into a rudimentary explosive cartridge.[24] The 1841 *Ordnance Manual for the Use of the Officers of the United States Army*—the first such directive issued on the proper implementation of military ordnance— goes into exacting detail about the composition of these cartridges, the structure in which they would be forged, and the implements used in their manufacture. If the nominative enclosure of the lead region and lead mines gave impetus to the imagination of extraction as a framework for property and ownership, the increasingly sophisticated formulae for the production of small arms ammunition provided a way of thinking property and enclosure, whiteness and self-possession, in relationship to the question of bullets as a mechanism for tracing lines of division and lines of ownership; and the capacity to pull the trigger as proof of otherwise ineffable claims to title, whiteness, or—more often than not—manhood.

The rooms required for a laboratory included:

1. *Furnace room*, for casting bullets and making compositions requiring the use of fire.
2. *Cartridge room*, for making paper and flannel cartridges of all kind.
3. *Filling room*, for filling cartridges for cannon and small arms.
4. *Composition room*, for mixing compositions.
5. *Driving room*, for driving rockets, portfires, fuzes, &c.
6. *Packing room*, for putting up ammunition for transportation and storage.
7. *Magazine*, or storehouse for powder and fixed ammunition, &c.

Dividing processes for the smelting of lead and the production of munitions into a series of readily digestible steps, the manual effectuates the state as a prefabrication, a model to be assembled in imitation of the image on the box. Itemizing each step of the process by which ammunition was to be manufactured and stored, including an excursus on the arrangement of the rooms in question, the state is generated out of moments of profound banality, instances where the sublime violence that underwrites the manifestation of the state is very nearly undermined through its appearance in the gestural and the procedural, the pathetically unheroic cording of wood and disposition of tools. "These rooms are sometimes arranged, for greater security, in several separate buildings, protected by trees or traverses of earth; but it is more convenient to have them under one room, (except the furnace room and the magazine,) or connected by covered passages. The laboratory should be apart from inhabited buildings."[25] The process of casting shot is treated at even greater length—with the same sense of calculation and replication, of the melancholy repetitions of capital, that underlie the descriptions of geology, geography, and the geophysicality of extraction as enabled by the furnace.

> TOOLS AND UTENSILS. 1 Iron kettle, fixed in a furnace as before described—2 iron ladels, 0.10 in. thick, 3.5 in. diameter, with a lip on the left side and a handle 18 in. long a little bent—1 bench, of 4 in. plank—6 moulds, (brass,) with double rows for 6 or 8 balls on each side, or for 8 balls and 15 buckshot; placed on the bench—1 mallet—1 double ball-gauge; the diameter of one ring is 0.002 in. greater, that of the other 0.0015 less, than the true calibre of the ball—3 nippers, one arm is bent and fixed in the bench, the other is about 5 in. longer and has a wooden handle; the jaws are of steel, two inches wide, tempered and ground sharp; they may be so formed as to cut the gate according to the spherical surface of the ball.

The description of the tools needed to produce shot continues, at length, before coming to the process by which the balls are cast.

> Weigh the lead; fill the kettle and cover it; as the lead melts add more, until it comes within 3 inches of the edge of the kettle; the cover it with a layer of powdered charcoal 1 in. thick; push the heat until paper in contact with the lead is inflamed by it; this requires from 1 to 2 hours.
>
> Immerse the ladle and fill it about ¾ full of lead covered with charcoal, which is kept back with a piece of wood, in running the lead; fill all the moulds on one side, then turn them and fill the other

side; the first castings are thrown back into the kettle, being imperfect from the moulds being cold; the diameter of some of the balls is verified from time to time, with the gauges; the moulds must be carefully cleaned when it is perceived the lead sticks to them, and if any moulds give imperfect balls, they must be filled with copper.

Extract the balls and trim them; in cutting, the ball should be gently pressed with the left fore-finger against the nippers, the gate being placed between the jaws.[26]

In total, the 1841 *Ordnance Manual* devotes approximately 60 of its 357 pages to the manufacture of ammunition, including detailed instructions for its preparation in the field. The pedantry of its diction is consistent throughout and is reflected in the exactitude with which the manual treats the capacities of the armaments it describes. "At the distance of 24 yards, a musket ball penetrates 20 in. into a gabion stuffed with sap fagots [*sic*]; the ball from a wall piece, 23.63 in. The resistance of fascines decreases very rapidly by the twigs being broken or separated by the balls. . . . The penetration of balls in wool is more than double of that in compact earth, even when the wool is contained in close, well quilted mattresses."[27] What is striking about this language, both here, and throughout the manual, is the extent to which it alienates tasks that would have been intimately familiar to many if not most Americans of the era—the preparation of shot, the discharge of a bullet—and turns them into processes to be analyzed, or steps to be followed, matters composed of nothing so much as a dense network of tedious minutiae. The 1792 Militia Act, signed into law by George Washington, had been far more direct in its approach: "Every citizen [must] provide himself with a good musket or firelock, a sufficient bayonet . . . a pouch with a box therein to contain not less than twenty-four cartridges, suited to the bore of his musket or firelock, each cartridge to contain a proper quantity of powder and ball . . . [and] twenty balls suited to the bore of his rifle."[28] The intervening years, of course, had seen the professionalization of the military and of military service; yet, the language of the *Ordnance Manual* betrays also a measure of its routinization: the slow drift from the romantic, republican ideal of the citizen-soldier toward a more standardized vision of military practice, one organized around a hierarchical chain of command in which all of the pieces are effectively interchangeable. While this, itself, might be seen as a symptom of the professionalization of the military, it is perhaps better understood as a mark of the biopolitical state, less a radiant sovereignty than a calculating machine, bent on the management of life and the expression of its proper modes. The *Ordnance Manual* treats people much as it treats bullets: as pieces of a larger assemblage, a rational machine taken apart, and put together, without meaningful consequence for the parts or the whole.

Black Hawk's Burial

This approach to enclosure, to extraction and possession, was the one that was brought to bear upon Makataimeshekiakiak's grave in November 1838. Continuities between the ecological metabolic of history, memory, and of kinship, as well as the dramatic fissure imposed upon that relation, the refusal of the reciprocities of kinship and the articulation of resource materialities as mineral and agricultural commodities, is staged in an 1890 autobiographical sketch composed by early settler to Iowa, Sarah Welch Nossaman. The only eyewitness to leave testimony of the violation of Makataimeshekiakiak's burial and the theft of his remains, Nossaman described, in detail, the circumstances of the night Turner went to steal the body: "Black Hawk's burial place was near old Iowaville, on the north side of the Des Moines River, under a big sugar tree. It was there Dr. Turner severed the head from the body." This altogether perfunctory description of the circumstances surrounding the violation of Makataimeshekiakiak's burial gestures toward a sense of its significance within a larger ecosystem of indigenous place and memory, while preserving an image of both the brutality and the utter banality of Turner's act with respect to the normative protocols of settler colonialism and the quotidian violence of enclosure and extraction. Between the first and second sentence in this statement, Nossaman's statement moves from a tacit invocation of Native sovereignty and an ethics of kinship expressed through relations between people and place, to a blunt characterization of the techniques of enclosure and extraction as techniques of US countersovereignty. The conscientious refusal of the ethical imperative to make kin and to observe the reciprocities constitutive of kin relations is captured by the declarative economy with which she dispenses with the fact of Turner's cruel vivisection and its obscene epilogue. "He got in with [the head] at four o'clock the next morning and hid it till the afternoon of the same day, when he cooked the flesh off the skull."[29]

Removed from the semiotic dynamics born of its social and ecological relations to place and people, the extraction and excarnation of Makataimeshekiakiak's skull rendered literal the geological presumptions that underwrote the colonial structure of settler rapine, effacing the vitality of Makataimeshekiakiak's being within the ecologies of Sauk kinship through a claim upon the mineral as nondynamic, without inherent semantic relevance. Makataimeshekiakiak's remains do not decay; his body does not become new life, enfolded within the metabolic of Indigenous place. Instead, Black Hawk is literally extracted, objectified, made thing; a moveable and transferrable, if unusual, object that is subject to possession and disposal. Torn from the ecological terrain of Sauk sovereignty, the extraction of Makataimeshekiakiak's remains as the body of Black Hawk instantiates an imperial, geological relationship to the resource vitalities of the Upper Mississippi River Valley, assemblages to which the expression of Sauk sovereignty and self-determination were necessarily beholden.

Torn from his ecological context and made over as *memento mori*, Makataimeshekiakiak's skull could not speak for itself; it had to be made to speak. The less visceral counterpart to the violence of excarnation was most clearly expressed in the voice of phrenology, with its emphasis on the immutability of bone as evidence for the structure of character. Some of the most revealing of these settler fantasies are evident in the account left by Oswald and Lorenzo Fowler in the *American Phrenological Journal and Miscellany*: "His head is large, giving much more than an ordinary amount of intellect and feeling, and indicative also of weight of character and extent of influence." This extraordinary head, whatever its powers of mental acuity, is almost immediately countered by more immaterial considerations of character. "His temperament is bilious-nervous, combining great strength with great mental and physical activity, and power of endurance." Employing a descriptive that implies, in equal portion, a feisty bad temper, as well as a tendency toward vomiting, the Fowlers' description of Black Hawk's mental activity becomes entwined with a strange array of meanings drawing together physical illness with mental disturbance, figuring him as a sort of martyr hysteric, a person whose mental and physical capacities were drawn not from his experience, training, or skill but from some preternatural well of unaccountable racial capacity. This was further expressed through his dedication to conflict and war. "Combatitiveness, and the domestic organs, is indicated by the immense breadth of the head, behind the ears, rather than by posterior length. . . . These, being very large, give to this portion of the head a spherical, bulging appearance." The horizontality of Black Hawk's head becomes, here, the seat of his malice. "It embraces the organs of Combatitiveness, Destructiveness, Secretiveness, Cautiousness, and Acquisitiveness. These organs, when large, or very large, always give great energy and force of character, and, in a savage state, would give cruelty, cunning, and revenge; would make an Indian a bold and desperate warrior, and tend to raise such a one to be a leader, or chief, where physical power and bravery are the most important requisites." The organs of his malice are further amplified by those of the domestic plane. "His domestic organs are unusually large for a male Indian, as may be seen by the length and breadth of the posterior portion of his head, as exhibited in the cuts, but more strikingly on the bust, or living head." The Fowlers conclude with a foreboding explication of what the size of these domestic organs imply. "These would give a very strong love of home, family, friends, children, wife, and with very large Self-Esteem, his tribe; and, combined with Combativeness and Destructiveness, would create the most unyielding resistance to ward off all attacks on their peace and happiness, and the most indomitable perseverance and insatiable thirst to revenge all assaults."[30] All of those characteristics of civic pride and filial affection typically reserved for settlers, here become the source of an incipient horror, a refusal to give way to the settler and the settler home, and a fidelity to people and place that was more than merely circumstantial.

These "observations" of Makataimeshekiakiak's character were made from a bust of his head cast by the Fowlers during Black Hawk's 1837 visit to New York City. Published the same month as the violation of Makataimeshekiakiak's burial and the theft of his body, the study provides an uncanny, pseudo-intellectual reflection of the grisly excarnation performed upon his skull, the ostensibly more elevated counterpart to the execrable work of body-snatching. Carved up into thirty-seven distinct "zones" that constitute the legible organs of human character, the phrenological dissection of Makataimeshekiakiak's bust provided a schema of his personality caught up in an ouroboric relationship to his public persona and substantiated through reference to discrete passages of Black Hawk's *Narrative*. In what might likely be the first literary critical engagement with that text, the phrenologist's report concluded with a close reading of the *Narrative* through phrenological theory, highlighting passages in which Black Hawk's character was revealed in words or actions that corresponded with the findings of the phrenological analysis. Like the excarnation of his remains, this evisceration of Black Hawk's text subverted its semiotic relationship to the larger history and practice of Sauk sovereignty, severing its connective tissues in the process of serving it up for display in a scientistic grid of legibility.

Makataimeshekiakiak's burial would meet a similar fate, torn up by the notional construct of the Public Land Survey. "While performing the public surveys of the District in 1843, one of my section lines ran directly across the remains of the wigwam in which this great warrior closed his earthly career, which I marked upon my map, and from his grave took bearings to suitable land-marks; recorded them in my regular field notes, and transmitted them to the Surveyor General."[31] Published in the first issue of *Annals of Iowa*, the nominally scholastic vehicle launched by the State Historical Society of Iowa in 1863, this account from Willard Barrows, agent of the public land office, illustrates Jodi Byrd's reading of indigenous kinship as a transit for the realization of settler sovereignty, inasmuch as Makataimeshekiakiak's burial is figuratively unearthed, forced to express its identity in relation to the abstractive technologies of the cadastral survey, the museum, and the monograph. "The grave of Chief Black Hawk is upon the s.e. ¼ of section 2, from which bears a maple 20 inches in diameter, south 38 ¼ [degrees] west 784 links; ash 20 . . . south 84 1/4 [degrees] west 866 links, burr oak 30 . . . s. 71 ½ [degrees] west 835 links."[32] Taken from Barrows's survey notes, these measurements translate the ecologies of indigenous place into the academic matter of political geography, inasmuch as they insist upon the numeric as a vector of relationality pressed into service in the constitution of a settler space. Within Barrows's history of Scott County and the work of the public survey, the physicality of Makataimeshekiakiak's remains is figuratively displaced from within an infrastructure of indigenous place tethered to the geophysicality of a living ecosystem, both transparently disregarded for a preferred emphasis on Black Hawk as an inert, if not reified object.

"Black Hawk's war club was then standing at the head of his grave," Barrows's account continues, "having been often renewed with paint and wampum, after the fashion of his tribe. At a later period, it is said that a certain Dr. ____, of Warsaw, Illinois, disinterred the body, and took the bones to Warsaw. Gov. Lucas, learning this, required their return to him, when they were placed in the hall of the Historical society at Burlington, and finally consumed by fire with the rest of the society's valuable collections." Circulating between different zones of intelligibility, as Black Hawk, Makataimeshekiakiak's remains take on a range of complementary meanings, suturing the natural and the national through disciplinary techniques predicated upon the abstraction of the visible from the experiential, as expressed in the coordinates organizing the work of the land survey office as the agent of a notional nationality. "Black Hawk was buried on the N.E. qr. of the S.E. qr. of Sec. 2, township 70, range 12, Davis county, Iowa, near the northeastern corner of the county, on the Des Moines River bottom, about ninety rods from where he lived at the time he died, on the north side of the river. I have the ground he lived for a door yard, it being between my house and the river."[33] Recorded some twenty years after Barrows's account of his own work as surveyor, Captain James Jordan's description of the burial effectively completes its disintegration from the topography of local memory, situating it within a calculus of property whose only affective remnant is its situation with respect to his "door yard."

Dislodged from its place within the social and cultural practices animating the ecologies of Indigenous kinship, Barrows's notes from the federal land survey bureaucratically reenact the violation of Makataimeshekiakiak's burial and the theft of his remains, dissolving its place within the ecologies of Indigenous sovereignty by inserting it as a single point within an otherwise abstractive register of property relations. Materially and ideologically registering the imaginary dimensions of the land survey, Barrows and Wittelsley and their fellows contributed to the substantiation of the fictions of US counter-sovereignty, tethering the future of the region to increasingly punitive forms of resource extraction, mineral exhaustion, and nutrient depletion. While the geophysical character of the Upper Mississippi River Valley, as well as the forms of Indigenous social relations that sustained—and were sustained—by it, had been decisively altered by the practices of the fur trade, the commercial imperatives that animated settler rapine would come to have far more deleterious consequences for its ecologies and the forms of life they maintained. These alterations made manifest, within the material configuration of the biome, the substance of US counter-sovereignty, as well as its toxic relationship to the forms of racial capitalism that were sustained by enclosure and extraction.

The Violation of Burial and the Denial of Kinship

The closing discussion of the previous section draws attention to the question of kinship as the substance of Indigenous sovereignties. Kinship designates not only a relationship among people—and it need not, perhaps best not, designate lineal, sanguinary descent—but rather a set of relations of reciprocity that obtain, between and among people, reciprocities that bind people and constitute the matter of community. Moreover, kinship touches not merely human beings' relations to each other but human relations with animals, plants, minerals, and elements of all sorts—the whole of the myriad forms, which constitute the geophysical dynamic of the biome. Perhaps more prosaically, kinship provides a figure through which to think—with the Indigenous paradigm in historiography—the "actual history of our plural existence" in all its horror and beauty, violence and desire, and all the terrible punitive asymmetries, the advantages that have accrued to the settler as a function of his refusal of kinship. The reciprocities of kinship are part of what is destroyed, enclosed, expropriated, and extracted, with the violation of

Makataimeshekiakiak's grave. In this section, I want to give more attention to the substance of kinship, of reciprocity, and what was violated that
night in November 1838. Whereas the acquisitive histories of primitive accumulation and counter-sovereignty discussed above constitute so many
gross violations of the ethics and reciprocities of kinship, what I discuss
below are the mutualities and the obligations endemic to the expression
of Indigenous sovereignties, the ongoing purchase of Indigenous sovereignty as a model for rethinking "the history of our plural existence," and
the future of any existence, any life. To get there, however, we need to start
with mourning.

The twinned figures of death and mourning have never been far from
the settler hypostatization of Indigeneity and the problem of Indigenous
difference. As the Ojibwe writer and critic David Treuer has caustically
remarked, most non-Native Americans have encountered far more dead,
fictitious Indians than living Native peoples. For much of the nineteenth
century, settler representations of Native peoples and Native cultures entailed a deeply cathected relationship to the figure of the dying, disappearing Indian; it was a literary confabulation that served as an emissary
of absolution, effacing the violence-propelling settlement and accelerating the displacement and death of Indigenous peoples. Born in 1767, near
the end of the French and Indian war, Makataimeshekiakiak was well
suited to this role, because the circumstances of his life—like that of his
contemporary, Andrew Jackson—were entangled with the history of the
newly United States. Where Jackson would become the heroic figure most
necessary to Indian "removal" as a process of primitive accumulation and
national regeneration, as Black Hawk, Makataimeshekiakiak would become its tragic victim, less a sacrifice than a sad example of the enervation of Indigenous culture in the face of white civilization.[34]

As Laura Mielke has indicated, in the mid-nineteenth century, such
national sentiment was focused, in no small part, upon Makataimeshekiakiak's 1834 narrative, *Life of Makataimeshekiakiak, or Black Hawk*.[35]
Composed in tandem with Makataimeshekiakiak's long-time translator,
a French-Pottawattomie trader named Antoine LeClaire, and transcribed
by a Rock Island publisher named J. B. Patterson, *Life of Makataimeshekiakiak* is a multivocal text, joining Makataimeshekiakiak, LeClaire, and
Patterson in the act of giving life to Black Hawk, each voice bringing its
own sense of historical urgency, its own specific cultural orientation. As
a linguistic and cultural chorus, *Life of Makataimeshekiakiak* is a peculiar artifact of "the actual history of our plural existence" and the irreducibly complex relationships among settlers and Indigenous peoples as a
condition of their coexistence over generations. As a commodity made to

circulate within market networks overdetermined by the emerging protocols of commercial celebrity, the *Life of Makataimeshekiakiak* was taken
as little more than the *Autobiography of Black Hawk*, consumed as a memento of his exemplary heroism and unhappy demise. Situating the *Narrative* in relation to early nineteenth-century works addressed to the
historical condition of Native peoples as subjects of decline, Arnold
Krupat has argued that the *Narrative* serves as a point of contact and rup-
ture between indigenous and settler approaches to mourning; the narrative collapses culturally distinct structures of feeling that touch upon
expressions of the elegiac and the myriad sociological mediations enacted
through experiences of loss and its representation. For settlers, Krupat
argues, histories of Indigenous people contemporaneous with *Life of
Makataimeshekiakiak* offered mourning as a palliative through which an
imagined white reader might approach the equally contemporary forms of
violence underwriting Indian "removal" and US territorial expansion. By
engaging the fact of individual Native people's demise through the rhetoric of mourning, these works figured Indians as objects of loss as well as
lost objects, reified elements fixed within a socially and politically freighted
schema of grieving through which settlers sought to habituate themselves
to the unhomeliness of indigenous place through an ascription of kinship
with figurative Indians realized through rituals of death and remem-
brance. *Life of Makataimeshekiakiak*, Krupat goes on to suggest, was received by settlers in relation to this well-entrenched structure of feeling,
appearing as one of the many textual mediators whereby the unruly and
often violent negotiations characteristic of "the actual history of our plural
existence" was transposed onto a family romance of racial patriarchy
under the sign of the nation and the work of national mourning. Adopting
Indian peoples as surrogate parents, through the fantasy of the family
romance, settlers found an attachment through which to dissolve their
lineal relationship to Britain, even as they mourned their demise of their
adoptive families. In a ritualized course of communal overcoming, the
Indian family romance helped settlers move beyond the affectively inde-
terminate intensities attendant the existing history of settler conquest and
indigenous dispossession, toward a sense of emotional resolution underwritten by historical amnesia.

Questions of prophylactic national mourning do not, however, exhaust
the socio-symbolic processes routed through Black Hawk's narrative.
Reading the narrative in relation to contemporaneous traditions of Native American elegy, Krupat goes on to evoke the contours of an indigenous relation to loss that is less immediately bound to an effectively linear
course of national overcoming than to what Joseph Roach has described

as *surrogation*, a mode of cultural reproduction and transmission that "does not begin or end but continues as actual or perceived vacancies occur in the network of relations that constitutes the social fabric."[36] Where the cultural logic of national mourning sponsors a sense of resolution bound to a politically ordained course of forgetting, for Roach, surrogation implies the preservation of memory through acts of performance that preserve history through acts of citation, even as the historical or textual referent to which those performative rituals gesture becomes lost to purposeful memorialization. While not present to memory, in this sense, the materiality of history is preserved and transmitted in ways that echo Gerald Vizenor's characterization of Native survivance as that which "creates a sense of Native presence over absence, nihilitry, and victimry" bent toward the preservation of tradition as a nexus of historicity, improvisation, and futurity.[37] In Krupat's rendering, Native American elegy exemplifies these mutualities, in that "elegiac expression is itself an act intending the recovery, in whatever measure possible, of what has been lost. It offers consolation but moves rapidly toward recuperation and restoration."[38] Native elegy, moreover, "tends not to accept loss as final, and seeks to [use it] to renew the life of the People."[39] Approaching Black Hawk's text through its many references to mourning and its associated rituals, Krupat rereads the text as contributing to the renewal of Sauk nationality as structured through materially embodied forms of kinship. Citing Jace Weaver, Krupat ends on the suggestion that the *Narrative* might be understood as such an act of ritual mourning, insofar as it "participates in the grief and sense of exile felt by Native communities and the pained individuals in them" as a means of renewal, of making "his life as a Sauk . . . whole once more in language."[40]

While focused primarily on the linguistic as a function of the textual, Krupat's reading of Black Hawk's narrative nonetheless helps to elucidate something of the corresponding strata of narrative figures and physical infrastructures enfolded within the topography of Makataimeshekiakiak's grave, because the extension and preservation of the dead as bearers of history and kinship is necessarily linked to the ecologies and geophysicalities instantiated by the act of burial. As Krupat notes, among Makataimeshekiakiak's Sauk contemporaries, maintenance of burial places assured the continuity of dead as bearers of history. This process, however, was not merely memorial but inscriptive, a means of secreting away the physical remains of the dead and enfolding them within new topographic arrangements of land, extending and enriching their lives through their articulation with local ecologies and cosmologies, writing the dead and their memory into the land, and into the kinship networks that sustained multifarious forms of interdependent life. Black Hawk suggests as much in one, seemingly inconsequential, passage of his *Narrative*, where he describes the medicine feast that marks the end of the winter hunt and the beginning of spring planting. Dispersed into lineal family units during the winter months, the spring medicine feast occasioned the Sauks' return to their village, the beginning of a new year and a renewed sense of collectivity. "When we returned to our village in the spring, from our wintering grounds, we would finishing trading with our traders. . . . [T]he next thing to be done was to bury our dead, (such as had died during the year). This is a great medicine feast. The relations of those who have died, give all the goods they have purchased, as presents to their friends— thereby reducing themselves to poverty, to show the Great Spirit they are humble, so that he will take pity on them. We would next open the cashes, and take out corn and other provisions. . . . As soon as this is accomplished, we repair the fences around our fields, and clean them off, ready for planting corn."[41] While describing the labor that precedes planting and the renewal of communal life, Black Hawk's description of these otherwise seemingly mundane activities suggests their semiotic abundance, the ways in which they constitute a narrative inscribed through ecology and reinscribed through his printed text. As the preparation of the ground preceding planting echoes the burial of the dead as a condition of the renewal of communal life, the text metaphorically links the material regeneration of vegetable life to the renewal of ecological vitality and the nutrient life of the dead, just as the act of impoverishing oneself by giving away one's possessions substantiates relations of dependence and mutuality that maintain the community. Death and burial, as such, become ritually enfolded within narratives of cyclical time and seasonal renewal, part of an ongoing process of reanimation and restoration that, as Sarah Bezan has argued, "continually affirms the organic relations of decomposition as a radical mode of condition of being that extends beyond the moment of death itself."[42]

Black Hawk's account of the medicine feast goes on to establish relationships between the maintenance of memory as a dimension of Sauk kinship, the material, physical needs of the community, and the vegetable through which those needs are met and sustained. Ending his account of the feast with a reference to storytelling and the sociality of memory, he notes: "The men, during this time, are feasting on dried venison, bear's meat, wild fowl, and corn . . . and recounting to each other what took place during the winter."[43] While his previous descriptions of the feast established a relationship between death, burial, and vegetable renewal, Black Hawk's reference to these seemingly casual conversations suggests their significance to the life of their community as a function of the relationship between food and narrative, as well as the ways in which the fragmentary traces of narrative participate within a range of sedimentary practices constitutive of the vitality of land and its associated living forms. Inasmuch as the stories that pass between people give shape to the mundane work of rebuilding communal life, it becomes bound up with the stuff of the earth, part of the ecology—as much as the sociality—that sustains them, while the produce of their mutual labor, their transfiguration of the sacred dead, returns their memory in the form of sustenance. While glossed over lightly as idle gossip, the full significance of such exchanges emerges when considered in relation to an earlier passage in which Black Hawk expands upon the affective contours of what it means to have been removed from the graves of his relations. "There is no place like that where the bones of our forefathers life, to go to when in grief. . . . [H]ow different is our situation now, from what it was in those days! Then we were as happy as the buffalo on the plains—but now we are as miserable as the hungry, howling wolf in the prairie!" Characterizing the condition of the Sauk community as one of unrelenting mourning, here, Black Hawk describes their spiritual sorrow in terms of physical hunger, contrasting both to the former condition of the community during a time when care shown for the grave provided a vehicle of communion with the material aspect of the dead, both related to a familiar predator and prey. While the buffalo dines upon the abundant grass of the prairie, providing sustenance for the hunt and for its community, the wolf wails in sorrow as game disappears, unable to satiate its hunger.

In posing a relationship between sorrow and hunger, this passage of Black Hawk's narrative evokes a consubstantiality that should be taken as literal rather than metaphoric. From the perspective of what Seminole scholar Susan A. Miller has called the "indigenous paradigm in historiography," history is less an inert record of the past than a dimension of that which sustains indigenous sovereignty, kinship, and self-determination. As such, it cannot be disentangled from the physical substance of the earth, nor can it be severed from the conditions of relationality that obtain between the earth and the multitudinous forms of life that constitute some component of its geophysical dynamic. For Miller, within the "living cosmos" presumed as the core of indigenous lifeworlds, "every element has rights that one must respect." This ethical imperative is broadly resonant with the relational approach to law and justice outlined by former Chief Justice of the Navajo Nation, Robert Yazzie, for whom "justice" names the restoration of that form of solidarity by which individual elements of the living cosmos are reconciled to one another. Justice, in this sense, becomes a process of what Yazzie calls peacemaking, the negotiation of "a system of relationships where there is no need for force, coercion or control." Yazzie goes on to emphasize the consubstantiality of the elements of this relation with the law as a substance: "Navajos," he writes, "do not think of equality as treating people as equal *before* the law; they are equal *in* the law."[44] Within this ethical milieu, rights are broadly distributed, and among these rights are those granted a "deceased person . . . to rest unmolested in the grave while his or her spirit follows the natural course of the afterlife." Moreover, the afterlife does not name some ethereal transcendence, but the persistence of the dead within an ecosystem based upon an ethics of kinship among human and nonhuman constituents. "The relationship between the Earth and buried remains can be seen within the greater context of a community of interrelated beings that include the plants, animals, and other spirits in the neighborhood of the grave. . . . Within this cosmos, the remains of a community's dead are inseparable from the land itself, and their spirits are inseparable from the living community."[45] Burials, within this framework, structure a circuit whereby affect is given orientation and kinship is nurtured in its relation to ecology as a mode of relation to place. Burial organizes, enfolds, and arranges history as a socially meaningful, physically material presence that imprints itself upon the life of the land by respecting the right of the Earth to "receive and shelter her children's remains" as part of an ecological metabolic of kinship and Indigenous sovereignty.[46]

Given the centrality of burial to the entanglements that constitute the imminence of Indigenous sovereignty, the theft of Makataimeshekiakiak's remains constituted a direct assault on the Rock River Sauk community, because it violated the sedimentary processes by which they sought to negotiate belonging as a function of ecological and geophysical mutuality. The ecologies instantiated by Makataimeshekiakiak's burial enfolded history and memory as part of an ecological metabolic inseparable from Sauk expressions of kinship with one another and with land understood as a form of life present to the negotiation of social and political relations. In the Algonquian language family spoken by the Sauk, historically, the proper name for the nation was *Oθaakiiwaki*, or "people of yellow earth," an autonym derived from the color of the soil near their ancestral home on Saginaw Bay in present-day Michigan. For Makataimeshekiakiak's contemporaries among the Rock Island Sauk, the history of the people was the history of the land; not for a single piece of land, but for land as a medium of continuity for the people over time and through space. As such, reverence for the land, expressed through a grammar of care, sustained a living record of the people, just as it sustained the people. Only recently banished from their homes in Western Illinois, for the Rock Island Sauks, Makataimeshekiakiak's grave was not a tomb, a monument through which to calcify his remains and his memory, but a point of orientation; a means of substantiating both their relations with one another and the substance of their community as it constituted itself in relation to the vitality of land as the substance of their capacity for self-determination and the maintenance of their peoplehood. In burying Makataimeshekiakiak and performing the rituals through which he was mourned and remembered, the Sauks initiated a new ecology of memory, one coextensive with earlier histories of Indigenous place-making, but anchored to a specific place, time, and people, while expressive of a renewed trajectory for Sauk nationality and futurity.

Black Hawk's burial was a multivalent, multivocal text, an inscription meant to orient, to instruct and to narrate, and to console through narration. A site of entwined Indigenous and settler meaning-making, the Sauks constructed Makataimeshekiakiak's burial so as to enfold "the actual history of our plural existence" as a testimony to the ethics of kinship among settlers and Native peoples; an ethics to which Native peoples maintained an immoderate fidelity, despite the persistent, punitive transgressions of the settler neighbors. "Prior to his death [Black Hawk] expressed a desire to be buried on the spot where he had held his last council with the Iowas. . . . [H]is request was complied with."[47] As a gesture toward the prior inhabitants of the land to which he and his people had been removed, Makataimeshekiakiak's request to be buried on the site of this council indexes a sense of kinship that recognized the ongoing right and obligation of the Iowas, as a sovereign people, to negotiate the terms upon which cohabitation among multifarious forms of life would take place. Even as the request was directed toward local settlers and Indian traders, it reveals a sense of the entanglements constitutive of "the actual history of our plural existence," and thus, the negotiations through which the terms of kinship and sovereignty were made manifest.

Later testimonies concerning the circumstances of Makataimeshekiakiak's burial provide a glimpse into these interrelated sets of kinship obligations, even as they reveal an utter lack of faith, on the part of settlers, to the forms by which such mutuality was to be recognized and reciprocated. Some portion of this mutuality is most powerfully inscribed through attention to sartorial effulgence. "He was dressed in the military uniform of a colonel of the regular army, said to have been presented to him by a member of President Jackson's cabinet, with a cap on his head elaborately ornamented in Indian style with feathers." Layering the military garb of his enemy and erstwhile conqueror, the uniform and the cap, adorned with feathers, evokes the entwined, overlapping histories of Indigenous peoples and settlers, even as the seemingly inconsequential accent of plumage against the raiment of military costume evokes something of the overbearing might of empire. The entwinement of Black Hawk's life, and the lives of his people, with imperial forces, in relation with imperial elements, is further evoked by the artifacts he bears with him. "At his left side was a sword, which had been presented to him by Gen. Jackson; and at his right side were placed two canes, one of which he had received from Hon. Henry Clay, the other was the gift of an officer of the British army." Symbols of virility and debility, sword and cane represent overlapping histories of victory and life; they are also harbingers of power in decline, of the body in decay unto death. These mementos of empire and its relationship to the historical lives of Native peoples as well as of Native peoples to empire are further inscribed through the array of peace medals that festoon Black Hawk's neck. "Besides these were deposited on either side other presents and trophies, highly prized by him as mementos of his valor and greatness. About his neck were ribbons suspending three medals, one the gift of President Jackson, another was presented to him by ex-President John Quincy Adams, and the third by the city of Boston." Describing the medals as "deposited," the text draws out the medals' similarity to money, as the composition of the grave suggests the association with money and the circulation of money, the accumulation of capital, as the end of empire, and the cause of enormous human, Indigenous misery. The ironies of the plurality, the mutuality, of Indigenous and settler histories are further underscored by the tattered rag that stands as sentinel over all. "At the head [of the grave] was a flag-staff thirty-five feet high, which bore an American flag worn out by exposure, and near by was the usual hewn post inscribed with Indian characters, representing his deeds of bravery, and record as a warrior."[48] A palimpsest of histories, the plurality evoked in this gesture tells of the uneasiness of plurality, its inconveniences and problems, its inevitable failures, ironizing the flag as a symbol of victory by hanging it faded, from a post, adorned with the story of Black Hawk and his victories, inscribed with "his record as a warrior."

Recorded by land surveyor, amateur geologist, and historian Willard Barrows—a name, of course, that was deeply ironic, given his preoccupation with Indigenous burial monuments—this description of Makataimeshekiakiak's burial offers an unwitting insight into the ways in which the arrangement of the site was meant to enfold "the actual history of our plural existence" through a conscientious observation of the obligations of kinship. In this passage, dress provides the most immediately legible sign of Sauk fidelity to these obligations, because the raiment adorning Makataimeshekiakiak's body suggests a ceremonial and deliberative relationship to successive imperial powers—including the United States—and their subjects. Outfitted in a US military uniform but crowned by Native millinery, Makataimeshekiakiak's burial clothes conveyed a shared history through sartorial choices, gesturing to legacies of trade— but also battle, conquest, and defeat—of Native men acquiring settler clothing as trophies of war, and of acknowledging respect for their enemies by adopting their insignia even after they had been bested. By a similar token, the inclusion of the multiple gifts—the sword and cane— and, in particular, the peace medals stood as tokens of Makataimeshekiakiak's recognition, even among his foes, of his greatness in battle, and his stature as a leader, while acknowledging the overlapping histories of empire to which the Sauk were party, as well as the negotiation of kinship relations between the Sauks and their imperial foes. The burial enfolded the material history of Sauk sovereignty as an ecological and social force, one bound in complex and contractor relations to histories of imperial rapine, successive histories of settlement, and the ongoing renegotiation of their mutual obligations.

> He was rigged out in a full suit of regimentals; frock coat with gold
> epaulettes, worth several hundred dollars; a cocked hat; sword and
> belt and spear cane; and fastened about him were there medals, each
> near the size of a dinner plate—one presented to him by General
> Jackson, one by President Madison, and one by the British Government. They were valuable, but whether of silver or gold I have forgotten, although Mr. Jordan stated the kind of metal to me. The sword
> and the cane came into Mr. Jordan's hands, and the sword was by
> him presented to the Masonic Lodge at Keosauqua, in whose possession it now is. The sword was also a present from General Jackson.[49]

Composed as part of an 1873 investigation into the disposition of Black Hawk's remains, as in the previous passage, military raiment is highlighted, gesturing toward the martial as a complicated space of intimacy, a contact zone staged between cultures and histories forged in and through asymmetrical relations of power. The burial, here described by local lawyer and businessman D. C. Beaman, effectively echoes and recapitulates the ceremonial gesture by which Makataimeshekiakiak opens his *Narrative*, where he dedicates the work to Brigadier General Henry Atkinson, the man who was credited with defeating him in battle. "The changes of fortune, and vicissitudes of war, made you my conqueror. When my last resources were exhausted, my warriors worn down with long and toilsome marches, we yielded, and I became your prisoner. . . . The story of my life is told in the following pages; it is intimately connected, and in some measure, identified with a part of the history of your own: I have therefore dedicated it to you."[50] Here, conquest and defeat become the condition of an identification that supposes an entanglement between Makataimeshekiakiak and Atkinson as the physical embodiment of their mutual histories, and the larger kinship relations to which each was beholden. As exemplified by the flagstaff planted at the head of his grave, this intimacy is moreover referenced and recorded through the inclusion of ceremonial objects within the ecology of Makataimeshekiakiak's burial, effectively suturing Makataimeshekiakiak and the Rock River Sauk, as well as the geophysical forms of their historical record, to friendship extended by successive imperial governments, including the "Great Father," Andrew Jackson.[51] Yet, in its emphasis on the value of the items placed within the burial, their probable composition of silver or gold, Beaman's description of the site stages its archaeological stratification, the evisceration of its sedimented components into commodities, reified as objects of scientific and commercial logics by which they might be rendered comparable as evidence, or fungible as goods for trade.

Conclusion

The forms of extractive capitalism that took shape in the Upper Mississippi River Valley in the wake of the so-called Black Hawk War were predicated upon the production of lead and the instrumentality of lead as an implement for the distribution of violence, for the substantiation of the fiction of the state through the unbidden penetration of the body of another. The application of state power in control over lead was abetted by forms of science beholden to Malthusian provocations regarding the need for labor and the inherent limitations of the natural world as that which provides for the maintenance of populations.

2 / "Dressed in a strange fantasy": The Dialectics of Seeing and the Secret Passages of Desire

What is the weight of forgetting? How do we trace the proliferations of disavowal within settler colonialism, the ways in which legacies of mutuality and need give way to fantasies of categorical independence and self-sufficiency? By what monstrous dialectic must the formation of the self through the refusal of the other unfold as aimlessly destructive hatred? In chapter 1, I explore the settler disavowal of Indigenous sovereignty and the associated obligations of kinship through a consideration of Makataimeshekiakiak's burial and the violation of his remains. I read Makataimeshekiakiak's burial as part of the composition of Sauk sovereignty as geophysical narrative, a form of political expression manifest in the cultural secretions that constitute the sensuality of place and the historicity of place; the ways in which sovereignty inheres in the geophysical arrangement of place as a vector for the orientation of memory. The theft of Makataimeshekiakiak's remains, I argue, was contiguous with the forms of enclosure and extraction by which the mineral, agronomical, and terrestrial resources of the Upper Mississippi River Valley were fashioned as commodities. Makataimeshekiakiak the man—affiliated, intimated, enfleshed—belonged to the narrative figures by which the Sauk sustained their relation to place, by which they shaped the geophysics of place, by which place was made a technology of memory. Removed from the sensuous conditions of Indigenous narrative and the myriad forms of life—animal, mineral, plant, human—his burial sustained, Makataimeshekiakiak's remains were made over, among settlers, as just another resource, one equivalent to the forms of terrestrial lead settlers so eagerly fashioned into the bullets by which they carved out a cruelly narcissistic grammar of property. As resource, Makataimeshekiakiak's remains were made to serve as data, matériel from which to enact the bureaucratic reconfiguration of Indigenous life and land through the application of ethnologically interested geology. The connection between Sauk sovereignty, the geophysicality of place, and the overlapping histories of the recomposition of place were effaced—if only in part—through the imposition of an abstracted topography that was conducive to the commodification and extraction of entangled resource vitalities through the enactment of property as a measure in law; one enforced by the material distribution of force over space, the calculation of velocity and trajectory as elements of an ecology of state-sanctioned killing. Disconnected from meaningful histories of use or occupation, the topography of ownership and aspiration etched itself into the land through the erratic inscription of US counter-sovereignty through the application of terrestrial lead in the form of bullets. Lead extraction and its employment in the service of the fiction of the state, I suggest, composes a form of writing dedicated to the realization of the spectacular, the conversion of the fictions of the state into a socially meaningful fact, manifest through the military as the avatar of the technological sublime. I argue that what Manu Karuka has called "the prose of counter-sovereignty"—the forms of literature by which the fictions of US sovereignty have been forged from the irregularly shaped pieces of the state and its destructive engagements with living expressions of Indigenous sovereignties—counter-sovereignty becomes written into the shape of the land, while the composition of the land becomes a subject of political contestation.

The previous chapter traces relations constitutive of the substantive materiality of Indigenous sovereignty as a means of highlighting the forms of disavowal—of abject, calculated narcissism—by which settler colonialism was realized as an extractive culture of violently enforced resource ownership. I looked to bullets as instruments by which settlers write, technologies by which they tell their stories, as well as elements of a language, a grammar of the nation and the state. In this chapter, I follow the permutation of lead along a different trajectory in the commodity chain, moving toward a more conventional form of writing, more congenial instances of story and narrative. While the majority of the lead extracted from the mines of the Upper Mississippi River Valley was fashioned into bullets, here I approach lead—and the relations between its enclosure, extraction, and elimination—through a consideration of its transmutation through the culture of print, through something that might provisionally be referred to as journalism. A form of literature not meant to be savored but consumed, journalism harnessed printing and reading as instruments of entertainment and information, a way of giving shape to the day, to the week or month, and to time as it relates to the manifestation of place.[1] One of three soft metals that, historically, have composed the basis for type alloy or type metal, lead drawn from the mines of the Upper Mississippi region, facilitated by the military and juridical enclosure of the valley, lent new vitality to print as a medium, providing a previously unknown source of raw material through which printers might expand their technological capacities at a moment in which the infrastructures of the market—highways, canals, steamboats, railways, and other innovations in transportation and shipping—allowed for the expansion of the empire of print, now ever more closely allied with capital and the state. As Mississippian lead saturated the market in the years after 1816, the domestic price of lead saw a significant decrease, allowing for the expansion of printing and print-related industries, including a professional coterie of type-makers that dedicated itself to the service of the publishing industry. Making printed material more available to a wider variety of consumers by reducing the costs associated with the implements of printing, the lead captured in the wake of the so-called Black Hawk War was, I argue, one of the most significant—if largely unexplored—variables in the growth of the US print media in the early nineteenth century; as well as one of the most significant ancillary factors to the elaboration of those literary forms and media ecologies that would come to suture the affective ligaments of the incipient nation.

In what follows, I explore the ways in which such processes were themselves coextensive with literary techniques of enclosure that abetted the progress of settler colonialism; of the ways in which print, as a vehicle for the circulation of affect, collaborated in the forms of enclosure that accompanied and facilitated the expropriation of Native land and resources, while refusing modes of affinity between Native peoples and settlers.[2] I look at the ways in which artifacts of the culture of print record glimpses of different forms of collectivity, desires touching upon unlikely, unfamiliar ideas about belonging and the companionate negotiations of social and political life. I hold to these brief irruptions, these transient flashes of illumination, despite all the ways in which print has collaborated in the foreclosure of these other visions of collectivity. Drawn from the mines and cast as bullets, lead would contribute to the material instantiation of the fictions of state, sovereignty, and capital through a practical monopoly on the means of violence. Cast as type, lead hewn from those same mines would provide the mechanism whereby print and printing, writers and writing, would come to play a role as apologists for empire. Poets of the nation, bards celebrating the muscularity of the state, through access to print, writers and writing participated in the scholastic formality that gave credence to pseudo-scientific formulations of racial difference and white superiority, including questions touching upon the proper arrangement of kinship and the appropriate channels for the expression of desire. Where the extraction of lead and its manufacture as bullets composed a story about the land and upon the land through the immediate alteration of its geophysical metabolic, fashioned as type, lead was used to tell a story about the land that—while not unconstrained by the physical geography of the terrestrial surface—was not bound by place; a story that could move and be repeated, that could serve to mediate the experience of physical place in ways that overwrote the sensual conditions manifest in place. This was a story that could tell people about their relationship to place and to each other; a story that undermined the continuities of Indigenous sovereignties and Indigenous lives, while foreclosing the possibility of solidarities that might generate different ways of living together, of imagining the present, the future, and the past.

Moreover, I approach the relationship of print to the history of enclosure through a consideration of contemporaneous media coverage of the events of the so-called Black Hawk War. Specifically, I analyze the archive of war and its aftermath—the surrender and arrest of Black Hawk and Black Hawk's subsequent 1833 tour of the eastern United States—as a means to elucidate the ways in which print served as a means to orient and organize affect. I am not interested in all the ways in which the representation of the Black Hawk War or the techniques of their dissemination might have contributed to the formation of a national public.[3] Rather, I am interested in the ways in which the enclosure of the circumstances of the conflict within the culture of print was part of a broader articulation and enclosure of Indigeneity through the logic of the commodity, the reification of Indigeneity through the production of "Indianness" as something to be possessed; a thing that could be split off from the specific material forms of Indigenous peoples' sovereignties and modes of self-determination and made an object for the possession of white people. The enclosure of the conflict within print, I argue, produced the war; just as the enclosure of Makataimeshekiakiak, his paper confinement an echo of his physical constraint, produced Black Hawk as an object of historical scrutiny. I will elucidate the myriad ways in which the reified Indian, like the pretense of US sovereignty, was punctured by the continuities of Indigeneity and Indigenous sovereignty, as well as the irrepressibly unruly forms of desire that have shaped "the actual history of our plural existence."

These forms of desire, I argue, have been continuously and persistently suppressed, part of an ill-coordinated assault on new visions of a collective future, forged in an anticolonial movement toward justice. By trapping desire within the social life of dead labor, I argue that the structure of the commodity and commodity fetishism effectively forecloses the possibility that desire might find expression through nonhierarchical appointments for social organization, ways of setting the table to better share the meal. As such, I look at forms of desire that find some expression within the field of the commodity as a means of elucidating a desire for the otherwise, a desire to illuminate relationships among people that were not so neatly subsumed by patriarchal forms of social reproduction dedicated to the expansion of capital and fantasies of whiteness, forms all-too-neatly coextensive with the formal structure of capital as a model for the elaboration of settler colonialism. In exploring the briefly effervescent irruptions of the otherwise, I am most specifically attuned to the question of seeing, to vision, to the optic and all the ways in which it orients theories of sovereignty, even as the necessarily erotic aspects of seeing and being seen complicate notions of the majestic, the auratic, the spectacular, or the mundane. Made a spectacle for eastern audiences, an entertainment to be consumed—casually, mindlessly—the enthusiasm with which Black Hawk was greeted during his 1833 tour evokes an inchoate and perhaps inexpressible, inadmissible desire to live life in common, to live in common differently. I read representations of the 1833 tour by the thin light of these near cold embers, searching for expressions of desire that suggest the possibility of new ways of being together, of experiencing together, new rituals by which to honor and express the plurality of our histories, while turning our gaze toward the restitution of Indigenous sovereignties, and the expression of Indigenous sovereignty as a social and political framework for the realization of justice.[4]

Beginning with media accounts from the scene of the Black Hawk War, news reports that sought to present scenes of the war to a wide array of readers distant from the action, I look at the ways in which stories from the militarized frontier participated in a logic of security that sought to affirm the socioeconomic viability of those enterprises tethered to the political continuity of settlement; to assure investors that markets were not indelibly corrupted by the threat of Indian violence and its capacity to disrupt the forms of development by which eastern municipalities sought to direct the movement of resources. Starting with scenes of the representation of the massacre of Black Hawk's forces at the Battle of Bad Axe, I explore an inchoate desire to see that marks contemporaneous media accounts of the conflict and its aftermath by looking at the portraits sketched by reporters and editors who shaped the story of the war. Reports from the scene of the conflict, as well as stories about Black Hawk and his captivity in the year after the war, typically demonstrate a narrowing of the field of vision, an attenuation of focus and of depth, moving from panoramic images of battle to images of individuals and groups. Skimming flesh and faces to penetrate otherwise intransigent surfaces, reports from the scene of the Black Hawk War evoke the desire to peer beneath the integuments of skin, to see the eyes, and through the eyes, to know the other, his heart and mind. The desire to see appears here as a function of a hope for security, a means of imagining personal and material security through the ability to assess the visual field, the desire to see cradling an even more elemental desire to know and, through knowledge, to control. This desire to see, to see and know by seeing, I understand as necessarily emanating from within a narcissistic desire to consume, an erotic of the object as focal point of consumer longing. This desire, however, is not limited by the shape of the commodity as the form in which we subjects of capital have been taught to direct our longing. It presumes a desire not merely to see, or to possess through seeing, but to be seen, and—in being seen—to be possessed, to meet the eyes of another and to become, as it were, lost. The fantasy of the securely American self here unfolds as a fantasy of transformation as annihilation, of the annihilation of the self through the body of another, captured in the eyes of another. Drawing upon accounts written about the captivity of Black Hawk and his men, accounts that dwelled overlong on the physical comportment of their men and the ways in which contemporary writers luxuriated in the expressiveness of their bodies, a dimension of their physicality accessible only through the apprehensions of the visual, I trace the fantasy of annihilation as a desire for transformation, of physical and emotional conversion, through consideration of a suppressed homoeroticism a queer desire to be seen that reverses the gaze, inviting that of the Native to possess the settler, to make the settler his own.

Visualizing Battle, Inscribing War, Framing Black Hawk

After four months of privation, hunted by local militias and members of the federal infantry, the Rock River Sauk, under Makataimeshekiakiak's command, attempted to evade the combined forces of the settler military by crossing the Mississippi River, seeking refuge in the west. Projected, within Jacksonian-era Indian policy, as the physical, legal, and racial frontier marking the distance between civilization and savagery, the British Band hoped to find shelter among other, similarly displaced Native peoples as well as those who might be sympathetic to their cause. On August 1, at the mouth of the Bad Axe River—near present-day Victory,

Wisconsin—the four hundred remaining noncombatants who had followed Makataimeshekiakiak during his campaign began crossing the Mississippi on hastily assembled rafts. Their efforts were cut short by a patrolling US gunship, deployed from Fort Crawford, at Prairie du Chien. Despite Makataimeshekiakiak running up a white flag, the commander of the steamboat *Warrior*, Joseph Throckmorton, ordered his men to fire on the Sauks; the remaining Sauk warriors returned fire, in kind. After a two-hour battle, the *Warrior* withdrew to refuel. The next morning, an irregular company, composed of enthusiastic conscripts to the settler militia and some portion of the regular forces of the US infantry, stumbled upon the party of retreating Sauks; they attacked. Surprised by their charge and blocked from retreat to the river by the cannons of the refueled *Warrior*, the remnants of the British Band—warriors, women, old men, and children—were wiped out. With his comrade Wabokieshiek, the Winnebago Prophet, Makataimeshekiakiak fled, taking refuge among the Ho-Chunk, in the north, near present-day La Crosse, Wisconsin.

Of the battles fought during the Black Hawk War, none were so widely reported in the contemporary press as what came to be known as the "affair of the steamboat." Perhaps the most widely circulated journal of the times, *Niles' Weekly Register* published all intelligence it received on the subject, combing through less readily available western news sources to assemble a catalogue of miscellany, published for distribution among an ostensibly national audience. "Until too late to remedy it—we did not observe the omission of an account of a battle with, and complete defeat of the hostile Indians, on the bank of the Mississippi. . . . Black Hawk, before the battle was ended . . . left his people and absconded. . . . The war is, probably over! but 'take it all in all' it has been a severe one against us."[5] Reported in the August 25 edition of the *Register*, this was the first news of the battle to reach an eastern readership, and it echoed the report Hezekiah Niles had issued concerning the opening of the war earlier that spring. "We understand, that the Sac and Fox Indians have reoccupied the territory on the east side of the Mississippi, of which they were dispossessed last year. . . . They are guided now, as last year, by the noted chief Black Hawk, who is, indeed, the sole fomenter of all these disturbances."[6] Of three or four other reports of the war that appeared in the *Register* during the summer—in editions published on June 16, August 4, and August 11—one described the mutilation of the wounded and the dead following Sauk victory at Stillman's Run; two concerned the celerity with which federal troops had been mobilized to support regional militias; yet another touched on the progress of the cholera, which reached global pandemic status for the first time in the spring of 1832. Only one of these reports mentioned Black Hawk by name. "'Black Hawk, with near a thousand warriors had taken his station between Rock and Wisconsin rivers, and appeared determined to give battle.' . . . From the great superiority in number of the whites, it was supposed that an engagement would result *in a general massacre of the Indians*."[7]

Reports of the war in *Niles' Weekly Register* tell a simple story: a tale of invasion, repulsion, and victory; of beginning, middle, and end. What had transpired on the Mississippi frontier during the spring and summer of 1832 was, of course, immeasurably more complicated, touching upon a long history of friendship and enmity, of social and juridical arrangements extended then violated, of ongoing attacks on Indigenous peoples by settler communities seeking to secure otherwise dubious claims to property as well as a long-running campaign—by Makataimeshekiakiak and his comrades—to preserve the Sauks in their sovereignty over Rock Island. Generally ignoring the circumstances of Jacksonian-era Indian removal policy, to say nothing of the far longer and more baroque history of colonial relationships that had come to shape the social life of the Mississippi frontier, the version of events promulgated by Niles and other publishers dispensed with any sense of moral ambiguity or historical uncertainty, offering instead a categorical renunciation of the Sauks as partners in the mediation of regional expressions of social organization. Circulating reports from the western press to meet the rapturous demand of eastern readers, Niles's reportage conveyed a sense that the war had been waged with justice, righteousness, and purpose. Its end was unfortunate, but the means were justified. "There is no doubt but that Black Hawk is completely discouraged, and now hopes of nothing but escape. His army is in a state of sordid wretchedness. He, with his warriors, is said to be endeavoring to effect a retreat up the Mississippi, and, to effect this the more easily, has committed their women and children to the mercy of the whites. . . . It gives us much gratification to state that these miserable beings have generally been received and treated with humanity. . . . We war not with women and children."[8]

Published barely a month after the massacre at Bad Axe, Niles's report on Black Hawk's negligence with respect to women and children was drawn from a letter submitted to the *Saint Louis Times* by a Captain Loomis, identified here as a commander at Fort Crawford. Of a piece with a larger dispatch offering detailed accounts of the battle on the Mississippi, Niles's brief from Loomis's report drew upon well-entrenched mythologies about gender difference among Native peoples and the widespread belief, among settlers, that a general insensitivity to the obligations of patriarchy and the protection men owed to women was a congenital element of Native masculinity, an indication of its errancy and its failure. In reports such as these, "Black Hawk" the media confabulation first began to come into focus as a character for eastern readers, even as the attribution of the conflict under his name had, at best, only anecdotal support.

> BLACK HAWK'S INVASION . . . This bold fellow, who has occasioned so much distress on the north western frontier, for some months past, has paid pretty dearly for his temerity. His who loss down to the 3d August, is estimated at 400 killed and 150 prisoners. About 150 were killed in the engagement of the 2d . . . 23 to 25 in the affair of the steamboat Warrior on the 1st . . . Seventy prisoners were taken in the engagement of the 2d. . . . About 100 horses were also taken. In the affair of the steamboat it is estimated that the Indians fired from 1,500 to 2,000 balls. They however proved to be very bad marksmen, unless the boat was too distant for the range of their muskets, as only 60 of their shots struck her, and only one man on board was wounded. Nothing certain is known of the fate of Black Hawk. A prisoner reports, that the man who was standing next to him was killed by the first discharge of the six pounder on board the boat, and that, in the midst of the action, he himself retreated up the river.[9]

Presented through a series of descriptives, an otherwise inert set of statistics, Black Hawk appears here in the guise of an Indian barrow, subject to measurement, to study, to the ministrations of the anthropologists. Absent any more robust characterization, Black Hawk here is cast in a negative light, a creature of desire, a fantasy among settlers erected around a handful of stray, unrelated details that form an awkward collage. He emerges here as a figure saturated with hubris, arrogant enough to believe that he could do battle against the military of the United States, yet craven enough to abandon his people and their cause at the first sign of hardship. Black Hawk appears as a miserable tactician, motivated solely by ambition and justly penalized for his audacity by the decimation of his people. Represented here as a statistical table of living and dead, captured and killed, the Sauks are captured as little more than echoes of the bullets they so hastily and ineffectively fire into the hull of the Warrior: powerful matériel wasted through inefficient deployment. That Black Hawk might have survived the assault visited upon his people, that despite all reasonable expectations for his noble death in battle, he might have survived in retreat, leaving his company leaderless and without direction, was the ultimate demonstration of his perfidy. As a warrior, Black Hawk may have been brave, but he was utterly without honor.

This portrait of Black Hawk speaks to his fugitive status. He cannot be brought into focus because he remains concealed, hidden from the eyes of the state. As he came ever closer to the centers of state power, writers and printers would come to fill in this portrait of Black Hawk, to reverse the negative, setting his image and his persona into circulation as a condition of its capture and articulation within the body of the state.

> Black Hawk, a Potawatomy by birth, but raised by the Saukies, appears to be about 60 years old, has a small bunch of gray hair on the crown of his head, the rest is bare, has a high forehead, a Roman nose, a full mouth, which generally inclines to be a little open, has a sharp chin, no eyebrows, but a very fine eye; his head is thrown back upon his shoulders; he is about 5 feet 4 or 5 inches high; at present he is thin, and appears much dejected, but now and then assumes the aspect of command. He held in his left hand a white flag, in the other the tail, with the back-skin, head, and beak of the Calumet eagle; with this he frequently fans himself. His Indian name is Mascata-mish-Ka-kaek.[10]

Evoking the eye as an implement of enclosure, this passage produces Black Hawk from within a field of hysterical disseminations, producing the man by fixating on certain features of his person, of his bearing, and offering a visual grammar of bodily comportment as a means by which to evoke security, knowledge, and control. Immediately preceded by a lengthy report of a dialogue between Ho-Chunk leader One-Eyed Decorah, federal Indian agent General Joseph M. Street, and then-Colonel Zachary Taylor, this portrait of Black Hawk was recorded at the time of his surrender and arrest—at Fort Crawford, in Prairie du Chien—on August 27, 1832. Printed in *Niles' Weekly Register* little more than a month later, the dialogue among the leaders drew upon the rhetorical conventions of the family romance through which settlers had sought to understand the terms of Indigenous kinship as it related to their own social and cultural forms: Street addresses the Ho-Chunk as "[his] children," while the Ho-Chunk refer to Street as "[their] father." Street and Taylor, in this dialogue, make clear that they are merely local representatives of more distant "fathers," Andrew Jackson, "the great father . . . at Washington," and Winfield Scott, "a great war chief from the far east."[11] Behind these honorifics were rapidly diverging visions of how to negotiate cohabitation among settlers and Natives, even as the form of their performance maintained something of the illusion of a mutual commitment to the recognition of different, overlapping, and commensurate sovereignties. This shifting terrain is indirectly acknowledged in an appeal directed to Taylor from a Ho-Chunk warrior identified in the dialogue as Cheator: "Near the Dalle, on the Wisconsin, I took Black Hawk. No one did it but me,—I say this in the ears of all present, and they know it—and I now appeal to the Great Spirit, our grand father, and the earth our grand mother, for the truth of what I say. . . . That one, Wa-bo-kie-shiek is my relation—if he is to be hurt, I do not wish to see it. . . . Soldiers sometimes stick the ends of their guns, (bayonets) into the backs of Indian prisoners when they are going about in the hands of the guard. I hope this will not be done to these men."[12]

Claiming recognition—as well as the prerogatives of both acclamation and blame—for having delivered Black Hawk to the Ho-Chunk and, thus, into the hands of Taylor and Street, Scott and Jackson, Cheator's address nonetheless asserts a set of higher kin relations and ethical loyalties than those summoned by either representative of federal power, pointing to the Great Spirit and the earth as grandparents with a claim upon all who dwell upon them. Wrapping his understanding of kinship into a request for clemency or—at the very least—honor with respect to the treatment of these prisoners, he indicates a knowing fear that US soldiers are not to be trusted, making an appeal to their better natures without necessarily addressing or condemning their actions. Making clear that he has acted only to preserve his nation, the Ho-Chunk, in their relations with the United States, Cheator appeals to Taylor and Street that Black Hawk and the Prophet receive treatment—as prisoners—that accords with their status within the councils of their nations and their positions within networks of social and kin relations, that they might be preserved in their physical integrity, and returned to their families, in due course. Moreover, Cheator's discourse makes an appeal to Black Hawk's physical integrity, one that supersedes or suspends the ways in which the forms of physical confinement practiced by the military and the state effected the disintegration of the body, its parts, and their relation to larger environments, larger ecosystems. The description of Black Hawk and the Prophet recorded at the time of their surrender effected an image of this dissolution. The image of their captivity captured in the description of the men as a set of physiognomic and sartorial curiosities, articulated from within the space of Indigenous sovereignty; Cheator's appeal to the command at Fort Crawford, however, insisted upon the preservation of their bodies and their integrity, implicitly calling into question the implements of punishment among settlers: the cage, the ball and chain, the scourge, the wall.

Inasmuch as it preserved an image of the conditions of their captivity, the lengthy descriptions of both Black Hawk and the Prophet would suggest a less sensitive, less respectful end than the one Cheator had requested. The mimetic relationship between the conditions of their captivity and the conditions of their representation indicate the relay between enclosure in everyday life and enclosure in print; they also indicate the ways in which both express processes of primitive accumulation and of policing, which are endemic to the security of the state and the irregularity of its counter-sovereignty, as well as attendant formations of value. Held prisoner by the government of the United States and its military command, confined over the next nine months to cages in frigid cells, in winter, in military prisons, Makataimeshekiakiak and his comrade Wabokieshiek found themselves cut off from their friends and family, isolated as hostages, kept to ensure the docility of their remaining Sauk and Ho-Chunk allies. This was expressed, most acutely, through intimate, invasive descriptions of Makataimeshekiakiak and Wabokieshiek as captives. "The *Prophet*, a half Saukie and half Winnebago [Ho-Chunk], is about 40 years old, nearly six feet high; is stout and athletic; has a large broad face, short blunt nose, large full eyes, broad mouth, thick lips, with a full suit of hair." Where Oswald and Lorenzo Fowler had treated Black Hawk as a subject of phrenology, here Wabokieshiek become a subject of physiognomy. Yet where the calipers rendered Black Hawk's persona as an expression of pure bone, the engagement with the face—the texture of sinew, muscle, and flesh—renders Wabokieshiek subject of a curious erotics, the settler gaze transforming the man into an oblique object of desire. This is extended through the account of his dress. "He wore a white cloth head dress which rose several inches above the top of his head—the whole man exhibiting a deliberate savageness—not that he would seem to delight in honorable war, or fight; but making him as the priest of assassination or secret murder." Drawing the sartorial trappings of the headscarf as indication of a secret, murderous devotional, the settler gaze moves up from the face to linger in the violence of sexuality, in the inadmissibility of a passion for the other touched by the inevitability of death. This, however, is countered by a white flag, a sign of surrender in warfare now a sign of surrender in the passions. "He had in one hand a white flag, while the other hung carelessly by his side. They were both clothed in very white dressed dear skins, fringed at the seam with short cuttings of the same. His Indian name is Wa-bo-kie-shiek— (White Cloud.)"[13]

As Tena Helton has demonstrated, descriptions like these were common to the representational culture that grew up around Black Hawk's postwar tour of US cities.[14] Presented as bodies held fast in space, limited in their physical relations to their surrounding environment, passages like these projected the physical conditions of constraint through the functionality of block type, fixing both men in place as if their presences might spill out across the page. Through the mediation of print, here, Makataimeshekiakiak and Wabokieshiek are rendered as specimens; Black Hawk and the Prophet are subjects to be brought under observation, studied, looked at, watched. Beginning with evocations of their names as personae in the popular press—"Black Hawk," "The Prophet"—the accounts of the men and their appearance conclude with rough renderings of their ostensibly "Indian" names, bracketing the physicality of the men within a story about their translation as objects of ethnographic curiosity. Made into objects of scrutiny, items within a catalogue of Indian characters rather than comperes in an evolving dialogue, the cordial exchange that precedes these descriptions—in which the performative formality of treaty-making is preserved in practice if not in spirit or in law—is effectively abrogated: neither Makataimeshekiakiak nor Wabokieshiek are allowed to speak; or, rather, whatever they might have had to say has been expunged. They have been rendered mute, objects of pity to be absorbed, in their abjection, through the eye and not the voice. Enlivened on the page through the act of reading, whatever personality either man might have is made subordinate to the fantasies of the reader, elements within the fantasy of the consumer as subject, built around the expropriated image of the Indian as captive. Enclosed by a cage, the men are enclosed within print, their images set into circulation and made an object by which to effect the accumulation of value.

In these early accounts of Black Hawk's captivity, the fantasy indulged most regularly with respect to his capture was perhaps the fact of his capture and its circulation, in print, as an emblem of control; a signal to readers, wherever they were, that Black Hawk and his accomplices presented no threat to the social and economic interests beholden to the operation of western markets. Both mining and farming in the Northwest had been disrupted by the circumstances of the so-called Black Hawk War; and while regional agriculture had not yet become the economic force that it would become in decades to follow, the disruption in lead mining and shipping—as well as its necessary disposition as projectiles—occasioned a sudden, dramatic spike in the price of ore.[15] Moreover, the movement of Native communities—the Rock River Sauk among them—near and along riparian systems entailed a necessarily defensive posture with respect to the transport of goods and people; likewise, the inscrutability of Native peoples' relationships to the Sauk rebellion—the uncertainty of who might, at any moment, become an ally, or a foe—brought into question their reliability as trading partners, links within the market infrastructures that had taken shape—and shaped—the Upper Mississippi Valley over decades if not centuries. As subjects within a physical, embodied set of market relations, Native people had an extraordinary capacity to assert themselves politically by withholding labor or otherwise disrupting trade. This potential made even more urgent the development of competing infrastructures of trade, the railroads and canals that shifted the regional economy from the south to the east, even as conflict with Native peoples threatened the viability of those projects. Reports of the conclusion of the war, of Black Hawk's capture and imprisonment were, in this crude sense, means of forestalling anxieties over the economic prospects of the west, announcements to investors that all was well, and the economic forces brought to bear upon the region were secure, as was its civilian settler population. Where reports from the massacre at Bad Axe left obscure the possibility of Black Hawk's fate, descriptions of his person established that the threat represented by his person was contained, rhetorically subsumed in a manner that reflected the supposition of his enclosure within the colonial security apparatus.

While fantasies of security rested upon the representation of the visual as the cage through which Black Hawk and the Prophet might be contained, these descriptions were equally occupied by the question of their physicality and what it might reveal about the Indian character; a means of attaining a form of security that rested in a consideration of how the physical form of face and body composed a text that might be read for indications of personality beyond prevarication. Confronted by the questions of Native purpose and the supposed inscrutability of Native peoples, amateur forays in nineteenth-century US race science, abetted by renewed interest in the ostensibly learned discourse of physiognomy, sought to probe for insight into the Indian character through a focus on face and deportment, dress and demeanor. Leaning on physiology and the correlation it posited between "the expressions of the face, its muscular action, and the passion . . . which causes both action and expression," with particular attention given to the shape of the eyebrows, descriptions of Black Hawk and the Prophet began with rough approximations of their head and face: the shape of the nose, the breadth of the mouth, the fullness of the lips.[16] Presumed as a universal grammar of human interiority, the author of the report read the Prophet's "broad face, short blunt nose, large full eyes, broad mouth, thick lips, [and] . . . full suit of hair" as evidence of "deliberate savageness," a cultivated propensity to violence "making him as the priest of assassination or secret murder." Touching upon the honorific bestowed by his popular name, by implication, Wabokieshiek becomes a false prophet, member of an infernal clergy dedicated to rituals of blood. Black Hawk, in turn, becomes like a ravenous bird: crowned by a small bunch of gray hair and distinguished by a "Roman" or aquiline nose, the writer puns on the Latinate meaning of aquiline as "eagle-like" to convey upon Black Hawk the physical characteristics of a bird of prey, albeit one that, like the Calumet eagle fan he is said to hold in his right hand, is dead or near dead, "thin, and . . . much dejected." Hewing to the familiar association between Indian and nature, and nature with animal, this description of Black Hawk plays upon a common grammar of Indian racial difference, effectively abrogating his subjectivity and the forms of Indigenous sovereignty that sustained it by inserting him within an ethnological framework of ineffable but undeniable racial characteristics.

Similar descriptions would appear in the western press as Black Hawk and his comrades embarked upon their tour of eastern cities the following spring.

> On our return from Saint Louis, about two weeks after our visit to the Barracks, we happened to be fellow-passenger to this city with the six warriors who passed here under guard to Washington. It will perhaps gratify the curiosity of some of our readers to give some of their names, and a short description of their persons, &c. Mack-ad-tama-sic-ac-ac, or Black Hawk, is apparently 50 years of age, about 5 feet 8 or 9 inches high, with rather broad shoulders; he has a low retreating forehead, sharp nose, somewhat hooked, chin slightly receding, cheeks a little hollow, and eyes of a dark hazel color; his vision is impaired, and he occasionally wears spectacles. The expression of his countenance is reserved and thoughtful, but sometimes appears cheerful and converses with animation. He wears at his side the skin of the bird from which he is named, and uses its long feathers as a fan. . . . He was described to us, by persons who have known him for years, as a man of amiable disposition, kind in heart, and of strict integrity.[17]

If the earlier descriptions of Black Hawk and the Prophet struck a note of barely contained menace, in this brief from the *Cincinnati Mirror*, the character of Black Hawk begins his journey from scourge of the west to avuncular eminence. While physiognomy is highlighted as a visual mark of racial character, the more fearsome aspects of Black Hawk's face are

softened by his demeanor, equal parts melancholy, considerate, and cheer-
ful, as well as the good reports of his integrity and his kindness. Four to
five inches taller than he was a year before, and at least a decade younger,
this Black Hawk is not the sickly, dejected captive presented in the pages
of *Niles' Weekly Register,* mute and inscrutable, but a wholly amiable intelligence, as indicated by his occasional use of corrective lenses. Where
the fan of tailfeathers might have betrayed Black Hawk's place within the
order of nature, his glasses marked him as belonging to the world of manufacture, even as their inclusion in the description of his countenance
ironized his name by underscoring a visual impairment. Not so brilliantly
sighted as a bird of prey, Black Hawk is neither eagle nor hawk, but rather
an all-too-relatable, all-too-human figure, an old man suffering a common affliction that was part of the shared inheritance of the body and its
physical vulnerabilities.

Black Hawk on Display

Passing reference to Black Hawk's eyeglasses only serves to underscore
the centrality of vision—of seeing and being seen, of looking, being shown,
of reading and consuming through the mechanism of the eye—to the
myriad social and cultural processes, the forms of ideological confabulation, routed through the 1833 tour and printed reports of the tour. Without question, the express purpose of the tour was to convey to the Sauk
architects of the so-called Black Hawk War the sheer power and indomi-
tability of the United States through the animation of what Luke Gibbons has called the *colonial sublime,* the exemplification of imperial
purpose through explicitly visual demonstrations of national treasure,
military capacity, transportation infrastructure, cities, and the sheer op-
ulence of the nation as registered in its material alterations to the physical environment. The colonial sublime appears here as the capacity of
the state and capital, the power to command and control, to set into motion, but also to arrest, to design and build structures that might stand
against the forces of both entropy and evolution, physical edifices that
might harness nature and stand fast against her mercurial complexion.[18]
What was perhaps not anticipated, however, was the impact that Black
Hawk's appearance would have among settlers, the ways in which the
physical bearing of Black Hawk and his men would come to fascinate.
"When we got to Baltimore the streets were filled with folks as thick as
the spruce tree down in your swamp. There we found Black Hawk a little,
old, dried up Indian king. And I thought folks looked at him and the
prophet about as much as they did at me and the President."[19]

Writing under his *nom de plume*, Major Jack Downing, the celebrated humorist Seba Smith offered this characterization of the excitement that attended Black Hawk's appearance in the East as a means of getting in a dig at the newly reelected president, Andrew Jackson; but Smith's jibe captured something less conspicuous: not merely the dynamics of collective attention channeled through the act of looking but the act of looking as involuntary, something compelled and compulsive. A physical manifestation of his notoriety, the crowds that waited to see Black Hawk disembark from his steamer to his carriage and hotel in New York City were so massive as to choke the streets. Describing his arrival, Black Hawk recalled, "We had proceeded but a short distance, before the street was so crowded it was impossible for the carriage to pass. The war chief then directed the coachman to take another street, and stop at a different house than the one we had intended. On our arrival here, we were waited upon by a number of gentlemen, who seemed much pleased to see us."[20] Among settlers, Black Hawk's appearances along the route of the tour served as a form of popular entertainment, drawing enormous crowds among the less reputable as well as curious figures among the more genteel. The attention he compelled spoke to a certain kind of majesty, of magnetism, a fascination that he projected, a quality that was, among settlers, no doubt bound up with myriad fantasies of Indigeneity, of Indianness and race, and the commodity version of the Indian as a curio, an object to be collected. At the same time, the fascination he invited was not in any clear or simple way reducible to these fabulations. While the character of Black Hawk may have been one in a long line of "noble savages" through which settlers sought to make space for themselves in the Americas through the fabrication of a lineal relationship to place, treating the figurative "Indian" as a cipher for the nation, some portion of the interest in Black Hawk and his company as public, material, enfleshed presences was derived from the pleasure of looking, of seeing; of a quasi-erotic longing to see that, while shaped and constrained by any number of racialist discourses and ideological fantasies, was not—is not—wholly reducible to any purpose or agenda, evoking a range of desires and anxieties unconstrained by ideological articulation within the social. As in the earliest descriptions of Black Hawk and the Prophet, some portion of these desires were directed toward domination, toward a form of mastery clothed in a consumer relation, as well as toward exposure, the penetration of a mystery.

These descriptions of Black Hawk and his men are notable for what they reveal about the desire to see as gives way before the desire to know, as well as the relationship between the desire to know and the desire for mastery; the desire for control, but also the desire to be controlled, the desire to be made subject of a master. "At a little after ten, D——came to take us to see the savages. We drove down, D——, my father, he and I, to their hotel. We found, even at that early hour, the portico, passage, and staircase, thronged with gazers upon the same errand as ourselves." Drawn from the journals of Fanny Kemble, the celebrated English stage actor who had, from 1832 through 1834, toured the United States as a performer, the passage highlights the question of sight, of the desire to consume Black Hawk through seeing; as well as the frustration of that desire by the "throngs" of "gazers" who block her path, each composing a piece of the architecture of seclusion mediating her access to Black Hawk. Physical impediments concealing Black Hawk and his company, the "portico, passage, and staircase" preserve a fantasy of his invisibility, his spectral relationship to the world, while the movement of the fellow "gazers" provides a trajectory along which to proceed, the prospect of moving toward him in sequence of successive unveilings, passing from the outside within: exposure as substitute for interiority. "We made our way, at length, into the presence-chamber; a little narrow dark room, with all the windows shut, crowded with people, come to stare at their fellow wild beasts. Upon a sofa sat Black Hawk, a diminutive, shriveled-looking old man, with an appearance of much activity in his shrunk limbs and a calmness and dignified self-composure in his manner that, in spite of his want of size and comeliness, was very striking."[21]

Waiting in line, Kemble and her father move "at length" into what she describes as "the presence-chamber . . . a little narrow dark room, with all the windows shut, crowded with people, come to stare at their fellow wild beasts." Conjuring the architectural features of aristocratic pretense, at the end of her mission to see Black Hawk, Kemble places him, as herself, within a space of regal eminence, the "presence-room" that serves as a receiving area for monarchs, a space of encounter between the monarch and his subjects. Playing upon a sense of majesty as enhanced by its ineffability, its seclusion from the unadorned conventions of casual display, Kemble produces Black Hawk as sovereign in a distinctively antique, distinctively European sense, while nonetheless mocking the pretense of sovereignty and its dependence upon rituals of display and concealment, the need to preserve the illusion of the sovereign and his integrity through the invisibility of his physical body. Black Hawk's physical deterioration— diminutive, shriveled, old—reveals the hollow place within the fictions of European sovereignty, while the extraordinary fuss around the unexceptional scene betrays power in its relation to the operations of desire, the desire to see and to be seen, to expose and be exposed, lending itself to the auratic dimensions of power as a means of compelling allegiance.

If the desire to see Black Hawk was, in part, about containing and controlling, exploring ways of asserting mastery, Kemble's account of this scene illustrates a far nimbler sense of the ways in which seeing and being seen opened themselves onto less immediately admissible, less easily tractable elements of longing. Both a stage actor and an English subject, Kemble was well attuned to the dynamics of sovereignty not as a kind of democratic abstraction or legal conceit, a means of tendering and enacting control, but as bound up in the person or body of the sovereign as something to behold or to be concealed. Sovereignty here is not merely the capacity to command, but the capacity to command as a function of the ability to marshal affect and compel the gaze. Black Hawk, in Kemble's rendering, is both sovereign and savage; but so are those who have come to see him and be seen by him. Those who have come to gaze at "their fellow wild beasts" are necessarily prey as well as predators. In her rendering, to realize the desire to see through the act of seeing necessarily opens oneself up to exposure, while suggesting an unexpressed desire to be seen, to be exposed. The desire for mastery here opens onto the longing for submission, the longing for eyes to meet, and in meeting, to be enthralled, revealed, prone. As befitting her vocation, Kemble does not forget what most of the crowd that has come to see Black Hawk does not know: the audience may be there to see the performers, but the performers are looking back at the audience, as well.

Leering, Lingering, Wanting

Similar elements of desire were at play in many of the earlier, physically descriptive accounts of Black Hawk and his men—reports that, in seeking to display Black Hawk and his retinue to a readership, unwittingly revealed a complex of disparate, often antithetical, libidinal investments within the scene of encounter.

> We were politely attended by one of the officers, who acted as our cicerone on the occasion, and ushered us into the apartments of the prisoners, where we beheld a dozen red men, lolling in lazy indifference upon platforms, elevated a few feet above the floor, and serving in threefold capacities of bedsteads, tables, and chairs. We were immediately struck with admiration at the gigantic and symmetrical figures of most of the warriors, who seemed, as they reclined in native ease and gracefulness, with their half naked bodies exposed to view, rather like statues from some master hand than like beings of a race whom we had heard characterised [sic] as degenerate and debased.

We extended our hands, which they arose to grasp, and to our question, "How d'ye do?" they responded in the same words, accompanying them with a hearty shake.[22]

As in Kemble's description of her encounter with Black Hawk, this description from the *Cincinnati Mirror* begins with stagecraft, the writer eagerly "ushered" into the rooms where the men were held by an officer acting as "cicerone." Transforming a space of captivity and enclosure into a space of display, the word "usher" presents the scene as one of theatrical performance, of a curtain being raised, while "cicerone" renders the jailer as a guide and the men themselves antiquities for leisurely contemplation, "statues from some master hand" that have been salvaged from the debris of some ancient past. Summoning a Greco-Roman appreciation for the proportions of the male form (the descriptions of the men as "half naked bodies" "reclining in native ease and gracefulness" along surfaces that are simultaneously tables, chairs, and beds), the writer engages, simultaneously, in a racializing, ableist discourse of anatomical correctness—of symmetricality as a metric of beauty if not necessarily intelligence—while evoking a prurient, homoerotic interest that makes the men and the space of their captivity into objects of a discretely sexualized desire. Antiquarian intrigue becomes the guise in which erotic passion is manifest. Clasping hands with the reporters from the *Mirror*, the Native men are made into the subjects of this exchange, the unnamed writer overwhelmed by their purposeful demonstrations of seductive physicality.

After the salutations were over, we had leisure to observe more closely the appearances of these sons of nature: they were clad in leggins [*sic*] and moccasins of buckskin, and wore blankets which were thrown around them in the manner of the Roman toga, so as to leave their right arms bare; when reclining or lying down, they generally allowed the blankets to fall from them. The youngest among them were painted on their necks, with a bright vermillion color, and had their faces transversely streaked with red and black stripes. From their bodies, and from their faces and eyebrows, they pluck out the hair with the assiduous care; they also shave or pull it from their heads, with the exception of a tuft of about three fingers' width, extending from between the forehead and the crown to the back of the head; this they sometimes plait into a queue on the crown, and cut the edges of it down to an inch in length, and plaster it with vermillion paint, which keeps it erect and gives it the appearance of a cock's comb. The time and great care bestowed by them at their toilette, would put the foppery of the most civilized beau completely to the blush. . . . [The] slightest pimple visible on their faces awakens their anxious solicitude, and they proceed to eradicate, or erase it with all possible dispatch. . . . The hands of all of them are very delicate, and their feet very small; they walk erect and firmly, treading like freemen; some of them wear collars of brass around their necks, and bracelet of the same upon their arms. Their ears are bored all round the edges and strung with beads that cause them to bend with their weight. . . . They performed the duties of valet-de-chambre for each other, with a punctilious nicety, rendering every assistance with the utmost alacrity and good will.[23]

Within this weirdly, wildly homoerotic portrait of Black Hawk's compatriots, the half-naked reclining bodies become solicitous toward one another, commanding one another's attention through the fastidiousness of the toilette and the need to be assisted in the proper application of the physical, bodily, and sartorial trappings of foppery. Painting, plucking, pimples, and blush: the men engage in a mutual ablution through which they are feminized. This is figured through their attention to hair removal and makeup, depilation and paint, both elements necessary to the performative elaboration of femininity. No mere tokens, here, the significance of hair and makeup rest in the ways in which they solicit and command the gaze; the ways in which they are used to refigure the face and the body to compel people to look; and the ways in which the work of reconfiguring the visage necessitates looking as self-regard, looking into mirrors, seeing reflections.

The writer, of course, sees what the writer wants to see: longing does not emerge as a function of the object but through he who looks upon and consumes the object. Leaving aside, for the moment, the more sensational aspects of this portrait, what the writer sees, what the writer desires, may well be suffused by homoerotic longing; but it is a longing that emerges through a portrait of men engaged in a particularly affectionate form of community, a wildcat congress or impromptu senate, a space in which the "Roman toga" claims the conditions of their captivity as the substance of a balneum, a bath. The longing that informs and orients this textual portrait of Black Hawk and his men becomes even more explicit in the description that follows the misattributed characterization of Native foppery, as the writer dwells at length upon the body of Black Hawk's eldest son, a figure he identifies as "Jack."

The one among them who attracted our attention, perhaps more than any other, was JACK, the eldest son of Black Hawk. He is in his twenty-fourth year, about six feet and two inches in height, with a clear open countenance, high cheek bones, an aquiline nose, chiseled mouth and chin, and eyes the most brilliant, and the most frank in their expression, we have ever beheld. His figure seemed to be made up of Apollo and Hercules combined. He stood among the rest like a monarch among princes. We approached him, and he suffered us to take off his blanket, and at our intimation, he divested himself of one of his leggins, and placed himself in an attitude, with his head erect, his noble chest breasting out, his right arm as in the act of striking, and his body resting upon his right foot, with his left thrown back, and the ball of it slightly pressing the ground—his left arm hanging carelessly at his side. He smiled, evidently much pleased at our admiration of him, and as he smiled,

"He gave his lip that speaking air
As if a word were hovering there."

He appeared to be the very model of him, described by the Poet, as one on whom

"——— each god had set his seal
To give the world an assurance of a man."

Had there not been wanting in his countenance that peculiar expression which emanates from a cultivated intellect, and which education alone can give, we could have looked upon him as the living personification of our *beau ideal* of manly beauty and perfection.[24]

While the description of Jack's countenance ("high cheek bones, an aquiline nose, chiseled mouth and chin") displays the typical concern with the physiognomic rendition of the Sauk captives that occurred throughout print accounts of the 1833 tour, the delight the writer takes in Jack's eyes ("the most brilliant . . . the most frank in their expression") spills over into the delight the writer takes in letting his eyes linger over the surface of Jack's body. Content before to merely watch as the men lolled about, playfully exposing themselves before their guests, here, the writer crosses the proscenium and becomes a character in the play he has imagined himself watching, approaching Jack so to divest him of his blanket and his leggings, before commanding him to stand and assume a pose of command. Partially naked, if not fully exposed, the writer dwells upon the nobility and proportions of Jack's body, which again assumes the aspect of tumescence. "His head erect, his noble chest breasting out, his right arm as in the act of striking," Jack stands like "a monarch among princes," the physical embodiment of the phallus as a metaphor of patriarchal eminence, the strength of regal bearing. Pursuing his insistent translation of the space of captivity into one of theatricality and antiquarian intrigue, the writer presents the character of Jack as a statuesque figure, a graven effigy to the deity of manly beauty; unlike his beautiful but supine comrades, Jack stands rigid, stony, erect. Described as both "Apollo and Hercules combined," Jack is not merely handsome but near to the "*beau ideal*" of "manly beauty and perfection," a living image of the *kouroi*, the name later given to ancient Greek images of beardless boys of whom Apollo was the apotheosis. Ostensibly delighted by the attention he receives, for the writer, Jack is all too willing to assume a pose appropriate to Greco-Roman statuary as a means of soliciting admiration; his smile, he suggests, betrays his roguish amusement, the ghost of his desire, his appreciation at being seen, passing along the surface of his "chiseled mouth and chin."

Drawing upon the Greek lyric poet Anacreon and his ode to the slave dancer Bathyllus, the reporter offers a cheeky admission of his own longing to be consumed. While the couplet "He gave his lip that speaking air / As if a word were hovering there" suggests lips gently open, paused in contemplation—of a canny silence preceding eloquent speech—the lines immediately preceding this couplet evoke nothing quite so elevated as the desire to engage in forms of oral eroticism. "Then for his lips, that ripely gem— / But let thy mind imagine them! / Paint where the ruby cell uncloses, / Persuasion speaking among the roses."[25] Anacreon's meaning, in this passage, is not particularly obscure. Playing upon ancient techniques of manufacturing lip coloring from pulverized gems, as well as the contemporary Greek world's association of colored lips with prostitution and oral sex, in calling to Eros in ecstatic contemplation of Bathyllus's lips, Anacreon's request that the "ruby cell" be painted—presumably from the crushed pieces of his "ripely gem"—is a not-so-thinly veiled call for Bathyllus to be made sexually available to him as a receptive partner in oral copulation, to announce himself as a vessel for Anacreon's desire. "Persuasion speaking among the roses," likewise, speaks to the role of oral play in anal eroticism; the rose, in question, gesturing to the "unclosing" of the anus.

Omitting these elements of Anacreon's verse, the writer, in his description of Jack for the Cincinnati *Mirror*, elaborates the Greco-Roman frieze in which Black Hawk and his companions were presented for contemporary readers, while refusing to bring into account the necessarily homoerotic dimensions of that culture and its imagery; he is locking Jack and the others into a fantasy of aesthetic indifference for which the appreciation of the physical form of another entails no engagement with the realm of bodily sensation or physical gratification. Jack becomes a paragon; he is exemplary, a body whose surfaces preserve the objective ideal of charm and splendor. Beauty, here, is objectified, removed from any consideration of its ephemeral specificity, its emergence in the relationship between lover and beloved, and in the comportment of one to the other, the illumination of one by another. That Jack, for the writer, is the objective embodiment of a type is made clear by the otherwise unaccountable curiosity of his name and the ways in which it circumscribes his memory of these encounters with the Sauks. While identified as Black Hawk's eldest son, no man named Jack traveled with Black Hawk, and no person named Jack is identified by that name elsewhere in press accounts of the tour. Black Hawk's eldest son was named Naseaskuk, an appellation by which he was generally known in the press; indeed, he appears, under this name, later in the article from the *Mirror*, where he is described in less overtly flattering terms than his doppelganger. "His second son, Na-see-as-kuck, or the Thunder-cloud . . . bears a strong resemblance to his brother Jack, both in feature and in form, but is far from being so handsome."[26] Recorded after an encounter not more than two weeks following the reporter's initial meeting in Saint Louis, here, the reporter mistakes Naseaskuk for an entirely different person than the one he had so admired earlier. Where, as Jack, in Saint Louis, Naseaskuk had inspired an extraordinarily fulsome description of his physical beauty, encountered here, in Cincinnati, Naseaskuk is dismissed as the second son, an inferior likeness, less the radiant eminence of Jack than the "Thunder-cloud" that can only temporarily eclipse his brightness.

This instance is noteworthy for what it conveys about the relationship between the desire to see and what is seen, between wanting to see and seeing what one wants. In his description of Jack, the writer represents himself as in control of the scene. The men are imprisoned, lying prone; he is unencumbered, free to observe; he directs the action to his whim, "suffering" Jack to stand, to pose, to take off his clothes. He admires, and Jack is the glowing recipient of this admiration, taking pleasure in being appreciated unsullied by "a cultivated intellect." Unlike the anonymous writer, who would assert that his appreciation of Jack is of a wholly intellectual, aesthetic character, Jack experiences the pleasure of exposure as a form of arousal, the casual smile betraying his delight in being made an object for such contemplation. For the writer, Jack is not involved in the staging of this scene; he is possessed, a player who is merely carrying out his directions. This confidence in his capacity to direct the scene, to exert his control over the men, illuminates a fantasy of invisibility, his presence, at the scene, as the unseen, all-seeing eye, a fantasy underscored by his writerly anonymity, his material absence from the page as anything other than a narrative presence. By indulging this fantasy, however, he misses all the ways in which Jack is coauthor of this spectacle; all of the ways, that is, in which Jack's performance is calculated to delight the writer, the ways in which Jack makes himself the mirror of the writer's desire, reflecting that which he wishes to see. He does not see that he is being looked at; that he is being seen. Staging this vignette of encounter around the denial of an erotics of vision, the *Mirror* relays something of "the actual history of our plural existence" and the varieties of its deferral, the ways in which print replicated the structure of the enclosure through the unacknowledged narrative frame and the displacements through which it was produced. Figuratively transforming Black Hawk and his men, most especially his son "Jack," into antiquarian statuary, reports like these secured the Sauks not only as subjects of state authority, but as figures of unruly desire, refusing their entanglement with settlers as creatures of desire not fully reducible or captured by the logic of capital or the fictions of the state.

Some aspect of the coauthorship of these moments, of the mutuality of looking and looking back, is captured by anecdotes that were repeated throughout contemporary media correspondence, concerning the Sauk captives "sitting" for the infamous portraitist of Native people, George Catlin. Catlin made his first ethnological foray up the Missouri River in the year immediately prior to the so-called Black Hawk War, and he returned to Saint Louis during the months that Black Hawk and his companions were imprisoned at Jefferson Barracks. While in residence, Catlin finished portraits of Black Hawk as well as Naseaskuk, the Prophet, and his brother Neapope, and accounts of the sittings emphasized the ways in which the Native men were keen to persecute Catlin, emphasizing not merely the fact that they could see him but demanding to be portrayed, to be seen, in particular ways.

Naa-pope, or Broth, the brother of the Prophet, and some years his junior, resembles him in height and figure, though he is not so robust, and his face is more sharp; in wickedness of expression they are *par nobile fratrum*. We were informed that when Mr. Catlin, the artist, was about taking the portrait of Naa-Pope, he seized the ball and chain that were fastened to his leg, and raising them on high, exclaimed with a look of scorn, "make me so and show me to the great Father." On Mr. C's refusing to paint him as he wished, he kept

varying his countenance with grimaces, to prevent him from
catching a likeness.[27]

A similar report appeared in the *New-York Mirror.*

> [Black Hawk's] dress . . . is that which he wore during his confine-
> ment, and the pipe and fan which he holds in his hand, he was, for a
> long time, never seen without—believing, probably, that carrying
> these things, rather than anything like a weapon, would be thought
> by the officers under whose charge he was, as an evidence that he
> considered himself and his nation no longer at war. . . . As a proof of
> the matter, the following fact is stated: recently, while a painted of
> some celebrity (Catlin) was, with permission of the commanding
> officer, engaged in painting the likenesses of the principle chiefs who
> were confined at Jefferson barracks, he proposed to Black hawk, that
> he should be represented with a spear, as being more emblematical of
> his recent pursuits. "No!" said the Black Hawk, apparently indignant
> at the proposal, "no spear for me! I have forever done with spears!" . . .
> Nah-Pope, another Sauk chief, notorious for his bitter, implacable and
> unforgiving hatred of the white Americans . . . was deemed necessary
> to confine in chains. [Catlin], when about to commence the likeness
> of Nah-Pope, asked him if he chose to have his pipe (as the Black
> Hawk had done) represented! The chief stooped down, took up his
> chain, wound it round his arm, and struck it two or three times
> violently, "There," said he, "paint that! And let the Americans see
> that they have Nah-pope—a prisoner, and in irons!" The command-
> ing officer (General Atkinson) answered that there could not be the
> smallest objection to this, so that the painter also placed in the other
> hand, a representation of the scalps of women and children, taken by
> him during the war.[28]

Where much of the coverage of Black Hawk and his men was delivered by anonymous writers, staring longingly at supine figures and telling readers what they saw, in these passages, readers are presented with
a scene of seeing, of Catlin looking, and being looked at. Black Hawk and
Neapope, in these anecdotes, are not passive vessels of antiquarian interest, posed as objects of aesthetic contemplation; they are actively presenting themselves, soliciting the attention of others by taking command of
the scene of their exposure, contorting themselves into different shapes
in response to those who they imagine to be looking. With Catlin, they
are composing a record of their encounter, meeting his gaze and projecting what he wants, while considering how their images will appear

before others. As printed, these anecdotes seem to be meant as stories about duplicity, about Indians as mendacious cheats. As read, they tell a story about wanting to see and wanting to know, of the longing to know as it is met and arrested in the unknowability of another; of the longing that emerges in that moment, and the fear. Whatever his pretense of anthropological integrity, Catlin is entangled in a relationship in which the objectivity of his portrait is inherently corrupted by the desire of the other. Not only is he looking and describing, sketching and coloring, he is being looked at, wearing the burden of the hostility and the anger, the loneliness and the pain of defeat and captivity.

A significant portion of the coverage of the tour was dedicated to looking at Black Hawk looking, trying to discern what he was looking at, what he saw, and how he felt about it. In the July 13, 1833 issue of the *New-York Mirror*, a lengthy description of Black Hawk's travels along the East Coast were included with what purported to be the first lithographic reproduction of Black Hawk's image served to a reading public. "For this purpose we subsidized a genuine Boswell, the sole business of whose life for many years past has consisted in attaching himself to the skirts of great men, worming himself into their confidence, and placing a record all the foolish things they ever said or did in their lives. We flatter ourselves that the labours of this useful and industrious person . . . cannot but prove highly piquant."[29] Playfully referencing Dr. Johnson's haplessly well-fated, if ill-regarded biographer, the *Mirror* elevates Black Hawk to a man of some distinction, one worthy of being made the subject of a biography by another distinguished personality, no matter how thoroughly debased or ridiculous. Just as the image of Black Hawk reproduced by the *Mirror* was a far from reliable likeness of the person it sought to capture, their assigned Boswell's anecdotes are highly suspicious, written as comic anecdotes presenting Black Hawk as vulgar and gross, his misadventures offering a running commentary on the absurdity of presenting a savage with the trophies of civilization. Of these, many included anecdotes in which the charm and frivolity of bourgeois ladies, unaccustomed to common sense because of their socialization to the drawing room, found themselves on their receiving end of less than salutary overtures. "Among the ladies who honored him with their attention, was one remarkable for her fine hair, who made him a present of a tomahawk. Black Hawk patted her on the head and observed to his son, '*Ouascolendamauo*'—'What a beautiful head for scalping!'"[30]

Similar scenes were reported at almost every stop along the tour, as anecdotes about women coming to admire the men, presenting them gifts or being presented gifts in return, only to recoil in horror at having occasioned some unwanted solicitation. Boswell reports one such instance. "Being much pleased with the attentions of a lady, he presented her with a scalp of a white woman of the frontier, which adhered to a beautiful tuft of long black hair, desiring her to wear it for his sake, this being the quintessence of gallantry among his countrymen. Observing the lady shrink from the keepsake, he uttered in a great huff—'*Malatchiliche*'—'What a malicious squaw!'"[31] In Boswell's account, these instances were part of larger scenes in which Black Hawk and his retinue were confronted by crowds of admirers, none of whom he was fully able to appreciate.

> At Washington, Black Hawk was much annoyed by the ladies, who seem to have nothing to do but attend debates in congress, trials for murder, and run after great men. On one occasion he got out of all patience, and observed to the prophet—"*Debilinchbison jekoree manitou*"—What in the d[evi]l's name do these squaws want of me?
>
> He was still more savage at the crowds of men, who intruded into his room and stood gaping at him, as if he had been a mammoth. On one of these occasions he emphatically exclaimed—"*Eteone assin!*"—"What a pack of asses!"
>
> Black Hawk being carried away to the theater in Philadelphia, managed to sleep through the play, until the applauses of the audience at the song of "Jim Crow" waked him up. He endured the first repetition with tolerable resignation; but on its being encored for the fourth time louder than ever, cried out . . . "When those barbarians come to visit me I shall treat them to a concert of wild cats."[32]

As tales of Black Hawk's misadventures during the later stages of the tour, Boswell's observations are reliable evidence of nothing but their own racist preoccupations with Black Hawk as insufficiently capable of appreciating the scenes to which he was exposed, including that novel and inexplicably popular entertainment, blackface minstrelsy. Even in those instances when Black Hawk is sufficiently impressed by feminine charms as to be inspired to some act of gallantry, he is exposed in his incapacity for appreciating the norms of civilized courtship, presenting a grotesque trophy of his conquests from which all decent people recoil in horror. While related as a series of anecdotes about seeing Black Hawk, as read, what becomes notable is the extent to which Black Hawk's dismay, at every point, is roused in moments where he is exposed as seeing, whether that is to appreciate the beauty or frivolity of women—themselves disposed to lose themselves in a variety of entertainments and pastimes—or the gawking, admiring men who storm into his quarters; or, the absurdity of the Jim Crow as a spectacle of epidermal pigmentation, of cork-ash blackness, presented as popular entertainment. Although dismissive of Black Hawk's capacity as a subject of the gaze, Boswell's concern for what he was seeing, in what he was seeing and how he was reacting, was reflected in yet other accounts of the tour.

> THE SIAMESE TWINS, being at Cleveland, Ohio, were visited by Black Hawk and his party, who seemed much interested in seeing them, and asked many questions. Black Hawk addressed the twins, (through the interpreter), for five minutes or more. The substance of the address was—"That he and his friends had heard of the twins, and having been very anxious to see them that they felt pleased in having their wishes gratified."
>
> He said "the Great Spirit had made them as they were, and would protect them and be their guide and protector, should they again cross the great waters."—The concluding phrase was, "the Great Spirit will call both to him at once."
>
> The Indians sat with the twins for nearly fifteen minutes.
>
> He added "that he would show to his red bretheren the portrait which they had presented to him, and would tell them what he and his friends had seen."[33]

Like the anecdote of Black Hawk brought before the minstrel show, this story is compelling, in no small part, for the historical interest of people who had been made public curiosities meeting one another, the odd happenstance of Black Hawk and his men brought face-to-face with Chang and Eng Bunker, still relatively early in their careers as independent performers. Of more present interest, however, is the emphasis this report places upon Black Hawk's wanting to see—his "interest," his anxiety—as well the assurance he offers that he will present the twins' portrait to "his red brethren" with the promise that he will "tell them what he and his friends had seen." Less occupied by what the Sauks or the Bunkers might have thought of each other, the report is more concerned to illustrate the fact that the Sauks were interested in seeing the Bunkers, that the sight of the Bunkers provoked as much interest for the Sauks as it did for those settlers who had made an object of their image. Seeking absolution for their own prurient interest in the sight of the conjoined Chinese twins—a spectacle of disability and medical curiosity, as well as the racially alien—the report seems to convey an equally perverse interest on the part of the Sauks, a union expressed through the desire to consume the alien, the other; yet it also reports a concern with tracking the Sauks' line of sight, of seeing what they are seeing, and of evading their gaze. Looking at Chang and Eng, the Sauks do not see those who look at them. The settlers observing this spectacle of spectacularizing go unnoticed; or, at the very least, are able to maintain the pretense of being unseen.

A fantasy of mastery, within the desire to evade the gaze is enfolded an equally potent wish to be seen and to be known, just as they who look—who seek to efface their looking—look to know, to penetrate the mystery of the other, here conveyed as evidence of Native intransigence. "This old Indian Chief and his associates have been the 'Lions of the day,' for the last fortnight. . . . They exhibited but little emotion at the greater part of the curiosities they were induced to visit, but at times were aroused from the studied apathy of Indian character."[34] Cited as prelude to one of its accounts of Black Hawk's time in Philadelphia and New York, unlike the burlesque composed by Boswell, this passage from the *Saturday Evening Post* drew upon received wisdom of the impassive Indian to highlight the effectiveness of the tour as a deterrent, trying to gauge the impact of the colonial sublime through a consideration of the changed expressions of the otherwise inscrutable Native party.

> The Manufacture of glass, on their visit to Dyott's Glass Works, appear to gratify them more than anything else in the city. Immediately after their arrival at Congress Hall, they were placed at the front windows to gratify the immense crowd, which thronged the streets in a dense mass as far as the eye could reach. Black Hawk observing the extraordinary curiosity manifested by the people, made them [a] speech, through his interpreter. . . . He saw the strength of the white men. . . .
>
> In noticing the visit of Black Hawk and his companions to the Navy Yard, at Norfolk, the Herald observes:
> "They did not appear to be particularly struck with any thing they saw, until they were carried on board the Delaware 74, where they expressed their astonishment and delight by their gestures and their exclamations; and Black Hawk himself, even more affected at the wonders of the noble ship than his more youthful companions, asked to be shown the man who made this 'great canoe,' that he might take him by the hand! In passing the bow of the Delaware, in a barge, on their way back, the figurehead, which is a representation of a colossal Indian warrior, attracted their attention, and elicited from them the most extravagant manifestations of surprise and pleasure.[35]

Mastery over this scene—the sovereignty of the settler and, by extension, the sovereignty of the state—inheres in the capacity to distract, to compel the eye of another to observe that which one wishes or to present to another a sight that demands attention and appreciation. Command over the other emerges, here, in the substitution of the sublime for the self, the singular. Whether manufactured or monstrous, the things Black Hawk and his men are made to see, the things with which they are presented, are meant to tell a story about the state, a story told through substitution; a story told by distracting from the presence of the storytellers and by distracting the storytellers from their presence within the scene they have staged. Distracting the Sauks, the settlers that contrived these scenes are spared the burden of meeting their gaze, of being caught up in it, of meeting the fear of annihilation of looking as a form of violation, as well as the annihilation entailed in meeting the gaze as an expression of surrender, of being rendered supine before another, prone. This reading of the fiction of US sovereignty emerging through the purposeful misdirection of the gaze, of the refusal of seeing and being seen as an instance of encounter enfolding the material, embodied history of our plural existence, suggests a mode of seeing and being seen that encodes and enacts a purposefully abstracted, restricted field of vision, one resonant with the calculating machine of the state.

This aspect of the control of seeing and the expression of countersovereignty—of purposefully distracting from the fissures of countersovereignty—is addressed, obliquely, in the *Post*'s report from Philadelphia, which touches briefly on a visit Black Hawk and his men made to Eastern State Penitentiary. "The whole of the deputation visited the Water Works on Tuesday, and subsequently were taken to the Cherry Hill Prison, and shown the manner in which white men punish. The exhibition of arms and ships at the Navy Yard, led the Hawk to remark that he suspected the Great Father was getting ready for a war."[36] Moving between a site of municipal improvement, an early attempt at harnessing steam power to the engineering of an urban water system—an ostensibly progressive space of incarceration and punishment and a site dedicated to the mass and manufacture of weaponry—the Sauks, on one Tuesday in June, were directed to explore different monumental sites of state power and different instances of the biopolitical: the guardianship of health, the installation of self-discipline through punishment, and the instantiation of law through the spectacularization of the martial as a presence and a potential. Each a monument in itself, all of these sites are also spaces of misdirection, of camouflage and obstruction as used to obscure the workings of, the fissures within, the operations of power. Built on the Schuylkill River to direct and store water in reserve for Philadelphia, the Fairfield Water Works was constructed to provide a consistent source of water for the expanding city through an extraordinary feat of nineteenth century engineering, of steam and tubes and wheels; yet it was fronted by a spectacularly misleading Greco-Roman façade that obscured the mechanisms by which it carried out its purpose, hiding its necessarily unreliable technological apparatus behind a series of grand colonnades. For its part, the Eastern State or Cherry Hill Penitentiary was the first prison built upon the Quaker model of punishment as reform, an uncanny application of quasi-Benthamite principles of discipline through isolation and contemplation. Like the Panopticon Bentham proposed, Cherry Hill was designed to minimize prisoners' field of vision as a means of forcing them to look within, to search for the signs of the spirit and its movement as the seed of conscience, the beginning of true social and spiritual transformation.

Where Benthan imagined a Panoptic formation in which the fiction of being looked at was sufficient to condition the prisoner in his own regime of self-observation, the form of power suggested by the Eastern State Penitentiary, the techniques of observation directed toward Black Hawk and his men suggest a far more anxious relation to the totality of power, a greater concern with the fissures within social formations; the fissures that condition and constrain power, that constrain normative forms of political sovereignty, and its claims upon the social. Reference to "the studied apathy of Indian character," or "the Indian characteristic of being surprised at nothing," betray a mark of this anxiety, and the ways in which it troubles those who came into contact with Black Hawk, those who recorded his person and its relation with their ostensibly alien world. In contemporary news accounts, the writers who surround Black Hawk track his gaze obsessively as a means of evaluating how well the ruse holds up, how completely he and his men submit to the fictions which are set before them, the story that is being told about the United States as a sovereign power and, indirectly, the story that is being told about the poverty of Native peoples, the incapacity of Indigenous sovereignty to articulate a political community. The writers' oscillation between disappointment in the Sauks' reaction and their hyperbolic assessment of the Sauks' wonder—"their astonishment and delight"—suggest the shape of their own anxieties over the fictions of sovereignty and state power, their desperate need to assure themselves, through their Native captives, of the certainty of their claims, the assurance of their invulnerability. The threat of being looked at, of Black Hawk returning the gaze, here betokens not fear of attack but the fear of being exposed; the fear of ridicule and doubt; the fear of the raised eyebrow and sidelong glance of suspicion and disbeliefs.

Questions regarding mastery over the Sauks' field of vision, over what it is they see and how they interpret what they are seeing, trouble these reports as they reflect upon the mutual regard between Black Hawk and his men and the massive crowds that gathered to see them. Again, describing the throng that attended their arrival in Philadelphia, the *Evening Post* wrote:

> Not only were the house and yard thus blocked up, but the street itself was rendered almost impassable by the crowds that waited to catch a glimpse at Black Hawk or his son. All ages and conditions mingled in the crowd. . . . During the extraordinary manifestation of curiosity which the citizens displayed, the companions of Black Hawk sat near him, with features strongly marked, and wearing on their painted lips an expression very like that of scorn. The manner of these naties of the western wilds is majestic and serene. The Indian characteristic of being surprised at nothing, is plainly exhibited in the indifference which they manifest at anything which is passing about them.
>
> By a judicious stroke of policy, the tour of the chiefs, (who have been held as hostages for the good conduct of their countrymen,) has been arranged to follow in the wake of the President, to give them an idea of the strength and numbers of their white brethren.[37]

Like the miniatures sketched of Black Hawk and the Prophet earlier in their travels, the confidence with which this passage closes evokes a degree of control predicated on enclosure, the capture of the Sauks within a cage that restricts their gaze and allows them to see only that which they are allowed to see, only that which is presented to them, for their edification as subjects of the disciplinary regime of the state. The crowds that gather to see them, as such, appear before them as if summoned by command, dutifully following the coattails of Andrew Jackson so that the assembled whites might appear, for the Sauks, as yet another element of the colonial sublime, a corporate figure of state power embodied as a racialized body. This confidence is again shaken in the face of the studied impassivity of the Sauks who, for the writers observing and reporting on them, refuse to exhibit any degree of interest or concern, much less surprise. Confronted by their inability to read the Sauks, to see and to know, the writer retreats into the certainty that such a scene cannot help but convey, for the Sauks, a sense of the "strength and numbers of their white brethren." That the size of these crowds might inspire awe or fear is plausible enough yet undermined by reports of Black Hawk's routine attempts at extemporaneous public speaking, his—at times—overly solicitous addresses to public assemblies. "How do you do? How do you do all? The Great Spirit above knows that I love you and that my heart is with you all."[38] Reporting from Black Hawk's arrival in New York, upon disembarking his steamboat and ascending the Battery, the *Evening Post* reported these words as evidence of Black Hawk's awe in the face of the wonders of civilized Manhattan, having just witnessed a hot air balloon flight staged for his edification, and accompanied by requisite fireworks. Read as a sincere declaration of love, a solicitation of interest in the good of the other and of an expressed mutuality of feeling, the statement becomes much more deeply threatening, an expression of fidelity to a vision of communion with others that is not circumscribed by necessity or discipline, but that opens onto generosity and concern, an economy of the common. Looking out upon the crowds gathered to greet him, rather than fear, it is equally plausible that what Black Hawk felt was power; or, perhaps, the kind of intimacy that can only emerge in the space of the unadorned, the indiscrete, the improper and unregulated.

This is the fear that stalks each of these reports, the fear that draws together concern over the person of Black Hawk as objectified for the purposes of security and control, the fear that haunts the erotics of the gaze and the ways in which it troubles bodies, surfaces, and the ideologies that inhere within, whether they indicate something about the nature of gender or of race: the fear of the crowd—of the assembled—not as a disciplined subject of a racialized entertainment, a forced perspective glimpse upon the other, the different, but the crowd as the subject of the inchoate, the different; the subject of another form of sovereignty, one momentarily articulate in the instance of a seemingly chivalrous declaration of love. Violating all norms of propriety, the spaces brought into being by the presence of the Sauks were "crowded . . . by those who seemed to think that the importance of the occasion removed all considerations of private privileges." In these spaces, "all ages and conditions and both sexes mingled" in defiance of all conventions of social distinction, united and enthralled by one another, seeking something in one another that they themselves have not yet identified, tracing the limitations of the conventions to which they are beholden, and the spaces and possibilities of something otherwise, its image fleeting and indistinct, but nonetheless palpable in the moment of encounter.

Conclusion

The production of the Black Hawk War through its reproduction in print was coextensive with the forms of enclosure and extraction that emerged at the intersection of settler colonialism and capital. Part of a discourse of security, the language through which Black Hawk was captured in print reduced the socially relevant and necessarily unknow-able figure of Makataimeshekiakiak to a readily digestible object, a commodity fetish, cleaned, prepped, and ready for consumption. The commodity image of Black Hawk and his men participated in the enclo-sure of the visual, and the visual enclosure of Indigenous difference, ostensibly limiting the range of desires possible within the terms of in-dividual and social interactions, establishing the effectively racialized difference of Native peoples through their disqualification as objects of desire, through the foreclosure of desires that sought expression through the embrace of Native peoples. More vitally expansive than the frame of the commodity form, the desire to realize an otherwise, to live differently, continually undermined the forms of reification whereby the social world found its identity through a relationship with the continuity of property. The desire to see and be seen appears as the vexed realization of a queer desire for love and companionship and home that, as part of a nettle-some dialectical structure, find expression in the appearance of its op-posite, in the momentary resolution of the dialectic through the embrace of exile and awkwardness.

3 / Constantly at Their Weaving Work: Historiography and the Annihilation of the Body

Settler colonialism is an unending search for sustenance. Finding only meager offerings, a less than fulfilling meal, it refuses to eat. It becomes gaunt, pale, and grey. Frustrated, the desire for more sumptuous banquets finds consolation in the thin gruel of property, the settler home as the source of the least satisfactory aliment, nourishing but hardly inviting. Under these conditions, the settler stumbles into the house and bars the door. She makes amends with the dust. Drowsy yet sleepless, she settles into a dark corner, her face turned against the light. She watches the wall. She listens to the story the wall is telling. She looks for the lesson in the wall, finds solace in the wall, sees her own blank gaze reflected in the wall. She comes to recognize the wall as part of herself. She considers how these walls were built. She asks how she might build a better wall, a wall that is taller and stronger, a wall that one cannot see through or over or around. A wall behind which she might hide her wan visage, or the abject failures of those who promised to provide, their sorrows and their anger. She begins to build these walls with whatever is closest to hand. Her most available resource, the most rigid substance, she starts to recognize is the commons of language. She begins to build walls with words.

This chapter is about settler colonialism and the language by which settlers first built those walls. It is about the expropriation of words from the commons of language and their instrumentalization for purposes of colonialism and capital. It is about the words by which we sever relationships, the words by which we seek to be relieved of our obligations, to comfort ourselves for having given up our most sacred commitments to one another. It explores the words of disavowal, of refusal, the myriad forms of language by which "the actual history of our plural existence" was transformed into both a tragic fiction and a gothic romance. It examines the prose of counter-sovereignty through a consideration of the historiographic literature of the so-called Black Hawk War. It understands the prose of counter-sovereignty as shaped in reaction to the social and political continuities of Indigenous sovereignty, to the ways in which Indigenous sovereignty poses a material challenge to the principles of capitalism and liberalism as frameworks for the organization of social life around the drive for acquisition, possession, and accumulation. A technology of memory, part of a social and cultural struggle over the representation of the past that is contiguous with struggles over the reproduction of social relations in the present, this chapter takes the historiography of the Black Hawk War as a genre dedicated to the promulgation of a conceit, substantiating the fiction of the Black Hawk War as a means of stitching together the patchwork of US counter-sovereignty, overwriting and eclipsing the narrative techniques by which Indigenous peoples had long shaped, claimed, and inhabited place. As one element of an aggressively commercialized culture of print, the literature of the Black Hawk War, I argue, served as a staging ground through which to conjure the false intimacy of the nation through a fantasy of the social body as expressed by the family romance, mobilizing images of injury, pain, and blood to describe the feminized affectivity of the nation, while enacting the state as the bureaucratic terrestrial emissary of a righteous, patriarchal violence, an avatar of benevolent paternal solicitude. Confronted by social anxieties driven by contradictions of the market revolution—the continued valorization of yeoman agricultural independence in the face of the rampant concentration and proletarianization of agricultural labor within the slave plantations of the South as well as the collapse of customary forms of employment organized around apprenticeship as a pathway to proprietorship and mastery—the architects of racial capitalism sought remediation through the equation of identity with ownership; they tethered a vision of social and economic development to one of terrestrial expansion, while proffering a vision of patriarchal maturity manifest through the work, the material labor, of colonization. The subjects of settler colonialism were allowed to realize themselves as sovereign and self-possessed, recognized as mature citizens of a vibrant democracy, by collaborating in the debilitation of Native people and Native sovereignties; a debilitation that obscured the fissures endemic to the fictions of US counter-sovereignty through their articulation under the sign of the nation as a corporate body integrated through the patriarchal violence of the state. Haunted by the limits to their authority, both lineal and allegorical fathers trafficked in fantasies of disintegration and dismemberment, conjuring inebriate orgies and cannibal epicures gnawing away at the ligaments of the social body. The historiography of the Black Hawk War imagines this necrotic body, these cannibal rituals, as a means of collecting and assembling the broken pieces, putting them back together in the image of an ostensibly bloodless liberalism, united through the affective benevolence of the nation and sanctified by the righteous violence of the state.[1]

In what follows, I trace the articulation of this national body through three histories and one romance. The histories were published within the first decade after the conflict, some even as it was taking place; the romance appeared about fifteen years later, as the conflict with Black Hawk was swiftly becoming an object of nostalgia, its literature increasingly posed in the register of kitsch. Drawing upon William Edwards's setting of *The Narrative of the Capture and Providential Escape of Misses Frances and Elmira Hall* (1832), John Allen Wakefield's *History of the War Between the United States and the Sac and Fox Nation of Indians and Parts of Other Disaffected Tribes of Indians* (1834), Timothy Flint's *Indian Wars of the West* (1833), and Elbert Smith's *Ma-ka-tai-me-she-kia-kiak; or, Black Hawk, and Scenes in the West* (1838), I explore the relationships between rituals of blood and pain as well as ever more thoroughly redemptive visions of national collectivity, that is, visions of a nation sanctified through sacrifice and realized, defended, protected, and nurtured by the institutions of the state. The Hall narrative expresses the history of the so-called Black Hawk War as one of torture and rapine, barely restrained fantasies of annihilation, suffering, and murder that find resolution through the consolations of property and the state. Wakefield, in turn, refuses to countenance any suggestion that the conflict itself was not inherently defensive on the part of settlers, thus necessarily just, effectively projecting a vision of the west as the domain of a racial project dedicated to the prerogatives of whiteness as the antidote to class struggle. Flint, for his part, offers a theory of US history as a national history, one driven by the intractability of racial conflict. Sanctified in the crucible of Indian war, the settler, for Flint, appears as a redemptive force, an agent of empire who confronts the future as the eternal recurrence of race war, a force for regeneration that nonetheless tries the capacities of the nation and compels the diligent oversight of the state as the guardian of empire. Smith transforms this sanctified vision of nation and empire into a manual for investment and the redemption of capital, linking an erratic, if poetic vision of national sanctification and redemption to the realization of value through his own work and through his role as a booster for western development.

Rituals of Blood, Stories of Pain

Before it was known as the Black Hawk War, even as the events of the conflict were unfolding, accounts of what was transpiring on the Northwestern frontier had begun to circulate among an eastern readership. These accounts would shape the ways in which the conflict would be recalled—the ways in which it would be written about, told, remembered, alienated in language, and preserved for the future. Of these, perhaps the earliest and most significant—the one with the most immediate effect with respect to the organization of national conscience, to the formations of sympathy, and military policy—might well have been William P. Edwards's *The Narrative of the Capture and Providential Escape of Misses Frances and Elmira Hall*. Wildly sensational, chock-full of blood and gore and the intimation of sex, Edwards's *Narrative* was nonetheless packaged and sold as devotional literature, a latter-day contribution to the genre of the captivity narrative.[2] A modern synaxarion, the Hall narrative contributed to the sanctification of nation and state, drawing upon the trials and martyrdom of the Hall family as a means to articulate a national body, united in its vulnerability to violence and disease, made holy through the crucible of pain. The Hall narrative participated in the sanctification of the nation by illustrating its origins in rituals of bloodletting and sexual violence, attaching fantasies of annihilation to images of cannibal feasts and ritualized rape. "The preceding year . . . will be long remembered as a year of much human distress, and a peculiarly unfortunate one for the American nation—for while many of her most populous cities have been visited by that dreadful disease, the CHOLERA, and to which thousands have fallen victims, the merciless SAVAGES have been as industriously and fatally engaged in the work of human butchery on the frontiers." Likening Native demonstrations of martial force to the seemingly mercurial perambulations of *Vibrio cholerae*, the bacterium chiefly responsible for the transmission of Asiatic cholera, Edwards's introduction to the Hall sisters' narrative figures the former as a species of the latter, each an excrescence of the natural order, a pathogen to be eliminated from the biome. Both implacable foes, Native peoples, like cholera, are incapable of reason or restraint, transgressing frontiers and penetrating bodies, slowly but mercilessly undermining their integrity. Their broken bodies and the violence by which they were broken open the space for the birth of a new nation, a new body; a radiant figure, sutured through distress.

Drawing a parallel between Native violence and Asiatic cholera was both keenly racist and deeply ironic. The metaphorical relation Edwards posited drew upon all-too-common, colloquial, and pseudo-scientific associations between virulent illness and racial abjection; it obscured the historical, biophysical relationships that obtained between cholera and colonialism as well as the history of the geophysical secretions by which capital and empire had made those relationships particularly fecund. Although, in rare instances, cholera had been known to appear in eastern port cities, largely among sailors and stevedores, the spring and summer of 1832 saw the first ostensibly national cholera epidemic, one that impacted both the coast and the interior. Traveling along new pathways of transport and trade—the market infrastructures that drew the resources of the hinterland into communion with the port cities of the East Coast and the greater Atlantic world—weeks if not days after the first symptoms recorded in New York and Philadelphia, cases of cholera were reported in places like Buffalo, Detroit, and Chicago, all nodes in the transit network inaugurated by the completion of the Erie Canal seven years earlier. Part of a worldwide cholera pandemic occasioned, in no small part, by the acceleration of colonial resource extraction and the integration of global trade under the domination of the British empire, the 1832 US cholera epidemic was no doubt fueled by the increasingly routine and increasingly swift movement of goods and people across previously unimaginable distances and seemingly incongruous places. Among historians of epidemiology, there is general agreement that the speed with which cholera staked out its dominion in the United States was roughly proportional to the speed with which troops were mustered to meet Black Hawk on the battlefield; not content to follow the conduits of trade, cholera traveled with the infantry, making its way rapidly inland as a function of the movement of troops west along the infrastructures of capitalism and empire.[3]

A bacterial agent, indiscriminately sowing disease and death, cholera was a biogenic vector of US counter-sovereignty. Traveling along the routes of capitalist enterprise, it formed a piece of the biopolitical work of state formation, its epidemiology sketching the shape of the aspirant nation, mimicking the material and geophysical infrastructures that bound that polity, forming an inelegant, uncertain body. Contemporary ignorance concerning the disease and its etiology left cholera an exceedingly plastic trope, a vehicle serving the most unlikely and the most outrageous, speculative confabulations within literary culture, a ready metaphor linking illness and frailty, body and contagion, to nations, empires, injury, and invasion.[4] In his characterizations of Native peoples, Edwards took advantage of this trope and its elasticity, transposing expressions of Native sovereignty into acts of preternatural, savage villainy by evoking the inscrutability of the disease and its obstinate resistance to treatment. In its intransigence and implacability, cholera mirrored settler fantasies of Indians as vicious and bloodthirsty, indiscriminate in their choice of victims, utterly without sympathy, unwilling to entertain appeals. If cholera was, as many clergy insisted, a scourge sent by God to cleanse the nation of its sins, for Edwards, its avatar was the figure of the Indian. The diabolical instrument of divine will, the Indian was a demon set loose upon the earth to chastise the intemperate, the inebriate, the lecherous, and the faithless; to call the faithful to sobriety and resolve. Playing upon stereotypes of Indian drunkenness, in the narrative, Edwards underscores the association between settler intemperance and Indian malice, portraying the Pottawatomi raiding party as profligate inebriates venerating a savage god, infernal votaries to a Dionysian festival of blood. "On nothing did they seem to set so great a value, or view with so much satisfaction, as the bleeding scalps which they had, ere life had become extinct, torn from the mangled heads of their expiring victims! . . . [T]hese scalps, these shockgin [sic] proofs of savage Cannibalism, were those of [the Hall sisters'] parents! . . . [T]omahawks have, literally, been made drunk with innocent blood!"[5] Rendered as cannibals, Edwards's figurative Indians compound injury and murder through consumption, hailing readers through a fantasy of disintegration, a fear of the body undone, the illusion of its integrity corrupted.[6] This, in turn, unfolds a fantasy of consuming and being consumed, of the broken body, the social body, absorbed within the body of the other. Partaking of the flesh and blood of the settlers, Indians—like cholera—violate all frontiers, gnawing away at distinctions between inside and outside, man and woman, white and red, consecrating human life to an unholy communion with morbidity and decay, revealing the inescapable common destiny of all things.

While the figure of the body undone speaks to the material reality of the nation as forever aspirant, a collection geographically noncongruent places given reprieve from isolation through the fantasy of identity, Edwards's portrait of the shattered body of the settler—vulnerable, feminized—prefigures the fantasy of the national body integrated through the intervention of the state. Confronted by the injured, exenterated body of the nation, the state collects and preserves the discarded pieces, preventing them from being consumed, in preparation for some more suitable articulation. In the narrative, these secular metaphysics are entangled with Edwards's political theology, claiming temporal, terrestrial pain both as a portent of eternal suffering and pedagogical tool and as a series of exercises dedicated to the cultivation of virtue. "The horses on which the females were mounted, being each led by one of their number, while two more walked on each side with their blood-stained scalping knives and tomahawks. . . . [T]hey thus travelled for many hours, with as much speed as possible, through a dark and impenetrable wood; when reaching a still more dark and gloomy swamp, they came to a halt."[7] In a low if unmistakable echo of the *Inferno* and Dante's accidental descent into the underworld, Edwards's description of the sisters in thrall to the Indian raiding party finds them bound, on horseback, marching west—in company—on a journey into perdition. As for Dante, the dark wood and swamp they encounter appear as a carnivalesque space of nebulous indeterminacy, a zone of transit between the living and the dead, the creature comforts of home and family and the iniquitous agonies of the savage and the barbarous. Mimicking the figure of the Indian-as-cannibal, this scene plays upon the fear of being consumed, of disintegrating, of losing oneself—body and identity—through incorporation with the body of the other, in short, of losing oneself by becoming the other. This is, for Edwards, a vision of hell. Past this point in the text, the question of torture, of the deliberate and sadistic administration of pain upon the bodies of the captives, becomes a primary thematic concern, as the narrator teases the reader with the dire promise of unspeakable sufferings yet to be revealed. "No language can express the cruelties that were committed. . . . [These] feelings may be better imagined than described." Leaving unspoken the specific forms of violence and torture meted out upon the bodies of the women, Edwards's description of the Hall sisters' condition allows for a hysterically expansive encounter with the range of violence characteristic of temporal suffering, tethering the pregnant imaginary of their debasement into conversation with the eternal, presenting the loss of virtue and of whiteness, of being made a vessel for the reproduction of Indian villainy, as a living death and a premature burial, a death-in-life akin to the eternal death of damnation and the tortures met as a consequence of sin.

Artfully soliciting readerly compassion through an appeal to the salacious, Edwards's treatise on the goodness of Providence and the body of the nation here unfolds as a covert pornography of vicarious sadomasochistic pleasures.[8] The question of sin and salvation, of the captivity narrative as a vehicle through which to illuminate the theological elements of civic virtue, provides the opportunity for an illicit retreat into the contemplation of the forbidden and the obscene. "The poor unfortunate females, whose feelings as may be supposed, could be no other than such as bordered on distraction, and who had not ceased for a moment to weep most bitterly during the whole days, could not but believe that they were here destined to become the victims of savage outrage and abuse."[9] A ploy typical of the captivity genre, Edwards's presentation of the sisters lingers over their physical and emotional suffering as a means to elicit readers' sympathy as subjects of a common vulnerability, while nonetheless highlighting their racialized and gendered impotence as women whose whiteness makes them more than usually vulnerable to the capricious animal desires of non-white men. "Such were their dreadful forebodings—human imagination can hardly picture to itself a more deplorable situation; but, in their conjectures, they happily found themselves mistaken, as on the approach of night, instead of being made the subjects of brutal outrage, as they had fearfully apprehended, a place separate from that occupied by the main body of the savages, was allotted them . . . guarded by two aged squaws."[10] Unmolested by their male captors—but "doomed to become the victims of the most savage torture," haunted by the threat that the sisters are to be made wives to Native men—Edwards does not recognize the care bestowed upon the women as a measure of ethical judgment on the part of the Pottawatomi; instead he raises the presentiment of rape as a means to incense—and entice—the reader, while figuring the myriad violations perpetrated against settlers, by Native peoples, as the sign of a disordered relationship to the social mediations of gender and sexuality.[11] Feral and unsublimated, Edwards invites the reader to examine the dark perversions of their most secret, most inaccessible desires as a window onto the most social and most explicit expressions of Indian hunger.

The supposition of rape as a violent expression of sexual desire also supposes a violation of the proprietary and patriarchal negotiation of racial and national reproduction, as well as the forced attribution of a kin relation. Spared from death by the same people who had murdered their family, the sisters "could not believe that they were here destined to become the victims of savage outrage and abuse," so that they might become, "the adopted wives of the two young chiefs by whom they were first seized."[24] "If there was any thing calculated to add more horror to their feelings, it was this, which was indeed calculated to produce a greater shock than the intelligence that they were doomed to become the victims of the most savage torture!" Edwards's treatment of these noncustomary relationships revels in the illicit expression of polymorphous desire, even as they are presented as a parody of Indigenous kinship and the social and affective relations that suture Indigenous community. In Edwards's reckoning, for Native peoples, sex is violence: overwhelming and sadistic, luxuriating in the baroque trivialities of pain. As such, Indian sexuality necessarily summons its object as subordinate, debased, an effeminate caricature of womanly comportment whose physical violation damages the categorical distinctions by which sex and gender are organized and inhabited. Just as "no language can express the cruelties" of Indian warfare, a form of combat that recognizes "no distinction of age or sex," the violence of Indian sexuality composes a language that is properly unspeakable, a glamour corrosive of sexual difference as the ward of patriarchy.

Checked by the conventions of gender, of publicity and propriety, rather than touching upon the specifics of the tortures visited upon the bodies and the persons of the women, Edwards stages this deviant over-abundance of Indian sexuality through a protracted diversion into the story of Philip Brigdon, a young man he identifies as "the Kentuckian." Playing upon contemporary associations of Kentucky with a rugged frontier masculinity, Brigdon is introduced to the narrative artificially, appearing only that he might be unmanned by his captors, and that his body might serve to enumerate the agonies of captivity, as the Pottawatomi inflict considered pains upon him. "Immediately seized and pinioned . . . [Brigdon] was beset by a throng of natives, of both sexes and of all ages, armed with sticks and bludgeons, and who commenced beating him to a degree almost to deprive him of life! . . . [H]aving undergone this introductory discipline, he was (with the exception of his shirt and pantaloons) stripped of his clothing, and bound hand and foot to a tree. . . . [I]n one instance, he was so left bound for the space of twenty-four hours."[12] Bound and beaten, stripped, in these scenes, Brigdon is made to bear forms of confinement far more onerous and elaborate than those visited upon the Hall sisters, even as the conditions of his captivity appear accessible to language in ways elided by those of his counterparts. While threats of rape hang over Edwards's descriptions of the Hall sisters' confinement, those take the form of demure ellipses in the narrative, intimations that emerge in the absence of direct commentary. In his approach to Brigdon, however, Edwards renders sexual violation as literal as propriety will allow, his domination by the Pottawatomi playing out in the disposition of his limbs, the play of force along the surface of his body, the foreshadowed inversion of skin and viscera manifest through the penetration of his flesh. "Two posts were set firmly and perpendicularly in the ground, to which two cross pieces were fastened horizontally, with withes, one about two and the other about six feet from the ground, to which it is probable that his hands and feet were to be bound. Around the whole were piled dry fagots and other combustibles."[13]

Composed as a burlesque of the crucifixion, Brigdon's torture highlights cannibalism as a ritual of communion among his Indian captors, their union expressed through the satisfaction of their mutual bloodthirst. Bound, splayed, and set ablaze, Brigdon serves in the narrative as a holocaust, a sacrificial totem sanctified through his relation to violence, rendered sexless and abject. This display of infantile sexual exuberance illustrates the horror of a debased family relation, a parody of Indigenous kinship as a monstrous, all-consuming, unsustainable appetite. In posing a relationship between tomahawks "drunk with innocent blood" and the "cruelties perpetrated on the infant, the mother," the narrative evokes contemporaneous anxieties over gender and mothering attached to the question of breast-feeding; in Edwards's *Narrative*, Indian violence is figured as a nefarious mothering, a feast of bloodletting in which the mingled blood of the people is offered up as evidence of a common heritage and identity, a common nationality and racial patrimony. Throughout, the illiberality of Indian society is underscored by their incapacity for life-giving; that is, the manner in which their expression of culture and self is inevitably tethered to the auratics and execution of violence. Here, the threat of mutilation is used to illuminate the forms of sexual torture that cannot be named but that nonetheless emerge through the interstices of the narrative as depredations on the proprietary norms governing sexual and social reproduction; specifically, the forms of polymorphous animal desire that seek no discriminate object. Later evoking the tomahawks "made drunk with innocent blood" and the vampiric specter of Indian violence, the narrative calls upon the settlers of the western frontier to "revenge the cruelties perpetrated on the infant, the mother, and the defenceless . . . [to] unloose the spirit of revenge . . . in defence of his relatives and friends."[14] In the face of the "no future" wrought of Indian violence, the narrative calls for the restoration of the liberal protocols of domestic reproduction, and the forms of social mediation they enable. Appealing to the righteousness of vengeance in service of nation and state, in his preface, Edwards exhorted his readers: "Rise, fellow citizens of this city and country—let us no longer delay—talk no more, but act. To arms—unloose the spirit of revenge."[15]

Although Edwards's *Narrative* is at pains to emphasize the implied threat of the "blood-stained scalping knives and tomahawks" wielded by the sisters' captors, when stripped of these demotic invocations of sav-

CONSTANTLY AT THEIR WEAVING WORK / 99

agery, what is described in these passages is less a condition of captivity than a practice of guardianship, an act of attention born of an ethics of war-making as a dimension of social relations, within a history and practice of Indigenous sovereignty as a condition of ethical cohabitation. Framed by explicit reference to the myriad distresses visited upon "the American nation" during the year 1832, the regular invocation of "human butchery" carried out by "the merciless SAVAGES" makes a claim upon fear and desire as affective conditions that orient a sense of collective purpose; yet, in its trite repetition of these descriptions, Edwards's *Narrative* continually refuses to deliver, addressing only the most banal pains, while demonstrating—over and again—that the women are reasonably well treated by their captors. "The savages exhibited no disposition to harm or disturb them . . . food was offered them, but in consequence of the disturbed state of their minds and almost constant weeping, they had become too weak and indisposed to partake of it."[16] Moreover, when permitted rest, the sisters were allowed their own protected place of repose: "Instead of being made the subjects of brutal outrage, as they had fearfully apprehended, a place separate from the main body of the savages, was allotted them . . . guarded only by two aged squaws, who slept on each side of them . . . being unable to resist the calls of nature, they the morning ensuing felt much relieved by the undisturbed repose which they had been permitted to enjoy."[17] To the Native people present at the scene, the taking of prisoners and exchange of hostages exemplified what Michelle Pagni Stewart has called a "rite of war," a gesture of reciprocity between combatants that served also to proscribe the scope of allowable violence within combat. Hostage-taking was part of a larger, ongoing set of negotiations about the terms of warfare, how it would be conducted, and the extent of its damage: hostages served as guarantors of fidelity to those terms, and not as spoils of combat. Within the scope of Edwards's narrative of the Hall sister, however, captivity figured as injury is presented as an act of war, one that compounds the originary act of war-making, thus compelling a defensive response.

The story of the Hall sisters and their unfortunate family drew upon a common pool of settler testimonies that insisted upon the vulnerability of settlers in the face of Indigenous violence: these became fodder for the elaboration of the state as a defensive, protective agency. "We pray your protection against the Sac and Fox tribe of Indians, who have again taken possession of our lands near the mouth of the Rock River and its vicinity. They have, and now are, burning our fences, destroying our crops of wheat now growing, by turning in all their horses."[18] Signed by thirty-six prominent settlers who identified themselves as "citizens of Rock River and its vicinity," this petition was one of a series of depositions addressed to Illinois governor John Reynolds during the spring and summer of 1831. Asserting Native peoples' presence as a sign of their belligerence, documents like these translated otherwise commonplace acts of agricultural husbandry into barely restrained acts of malice.

The violence of settler testimony was not direct or immediate, yet it hailed an implacable force. In committing a representational violence, translating the forms of stewardship that sustained Sauk sovereignty into an idiom of assault, settlers invited a more visceral, more purposeful cruelty, one that bore the signature of the state.[19] Directed at relatively distant territorial authorities, reports from settlers described their circumstances in ways that denied their own complicity in local conflicts over resources, calling upon the state as the final arbiter of social relations. Foregoing any pretense of their ethical obligations to their Indigenous neighbors, settlers forged a story about their vulnerability in the face of Native aggression, and the liability of the state with respect to their remediation. "If not protected, [settlers] will be compelled to leave their habitations and homes from the actual injury that said Indians will commit on said inhabitants. That said band of Indians consists, as above stated, of about three hundred warriors, and that the whole band is actuated by the same hostile feelings toward the white inhabitants; and that, if not prevented by an armed force of men, will commit murders on said white inhabitants."[20] Insecure in their persons, settlers claimed to be defenseless in their homes, drawing upon the association between home and intimacy as a means of occluding the noncustomary forms of property—the juridical framework of property ownership mediated by the fiction of the state—that sustained both. Calling for military intervention as a means of effecting their physical deliverance from Indigenous violence, settlers' descriptions of events on the ground provided a rationale for the application of martial force as a means of imposing the civic norms of liberal statecraft as a socially meaningful standard for the organization of everyday life, thereby asserting both the legal validity and cultural authority of their otherwise ineffectual claims to ownership and the right to occupation.

The fiction of the Black Hawk War was initially forged in this moment, from these materials, as settlers promulgated a sense of grievance and injury, highlighting their attachment to place and to property, while calling upon the state as the avenging angel of their wounded devotions. These highly partisan instances of self-representation suggested nothing of the long history of US state intervention throughout the region— indeed, the long history of European colonial presence and negotiations among and between Native nations and European empires over the terms of mutual coexistence—and, despite the lasting material and moral consequences of their solicitations, betrayed no moment of hesitation or pangs of conscience. Fashioning themselves as victims of Sauk aggression, in testimony, settlers exaggerated their innocence, disregarding their complicity in the subversion of local social norms and social order, while seeking to forego the intimacies of Indigenous sovereignty and the "actual history of our plural existence" through appeals to the consolidation of the nation and the protection of the state. Binding themselves to the body of the nation through appeal to the infrastructures of state and state violence, settlers provided the rhetorical setting whereby to justify the extension of state sovereignty as the primary, insistent mode of social and political mediation throughout the Upper Mississippi River Valley, providing greater depths to the forms of US counter-sovereignty by working to efface—if not extinguish—multiple, overlapping instances of Native sovereignty and title, and long histories of Indigenous occupancy.

A Bureaucracy of Bloodlessness and Bloodletting

Reports from settlers helped to buoy the legitimacy of the treaty the United States eventually forced upon the Sauk and the Fox. Drawing upon the pretense of Sauk aggression, the 1832 treaty staked itself to the affected body of the settler-cum-citizen, the assumption of the settler and her vulnerability made opportunity for recompense, on the part of the Sauks and the Foxes, in the transfer of title in land. "Whereas under certain desperate and lawless leaders, a formidable band, constituting a large portion of the Sac and Fox nation, left their country in April last, and, in violation of treaties, commenced an unprovoked war upon unsuspecting and defenceless citizens of the United States, sparing neither age nor sex; and whereas, the United States, at a great expense of treasure, have subdued the said hostile band, killing or capturing all its principle Chiefs and Warriors—the said States, partly as an indemnity for the expense incurred, and partly to secure the future safety and tranquility of the invaded frontier, demand of the said tribes, to the use of the United States, a cession of a tract of the Sac and Fox country, bordering on said frontier, more than proportional to the numbers of the hostile band who have been so conquered and subdued." To justify the extension of its sovereignty over the region, the US government was necessarily dependent upon prior legal precedents that grudgingly acknowledged Native sovereignty; as such, the cession that the government demanded was a crazy-quilt, a hodgepodge composed from the remains of earlier treaties made between different nations and different authorities, long-standing customary arrangements over land tenure, and seemingly immutable geophysical aspects of the terrain, encompassing some fifteen million acres west of the Mississippi. Upon this unruly tapestry of legal and narrative protocols, US negotiators sought to impose a modicum of order, appealing to exact angles and straight lines that cut through the overgrowth of history. "Beginning on the Mississippi river at the Sac and Fox northern boundary line, as established by the second article of the treaty of Prairie du Chien . . . [as it] strikes said river; thence, up said boundary line to a point fifty miles from the Mississippi, measured on said line; thence, in a right line to the Red Cedar of the Iowa, forty miles from the Mississippi river; then in a right line to a point in the northern boundary line of the State of Missouri, fifty miles, measured on said boundary to the Mississippi River, and by the western shore of said river to the place of beginning."

The relationship between treaty and testimony, between settler accounts of events and the fabrication of a history of invasion, was more thoroughly effected through testimonials like these would come to figure prominently in the archive of the conflict, presented there as faithful descriptions of the conditions necessitating military intervention on behalf of settler interests as well as points of reference from which to establish a shared grammar of grievance, injury, and honor through which to demonstrate the justice of that intervention. Writing in 1834, John Allen Wakefield would cite such petitions in his *History of the War between the United States and the Sac and Fox Nations of Indians* as a means both to demonstrate the abuse suffered by settlers of the Mississippi frontier at the hands of Native predators and to leverage that abuse so that he might "show the cause of hostilities between those Indians and the United States [as well as] the course pursued to dissuade those Indians from their evil designs . . . without a resort to force of arms." For Wakefield, the injuries sustained by settlers demanded the intervention of the state as a matter of course; but not only were they justified, they were evidence of the nobility of the cause, or at the very least, of the people who were forced to prosecute the war against Black Hawk. In his accounting, not only was their participation necessary, but it was also measured and restrained, coming only after repeated appeals to the territorial government and careful deliberation on the part of its representatives.

> It will be seen that this [first] petition was sent to the Governor on the 30th of April. The citizens waited until 19th of May, when they found they would have to send a second embassy to his Excellency. . . . I will

trouble the reader with these documents to show that Governor Reynolds and Gen. Gaines did not act premature [*sic*], but acted with too much forbearance toward those Indians. . . . I think if they are to blame at all, it is for not calling out an armed force sooner than what they did, for the citizens certainly suffered very much by the annoyance of those Indians.

If the Edwards's narrative of the Hall sisters was meant to summon support for Indian removal through a depiction of war as an orgy of blood, Wakefield's history was meant as an intervention on contemporary party politics, a defense of those western settlers and economic interests who composed a large portion of electoral support for Jacksonian Democrats. Wakefield's 1834 volume on the history of the conflict is desperate to indicate the inherent justice of the state in prosecuting its war on Black Hawk and the British Band, a justice that emerges only after the authorial consideration of the Sauks' many "monstrous" depredations against settler communities. "Many false reports have gone abroad respecting the lands of those Indians, representing that the Government has not done justice. In giving an account of the frontier massacres by the Indians, the author has to depend on newspaper information; but it is his opinion that all have been found upon record, which were published in this state, are literally true, and may be relied upon as facts."[21] For Wakefield, the record of treaty negotiations by which US agents engaged the Sauks provided the framework by which to establish not only the illegality of Black Hawk's movements but also the principle by which the violence he wrought might be understood as in excess of conventional legal recourse. "The author, in order to show the cause of the difference between the United States and the Sac and the Fox Indians, thinks it best to lay before the reader many interesting documents, consisting of letters and a number of depositions, to show the necessity of the Executive in calling upon the militia of the state of Illinois, to protect its citizens: and he flatters himself that, after the perusal of those letters and depositions, none will have the hardihood to say, that Governor Reynolds did wrong in the course he pursued to subdue those Indians."[22] Wakefield's history thus engages the practices of the colonial state as a means of establishing the authenticity of his claims and the authority of his account; the documentary traces of the colonial state become the vehicle by which the truth of this historical moment might be established, even as the truth of Wakefield's claims—and the authority he asserts as a subject of this knowledge—retroactively rebounds to the state as the ideological figure that authorizes colonial governmentality as a mode of social mediation.[23] Wakefield's account thus evokes the tension between the techniques of mercantile economy and governmentality that had long underwritten life on the Mississippi frontier, and the emergence of a more recognizably national form of sovereignty as expressed through the self-possession of the settler as an extension of the military apparatus of the federal state.

The rhetorical gestures that open Wakefield's history of the war effectively establish the parameters of his authority. "In presenting this small volume to the world, the author is aware that he is exposing his name to the public calumny, by those who are ready at all times to find fault; but he hopes the candid, who will reflect a moment on the many difficulties attending the compiling such a work, will be charitable toward him."[24] Opening with words of apology that barely serve to obscure his ambition, Wakefield here participates in the conventions of authorship in the early republic, where the names of specific writers were almost necessarily effaced as a condition of entrance into print culture. Born from a long-standing suspicion of literature as an impediment to social order, a means of prejudicing the forms of embodied public engagement necessary to the health of a republican polity, such apologetics sought to establish the value of specific works of literature for public culture, presenting individual works as useful rather than fanciful or speculative. At the time of its composition in 1834, such gestures were increasingly on the wane; as such, Wakefield's indulgence in this mode of self-presentation might well be understood as a kind of literary affectation, a gesture toward the conventions that ruled an earlier generation of frustrated authors. Yet, the equivocation that opens the work ultimately serves his larger ends, as it allows Wakefield to position himself in a dialectical relationship to the multitude who were participants in the conflict. "[One] must reflect that the many actors in the late war have not all the same views of things that took place—as it is the nature of man to differ in opinions, and those that were eye witnesses of the events recorded in this narrative, (or history,) to have different opinions."[25] Wakefield here disappears into the multitude of participants in the conflict only to emerge, ultimately, as the arbiter who mediates the disparate accounts that emerge from within their polyphony; he becomes the sovereign who summons the abstract people from the incoherence of concrete peoples, a theorist of writing and of history as techniques for the extension and adjudication of sovereignty as command over time as well as space.

Wakefield's prefatory remarks evoke the trace of this procedure. Initially describing his intervention on the archive of the Black Hawk War as an act of "compiling," he goes on to describe the work as a "narrative," and then—parenthetically—as a "history," with the conjunction "or" signaling an easy exchangeability between the second and third terms of this sequence. Despite the equivalence implied by that conjunction, Wakefield's casual transit from compilation to narrative to history implies not just an increasingly authorial intervention within the space of the archive; it also implies an intervention that is increasingly justified in terms of institutional structures given to the mediation of claims made upon the past as an innately common pool of resources. Where "compilation" suggests a record born by a process of accumulation, "narrative" designates the articulation of a trajectory, the move from the incoherence of affect to emotion as a mimetic figure.[26] "Narrative," in this sense, designates relations of causality and a principle of economy that combine to exclude far more than they can ever include. Although Alexandra Vazquez has rightly indicated the ways in which the anthology, as a mode of compilation, is already ruled by a set of protocols and procedures that serve the ends of national formation, the move from compilation to narrative suggests the passage from an always incoherent and incomplete assemblage to a normative body, one that is no less sutured but that denies the possibility of further copula.[27] "History," by extension, indicates another degree of ossification, with the nominal equivocation of the word *narrative* now displaced by the authoritative and authorizing procedures of a disciplinary formation in service of a state project.

Wakefield's account thus assumes for itself that which it continuously denies the Sauks: notions of sovereign self-possession based upon normative projections of bodily capacity. Descriptions of the Sauks as animal or monstrous serve to confirm their dependence upon the state as a biopolitical agency, designating their incapacity for social reproduction absent the ministrations and disciplinary procedures of the liberal state. Crucially, in Wakefield's account, the event that precipitates the formation of the Illinois territorial militia occurs when a group of Menominee Indians are slaughtered, in their sleep, by members of an Indigenous company that Wakefield identifies as part of Black Hawk's band. First identifying the Menominees as a peaceable people that had always looked to the United States for their protection, Wakefield went on to report that, "[the Menominees] had been that day in an Indian frolic, and were nearly all drunk. It is a well known thing, that, when Indians get into one of those drunken frolics, they are dangerous, one to another." Here, the impact of alcohol on indigenous communities—particularly upon indigenous men—is registered not as the consequence of a colonial situation but rather as a circumstance that demands state intervention for the preservation of indigenous life. Wakefield goes on to link the debility of alcoholism to the forms of monstrosity represented by the Sauks, themselves.

"Those Menominees had just been gorging with this hydra monster of all evil . . . never dreaming or thinking that there was the least danger of being butchered by those hideous monsters that were of the same species of human beings with themselves."[28]

As above, in this passage, there is a sly elision of the categorical distinctions that might be made between the Menominees' drunkenness as a situational form of debility, the monstrosity of the Sauks as representatives of the limits of law, and notions of alcoholism as a particular "racial" characteristic of American indigenous peoples, all of which collapses into Wakefield's invocation of the Sauks and Menominees being "of the same species of human beings with themselves." With those final words, Wakefield invites the reader to conceive of these characteristics as part of the same set, one to which neither he nor his presumed reader belongs. His account, in this sense, elaborates an autopoetic course of becoming, whereby the figure of the sovereign emerges from the chaotic unknowability of desire, only to become the model for the constitution of a national people. His account negates the illegible, unruly course of desire and the possibility for a sociality of life lived outside the parameters of the biopolitical state, routing it through the Oedipal fiction of a national body organized by the gaze of the historian-as-sovereign. "[One] must reflect that the many actors in the late war have not all the same views of things that took place—as it is the nature of man to differ in opinions, and those that were eye witnesses of the events recorded in this narrative . . . to have different opinions." Here, Wakefield obscures the depth of his intervention by eliding distinctions between physically immediate instances of witnessing as bound to the capacity for sight and the metaphorical valence of "view" as mere opinion; suggesting that the latter corrupts the former, Wakefield goes on to assert the capacity of the historian as a model of reflection, whereby the documentary truth of the various traces of witnessing might be established. The desire to see, to consume, is here subverted, as the historian becomes the author of the text, and the arbiter of the way in which the text is to be read. The self-possession of the historian, the capacity of the historian to evaluate documentation and to pronounce upon the truth of particular narrative figurations, becomes the model for the whiteness of the settler, where whiteness is understood as a condition of being beyond the affective lability of the un-reasoning. "Many false reports have gone abroad respecting the lands of those Indians, representing that the Government has not done justice. In giving an account of the frontier massacres by the Indians, the author has to depend upon newspaper information; but it is his opinion that all that have been found upon record . . . are literally true, and may be relied upon as facts."[29] Claiming the extraordinary power of sorting misrepresentation from truth, Wakefield refuses the accumulation of miseries that subtend the settler state; choosing, rather, to absorb himself into the archival traces and documentary procedures that celebrate and defend the legitimacy of that state.

As with later histories of the Black Hawk War, Wakefield's had very immediate consequences with respect to policy. His repeated invocation of "false reports [that] have gone abroad," suggests something of the historical situation from which he wrote, where the prosecution of Indian removal was not merely a question of national significance for Jacksonian America, but for its adversaries. As Sean Harvey's work on the philological debate over Indigenous languages begins to suggest, the condition of Indigenous peoples and their treatment at the hands of the state was one of the questions that served to articulate party lines in the Jacksonian state; it also was a vehicle for international critiques of the United States as a fledgling republic. Reports on the robust linguistic structure of Indigenous languages were used, in London and elsewhere, as a means of scrutinizing the government of the United States, as well as the society that was emerging as a consequence of territorial expansion. Contrasting the richness of indigenous expression with the ostensibly crude dialect of white settlers, international actors sought to bring to light the rapaciousness of settler culture as a means of highlighting the ways in which American liberalism had become the guise for a pernicious liberality.[30] In both Wakefield and Stevens, the insistence upon the judiciousness of the settlers and the state in prosecuting the campaign against Black Hawk is intended as hedge against such claims, a salvo in a long running argument whereby the claimants to imperial prerogatives were judged by their treatment of populations deemed racially subordinate.

"Your honor no doubt is aware of the outrages that were committed by said Indians, heretofore. Particularly last fall, they almost destroyed all our crops, and made several attempts on the owners' lives when they attempted to prevent their depredations. . . . This spring they act in a much more outrageous and menacing manner, so that we consider ourselves compelled to beg protection of you."[31] While the frequency with which settlers addressed their complaints to state authorities belied their claim to imminent peril, they were nonetheless effective in translating the material forms of place-making practiced by the Sauks into an idiom of unredeemable savagery and atavistic malevolence. Understood as pieces of a vocabulary and a grammar dedicated to the expression of Indigenous sovereignty as the right to mediate conditions of belonging through the negotiation and narration of place, whatever actions Native peoples committed against settlers, in themselves, were less instances of aggression than attempts at reestablishing a prior composition of geophysical relations among human, animal, plant, and mineral, thus restoring infrastructural arrangements that supported the Sauks in the expression of their self-determination, while undermining the elements of social organization and nutrient extraction that supported the continuity of settler colonialism as a parasitic form of life. Agricultural practice composed a means of both sustenance and trade as well as a means to shape place and relations among the various forms of life that compose place; yet, in the reports offered by settlers, these actions were consistently represented as hostile. "They [are] . . . pasturing their horses in our fields; burning our fences, and have thrown the roof off one house. They shot arrows at our cattle, killed our hogs; and every mischief. [The] Indians say, if we plant we shall not reap, a proof of which we had last fall; they almost entirely destroyed all our crops of corn, potatoes, &c."[32]

To be sure, these actions were far from disinterested. Pulling down buildings, upsetting fences, killing livestock, and pasturing horses in already planted fields, the Sauks undermined the forms of agriculture and animal husbandry necessary to the sustenance of settler communities— while also revising, emending, and adapting those geophysical narratives of place derived from liberal conceptions of property-in-land that settlers hoped to impose upon the terrain, asserting the continuity of Indigenous presence through forms of stewardship that were not always wholly peaceable. Just as settlers sought to write their history upon the land through the fabrication of such "improvements," the Sauks meant to enact the same, recomposing the story of their legacies on the land by dismantling the infrastructures of agrarian settler occupation. This routinely involved attacks on houses and fencing as two of the more visible signatures of a property relation—as well as the most vulnerable pieces of the infrastructure of occupation. From 1830 to 1832, it also saw a series of seemingly isolated, uncoordinated attacks on local saw and grist mills, as Native communities protested the obstruction of river and streams with cumbersome dams that inhibited the free movement of fish and other wildlife. As the ever-increasing population of the Upper Mississippi region made consumables ever dearer, the inhibition of fish stock meant the disruption of Native fisheries and the place of fish within the Indigenous diet and agricultural economy. Moreover, mills were both a sign and a technology of settlers' intent to remain and to remake dramatic alterations of the landscape, as well as the course and rate of flow of local waterways, in service of the processing of timber and flour, the matériel from which to fabricate the stuff of home and hearth. Like most complaints against settler ingress, Native protests of these infrastructures were often quite measured, but tensions could escalate quickly, when settlers refused to recognize or countenance Indigenous concerns. The bloodiest massacre of settlers by Native peoples during the months of the so-called Black Hawk War began with a peaceful emissary from the Pottawatomi village on Indian Creek to a nearby settler community that had dammed the stream. After settlers attacked Pottawatomi men who sought to remove the dam, the Pottawatomies responded, weeks later, with a raiding party that laid waste to the settler village and killing all but two of its inhabitants.

Settler Colonialism and the Mystery of Grace

Where Wakefield was concerned to enact certain interventions in terms of policy, establishing the role of the historian as sovereign through the development of an authorial ideal of truth-telling and adjudication—an idea of the historian as priest of a uniquely insidious American liturgy—Timothy Flint's *Indian Wars of the West* took the bones of a historical narrative and transformed them into the stuff of romance, a story about redemption and sanctification that knitted the story of the United States around a grandiloquent history of empire. First published in 1833, Flint's account of the military campaign against Black Hawk composed merely one chapter of a larger study of the numerous campaigns by which the United States had cobbled together its hegemony over the riparian spaces of the trans-Appalachian west. Prefaced by the closing salvo from George Berkeley's *On the Prospect of Planting Arts and Learning in America*—"Westward the course of empire holds its way"—Flint's compendium folded numerous campaigns against indigenous populations into a general theory of American history, one that also served as a treatise on political economy and the prospects of the expanding nation. Whereas Berkeley saw the British American colonies as the proper inheritor of empire, the "seat of innocence" where "shall be sung another golden age" that precedes the fifth and closing act of human history, Flint sees the expansion of the United States as part of an epic of development and "improvement," one that was "unparalleled in the annals of colonization."[33] Crossing Berkeley's hope for a future redemption with a utopian vision of capitalist industry and its impact upon the land, Flint casts the Mississippi River Valley as the long-promised seat of prelapsarian abundance.

> Oppression and disease have no sooner banished man from the
> plains of Babylon, Persia, and Palestine, than the ground parches,

the trees disappear, the beasts, and even the birds depart into exile, and the country, abandoned to sterility, becomes a moving sand. In reverse of this order, when the thousands of square leagues of dry grass plains west of the Mississippi, shall become the resorts of husbandmen, the granges, the hedges, the young orchards, the mulberry groves, forming a new alliance with the sky, will generate showers, arrest the clouds, and pour innumerable rivulets over all these green wastes.[34]

Here, the liberality of American culture is amply repaid by inspiring a dynamism far in excess of those ancient and antique empires whose tyranny could only end in the evisceration of nature's vitality; in the American empire, the labor of industry would transcend the social contract, resulting in a contract with nature such that nature would bless the efforts of the husbandmen and, in turn, the efforts of the husbandmen would pay dividends to the elements of the natural world.

A portion of Flint's ambition is suggested by his book's full title, *Indian Wars of the West; Containing Biographical Sketches of Those Pioneers Who Headed the Western Settlers in Repelling the Attacks of the Savages; Together with a View of the Character, Manners, Monuments, and Antiquities of the Western Indians*. Not satisfied with one account of a single conflict, Flint aspired for a completest account of Indian warfare, one in which heroic individuals are forever warding off attacks from rapacious savages, who are portrayed as nothing less than a collection of cultural affectations, mannerisms, genealogical traits. In Flint's account, each conflict becomes the image of another, each account a synecdoche for the general, transhistorical manifestation of "savage" violence as an impediment to the historicity of the settler community, and the process by which land and resources were to be "redeemed from the wilderness" through their insertion into history.[35] Describing the expansion of settlements into the Mississippi and Ohio River Valleys in the decades prior to the conflict with Black Hawk, Flint would conclude that, "the north-western frontier of Michigan, Illinois, and Missouri, which all bound on the lead mine country, had become to the Indians what Kentucky and Ohio had been forty years ago."[36] Nursing a sense of injury, the Native peoples of the river valley began taking exacting small vengeances against their white neighbors, "precisely the same harbingers that used to accompany the Indian wars [of earlier days]."[37] His account effectively transformed the indigenous communities of the trans-Appalachian west into a variable of the land, less a participant in the husbandry he saw as the future of the land than an impediment to the realization of that future vision; the

Indian was, from this perspective, another figure of the wilderness waiting to be redeemed, a barrier to the expansion of value that would emerge in the contract between the settler and nature.

Against Flint's dismissive reduction of the "Indian" to an accumulation of manners and customs with no real reflexivity or inherent value, his volume promised to treat the pioneer defenders of human life and liberty through biographical sketches that reveal the depths of their suffering and the heights of their joys as measures of their heroism. Here, the "biographical sketches" referenced by the title should be read as the device by which the settler was most immediately humanized as a bearer of the virtues resonant with the liberality of the nation-state and its manifest sovereignty, a technique by which the settler—unlike the Indian or Indian violence—was afforded a singularity and a specificity more than their status as legal abstractions. "We will cause [our children's] eyes to glisten by the recital of [the pioneers'] deeds of daring, their spirit of self sacrifice, their heroic conflicts, and their lonely toils." Against those empires that would elevate their founders to the status of "demi-gods . . . their achievements . . . inscribed upon monumental marble and brass," Flint suggested that the United States would account for its citizens' great deeds and great characters so to "present a new and more elevated standard of imitation [than those] born in times and under circumstances tending to foster effeminacy and selfishness." Where histories of previous generations had taken solace in the heroism of the past, Flint assured his readers that "[it] can never be useless to contemplate these images of stern self control, of sublime vigor and perseverance. In seeing what men have done, and may be, we find the best incitements to arrest the downward tendency to indolence, self-indulgence, and pusillanimity."[38] History, in this sense, was to be deployed as a means of properly patriarchal capacitation, the enervation of a declaratively masculine sense of vigor expressed through a continuous course of primitive accumulation. The contemplation of the past, in other words, was a guarantee against the forms of decline that had been always the fate of empires, a means of compelling the discipline of the subject as one oriented to the horizon of the future.

The historical drama Flint develops plays out against an expansive tableau of natural wonders which, in his account, becomes the stage upon which history will unfold, as well as the determinate factor in the shape of settler character. "The peculiar configuration, climate, physical character, fertility, and modes of communication of this wide region, circumstances all having a peculiar bearing upon the character of its inhabitants, have not failed to form a language, and a mode of thinking, and manners peculiar to the west."[39] Taking issue with those who would expose the language of the settlers as a measure of their degree of "civilization," Flint embeds that language within a theory of space, where the customs of his heroic pioneers emerge in a dialogue with the physical dimensions of the earth. Insofar as the land of the West is taken as the space of a new contract between man and nature, where both find renewal through their mutual implication, Flint evokes a progressive history of settler character, one in which the dynamic of settler character emerges in a dialectical relation to labor, and in relation to the chromonormative temporality of the reproductive nation-state. Here, there is an implicit critique of the "Indian" as living "off" the land rather than in relation to it. The "Indian" is of the land and shaped by the land but does not engage in any reciprocal intervention. The settler, by contrast, is the germ of a new sociality, of mutually constitutive relations between the human and the natural; the settler becomes indigenous to a place, in this sense, through the modes of labor by which he intervenes upon it, rendering it a space of inordinate fecundity.[40]

This perhaps accounts for Flint's insistence on the fertility of the region under consideration. "The fertility of the greater portion of this valley is as surprising as its extent. Apparently of more recent formation that the remainder of the continent, it seems less marked with the curse of sterility." This fertility, he suggests, is itself the cause of the increase in the settler population throughout the river valley which, as he puts it, "is without any example or parallel in the records of other colonies in ancient or modern times; not excepting even the annals of event the advancement of the Atlantic country."[41] At the same time, he assures his readers that this exceptionality is conditioned by the peculiarity of national character. "[Give] Americans a fertile soil, and a mild climate, and their native enterprise, fostered by the stimulant effect of freedom and milt laws, will overcome every impediment."[42] Flint's catalog of these impediments again transposes the indigenous presence upon the land into a feature to be overcome through its transformation, thus evoking the policy considerations that underwrite his approach to regional history. "Sickness, solitude, mountains, the war-whoop, the merciless tomahawk, wolves, panthers, bears, dear and distant homes, forsaken forever, will come over their waking thoughts, and revisit their dreams in vain, to prevent the young, florid, and unportioned pair from scaling remote mountains, descending long rivers, and finally selecting their spot in the forests, and consecrating their solitary cabin with the dear and sacred name of home."[43] Here, home is the reward for the endurance of a range of natural hardships, from physical infirmity, and affective lability, to the incoherence of an unfamiliar ecology, including the unearthly cry of the "war-whoop" and the ever-present threat of the "merciless tomahawk."

Given the overall tone of Flint's account, it is not at all surprising that these ostensibly human instrumentalities should be included with an inventory of natural impediments to the progress of settler colonization; it is, after all, against the backdrop of this nature, a nature in which the "civilization" of the settler is always threatened with its own devolution, that the true heroism of the pioneer emerges, inasmuch as the pioneer who survives nature becomes entitled to claim his sovereignty as master of himself and the elements about him. It is to the augmentation of this sovereignty that Flint's history gestures, with his implicit suggestion that the state intervene, insofar as it could, to further rationalize the process of settlement by removing the tomahawk as an impediment; by carrying out the course of Indian removal that was, at the time of his writing, just becoming policy. "It is now a vexed question, debated with intense interest, and no little asperity, whether the remaining Indians in the limits of Georgia, Alabama, Mississippi, and Tennessee, ought or ought not to be compelled to join their brethren, who have already removed to the country assigned them west of the Mississippi." After reviewing the poles of this opposition, Flint offers a cagey endorsement. "[It] is impossible, that the Indians should exist, as an independent people, within the populous limits of the whites. . . . [F]euds, quarrels, and retaliations . . . [will] never cease until one of the parties becomes extinct."[44] While closing his account of the Black Hawk War with the Latin expression "*Non nobis tantas componere lites* [it is not for us to settle such high disputes]," Flint nonetheless leaves little room for equivocation. Surveying the prospects of the "Indians" in the west, Flint leaves his readers with no option other than to endorse the plan for removal. "Here [in the west] they are to grow up distinct red nations, with schools and churches, and anvil, the loom, and the plough—a sort of Arcadian race between our borders and the Rocky mountains, standing memorials of the kindness and good faith of our government."[45]

Home, in this sense, is the result for the settler's self-fashioning; it is the reward for his nimbly charting a course for others to follow, one which does not find its satisfaction in identification with the natural but through transcendence of it; transcendence, here, is to be understood as transformation, a course of transformation that becomes the mechanism by which the settler will attain his sovereignty. Home, here, is the domain of the settler's sovereignty, the form by which it expresses its territorial ambition.[46] It is a form that can emerge only in relation to the "perfect sovereignty in [the] lands" of the states, an ideal that remains, in Flint's account, nothing more than a fiction, one to be realized through the transposition of indigenous populations to a space beyond the imaginary space of US sovereignty. The materialization of the fiction of US territorial sovereignty, in this sense, was coextensive with the action of indigenous population redistribution; the genocidal course of removal that proceeded after 1830 was both an auratic proof of that sovereignty, as well as a mechanism whereby that sovereignty might come to inhere within a material geography of military occupation.

History, Romance, and a Case of Hysteria

Elbert Smith's contribution to the historiography of the so-called Black Hawk War was by no means so elegantly conceived; yet it told a story of the nation—and most specifically, the Old Northwest and the Trans-Mississippi West—as spaces for the employment and redemption of capital, for the sanctification of money through its application in the expansion of the nation and the metaphysics of empire, an agent of salvation. Composed from an ungainly confusion of metrical patterns, cultural allusions, rhyme schemes, genres, and styles, *Ma-ka-tai-me-she-kia-kiak* is a truly irregular work, even as it luxuriates in the hoariest of conventions, including those of the elegiac and the Messianic, of civilization and the savage. The poem, at large, is undisciplined and uninspired. Despite his assurance that the book was relatively trim, *Ma-ka-tai-me-she-kia-kiak* is a *tome*, stuffed with unnecessarily antique allusions, metaphysical flourishes, metrical incompetencies, and narrative diversions. Meandering over six cantos, Smith begins with an invocation to his readers as an audience of Americans—"with hearts as warm, as generous and as free / As that pure atmosphere in which ye breathe"—that establishes the identity of the American with and through the mediation of nature, the atmosphere, and the breath. He goes on to exploit this all too typical conceit, giving body to the nation through an illustration of its physical geography and their infrastructural renovations, snaking along various paths of North American settlement, western expansion, and the Erie Canal, before digressing into a history of Mormonism and the Mormon prophet, Joseph Smith. Immediately, the narrative transports the reader to Nauvoo, Illinois; Council Bluffs, Iowa; and an ethereal California, before returning to Rochester, then proceeding to Buffalo, and dilating—at length—upon Niagara Falls. In Smith's account, the Falls are resplendent to a degree that reaches beyond the sublime. They are "the thunder's peal, the voice of Deity," "the consummation of all Earthly things," "eternity and never-ending time." Their majesty is a token of "the reign of liberty throughout the Earth. . . . The good Messiah's reign, and end of sin." Stacking description upon description with no apparent regard for the ways in which one might modify or enhance another, Smith's embellishment of Niagara traces no legible pattern, moving without purpose between the transcendental, the earthly, the sublime, and the mundane. Once the voice of God, in the next line they appear as the sound of a thousand cannons; once redolent with Eternity itself, next they collapse into the hideous transience of the temporal and the earthly: "Mount Aetna belching forth her liquid flame. . . . The lion's rage, the furious whirlwind's sweep."

The poem unfolds, more or less, in this vein. Moving between strict meter and free verse, events transpire, a story unfolds, the sublime and the wondrous are invoked so often as to become wearisome and mundane. While an earthly history of the so-called Black Hawk War makes up the spine of the narrative, in Smith's telling, it is preceded by a fabricated genealogy, one so thoroughly steeped in the metaphysical as to pass beyond the ridiculous. Tracing Black Hawk's lineage to the dawn of French colonization in North America, Smith invents two ancestors, Omaint-si-ar-nah and his intended wife, Gentle Dove, a humble woman who is evangelized and converted by the sainted Pere Marquette. Hoping to preserve her chastity from a would-be lover while Omaint-si-ar-nah is off to war, Gentle Doves hides in a cave, where she receives a visitation from an emissary of the Virgin Mary. "Greater than human, of a solemn mien / And dreadful aspect, awful revolting." Through her heavenly envoy, the Virgin warns Gentle Dove that she will face great privations and trials, and that her husband, in his jealousy, will turn against her. Despite this, she must nonetheless remain steadfast in her faith in the Lord if she hopes to survive her times of strife. Domestic affairs sorted, the angel continues:

> The Virgin has instructed to make known
> To thee, yet more; what else were under seal,
> Thy nation's future destiny reveal,
> And what will surely come to pass in years . . .
> A mighty struggle, not accounting life,
> Between thy people and a powerful race
> Of white men, far off, lately gained a place . . .
> But, waxing strong, to empire shall aspire,
> Sweep o'er, and subjugate the continent entire.
>
> They shall come, even here, with mighty hand,
> And, with their armies, overspread the land
> Of thy forefathers, and possess the same,

Not heeding, as they ought, thy people's claim.
But lo! thy nation shall not want renown!
Behold the prince that bears the laurel crown!
The prince that's yet to rise, Black Hawk by name;
The earth scarce proves a limit to his fame!
From thee descended, who shall, in his day,
O'er many chiefs and many tribes bear sway.
Shall fight successful battles in his prime,
Shall lead them forth to war, and, in his time,
Shall cause his enemies to fear and fly;
But numerous armies, that in ambush lie
Of whites, shall overcome him, and will bind
In chains his person, not his stubborn mind . . .
Yet he in peace shall die in his own ways,
And sympathizing nations give him praise;
And heap eulogisms on his injured name,
And thou shalt live forever in his fame!

Considering Smith's earlier excursus on the history of Joseph Smith and the Latter-Day Saints, it is tempting to read this counterfeit of a prophecy as partaking of contemporary enthusiasm for historical exegesis that cast Native peoples as descendants of the Ten Lost Tribes. As invoked in these passages from Elbert Smith's text, however, genealogy, prophecy, and later references to the Star of Bethlehem collapse the trajectory of Christian Messianism as it emerges in the relation between the patriarchs and the prophets of the Old Testament and the biographical fragments of the New, figuring Black Hawk as a Christ-like figure whose superhuman attributes include an uncanny return, even in death. The Black Hawk of history, much less of Smith's invention, fails to free his people, but his fame lives on, a portent of his inevitable resurrection. The implications of this revised Covenantalist history of US territorial expansion and Indigenous dispossession are never fully explored, much less incorporated within the structure of the narrative; nor does Smith seem much troubled by the implication of Calvinist doctrine within a history of Catholic evangelism and Marian iconography. Nonetheless, this prediction is not just a spectacular set piece, another piece of masonry within the baroque assembly of Smith's text. As with his descriptions of Niagara, the genealogy and prophecy of Black Hawk serve little purpose other than embellishment, the metaphorical elasticity of prophecy consecrating the material surplus Smith hopes to wring from the resource of his own imagination. In Smith's telling, Ma-ka-tai-me-she-kia-kiak the person dies only to be risen as the commodity, Black Hawk; while the exorcism of their person—the embodied figure and his living reputation as a military nuisance to the expansion of the settler state—makes way for the realization of the settler and the fantasy of unbridled commercial speculation.

While presenting his text in the guise of a historical epic—a form otherwise dedicated to the superlunary, the majestic, and the sublime— the most recurring and consequential preoccupation of Smith's *Ma-ka-tai-me-she-kiak-kiak* is far more prosaic: the enthusiastic celebration of the exceedingly terrestrial matter of speculation and commerce, the mundane alchemy of promise made profit. Addressed to "all the lovers of the arts of Poesy and the Belle Lettres, and to all the friends and patrons of American enterprise and home industry," from its opening dedication to its final stanzas, *Ma-ka-tai-me-she-kia-kiak* sutures poetic license and economic utility, justifying the superficiality of the former by invoking the materiality of the latter, certain in the hope that the work, "may prove useful and amusing" for those with the sensitivity to appreciate the relationship between art and artifice.

This comprehensive treatise portrays things as they were in the early settlement of Wisconsin and Northern Illinois, when civilization first dawned upon the beautiful forests and prairies, and the cultivation of the luxurious soil commenced; and shows this country's natural and abundant resources. Its fruitful mines of silver, lead, and copper, where men dig for hidden treasures in the bowels of the earth, and become rich, together with those of the Lake Superior country, where now is the rush of those who wish to make their futures; the cheapness of the soil, which produces so bountifully both the necessities and luxuries of life; the prospect of entering into a profitable business with a small capital, and the chances for speculation afforded by early and choice locations; the almost certain prospect of bettering one's condition and circumstances by a change of pace, and of living in the enjoyment of health, peace and competence in another clime, are just inducements, and are all things worthy to be inquired into. . . . The author might easily have swelled this volume to five times its present size—but this would, in a considerable degree, have defeated his object; which was, to make a useful work, comprehending much in little, whose low price would bring it within the reach of every-body. . . . To the admirers of the art of poesy, it is presumed this work will afford great pleasure and delight; while to those who are not in the same degree capable of perceiving and relishing its beauties, it cannot fail to be a source of information that will abundantly repay the cost.[47]

Confident in the assertion that *Ma-ka-tai-me-she-kiak-kiak* is consecrated to the practical and the earth-bound, Smith, in a preface, offers the text to his readers as an allegory of the occult power of capital to render fact from fiction, thereby transforming the ephemeral inventions of poesy into the substance of material wealth. While certain of the aesthetic worthiness of his text, for Smith, the final and incontrovertible measure of its value is in its function as a secular oracle, an almanac dedicated to the mundane art of encouraging investment and inflating fortunes, harnessing desire to purpose, and reconciling the contrivances of the imagination with the realization of capital. As a commentary on the socioeconomic utility of literary artifice, *Ma-ka-tai-me-she-kia-kiak* presents its readers with an uncanny sketch of the social forces that propelled Smith's fortunes. What reputation Smith enjoyed was born of an orgy of speculation, an unforeseeable irregularity within the literary marketplace that made many early investors conspicuous fortunes, but that was nonetheless eventually corrected, forgotten, erased. Swollen by gossip and innuendo, engorged by an avalanche of scrutiny that "comprehend[ed] much in little," the history of Smith's career mirrored the notional ideal of wealth realized through the act of speculation, offering an uncanny likeness of capital at its most mysterious and mundane. Drawn from Smith's preface, the aforementioned clause was meant ostensibly to convey his singular economy of purpose and of verse, his disciplined refusal of the turgid and the gross in pursuit of both metrical elegance and maximum affordability, as well as his insight into the big picture, his ability to divine the forest from a tree. Yet, as a mission statement for his literary work, it serves also, if unwittingly, to highlight the glaring discrepancy between Smith's ability and his fame, drawing attention to the distance separating his talents from his laurels and the myriad insinuations through which the latter were born. As with the story of the Black Hawk War, in general, through its mindless, unremitting repetition, Smith drew enormous credit from the counterfeit, as the fact of his celebrity was labored into being so was the fame of the war he sought to sing.

Conclusion

What is the weight of forgetting? What is its cost? The historiography of the Black Hawk War produced the fact of the Black Hawk War, marshaling a range of disparate events and sometimes unrelated circumstances and packaging them as a singularity, an event, something definitive of a moment in time and space. Fashioned as an event, the intertextual, citational culture of literary echoes expanded the influence of the fiction, in its eternal afterlife lending it a presence far more substantive than any it enjoyed during the months of its undead waking. Historiography cut the cord, severing the obligations of kinship within the structure of Indigenous sovereignty and offering the compensatory figment of the nation, that gloriously vulnerable ward of the state.

Writing history, settlers laid claim to themselves as self-reliant, self-valorizing by enacting the hatred of their dependency, of the actual history of our plural existence, through the embrace of a vicious, elemental destructiveness, through an intimacy with destruction that tore away at the healthy body of Indigenous sovereignty to bring forth the golem of the nation. A ritual of birth and death, historiography mobilizes a shapeless, nameless desire—the desire for an otherwise—and offers it consolation as realized in the arms of a substitute, a surrogate, the affected body of the nation cradled in the loving arms of the state. Historiography gives a name to this desire and thus a direction, a shape. But we do not know its name; nor do we know what it asks of us.

4 / Things Sweet to Taste: Corn and the Thin Gruel of Racial Capitalism

Born from the body of the land and fed by the nutrient matter of Indigenous sovereignty, the fledgling nation is fitted to the arms of the state, its body shaped under the pressure of its anxious fingers, pressing the misshapen and malformed into the approximation of an ideal. The previous chapters explored nineteenth-century histories of the Black Hawk War as a means to illustrate the ways in which "the actual history of our plural existence"—the long history of conflict and violence, amity and aggression, mutuality and distrust, hatred and respect, kinship and its violation—was enclosed within the propulsive dimensions of narrative and retold as a series of fables about warfare and the romance of the frontier, the inexorable tragedy of the Indian, and the redemption of the land from the blight of Indigenous degeneration. The extraction of lead and its manufacture as bullets gave life to necropolitical death worlds characterized by environmental deterioration, mineral toxicity, and organized killing; when fashioned as type, however, lead resources from the Upper Mississippi River Valley allowed for the promulgation of such fables as history, a genre of popular literature pressed into service as ideology in the guise of print. Transforming the history of the conflict into a device through which to suture the national body upon an imperial frame, histories of the Black Hawk War mediated anxieties that attended individuated bodies, tethering fears of physical vulnerability, of disintegration and injury, to a shared sense of historical uncertainty, of national debility, as well as the consolation of purpose to be found in the arms of the state. A vehicle for the capacitation of the nation, through revision, compilation, and memorialization, the historiography of the Black Hawk War harnessed "the actual history of our plural existence"—the history of colonialism, kinship, negotiation, trespass, and invasion—for the malign purposes of statecraft and economy; it claimed the material substance of Indigenous sovereignty as sustenance, a body harvested for its organs, its fluids drained into the arteries of capital and empire. Taken as a component of the prose of counter-sovereignty, historiography constituted one aspect of the infrastructure of settler colonialism and capital accumulation, a means of physical, material enclosure that contributed also to the foreclosure of different visions of association, of community, different ways of imagining how to live together, even in the assuredness of conflict, and the inevitability of harm.

In the previous chapters I suggest that lead and lead extraction provided a means to think the historical legacies of settler colonialism and empire as geophysical secretions, that is, as attempts at overwriting compelling histories of Indigenous place and peoplehood—expressions of Indigenous sovereignty—through the physical disaggregation of the terrestrial surface as a set of commodified resources. In this chapter, I explore the geophysical secretions of capital and empire through a consideration of settler agriculture. I am interested in the colonization of the Upper Mississippi River Valley and its subsequent development for purposes of commercial agriculture in relation to the socioeconomic, ecological, and biopolitical dimensions of what Jason Moore has designated "cheap food." For Moore, "cheap food" describes the agricultural surplus necessary for the reproduction of labor as the indispensable element of production and the consequent realization of surplus-value. "Cheap food," as such, is a means of sustaining the body, of replenishing it so it might again become enervated, its vitality poured into processes of production and valorized as capital. I take the settler capture of Indigenous land and the elaboration of a topography of commercial agriculture as an insidious geophysical intervention upon the terrain of Indigenous sovereignty and self-determination, a means of harnessing the historical and geophysical vitality of Indigenous lifeways to the biopolitical imperatives of capital through the expropriation and transfer of nutrients. Abetted by the mechanisms of the market, nutrients—captured through and transferred by the commercialization of agriculture and the commodification of its produce—were made the sustenance of loving, laboring, reproducing bodies; of the working classes—enslaved and free—preserved, however poorly, by the theft of Indigenous land and the consequent expropriation of the geophysical secretions by which the land had been made to sustain multifarious expressions of life. I situate the geophysical and geopolitical dynamics of cheap food production through the work of building and sustaining the settler home: a work, I argue, that is materially expressive of the refusal of Indigenous sovereignty and the obligations of kinship.

In this chapter, I explore settler agriculture and food cultures as theories of property. Assuming property as the primary organizing theory of the social, the settler home manifests the principle of fortification and possession that extends into the otherwise open fields of settler agriculture, the square lines and right angles of the boxy settler home mimicked by the organization and maintenance of fields. Silent and unbidden, these unassuming, prosaic lines describe a family relationship between the affective formations of settler colonialism, the topography of capitalist agriculture and nutrient extraction, and the global supply networks through which populations are sustained as labor through the production and consumption of cheap food. I trace these relationships through an object as ubiquitous as lead, though far more conspicuous: the myriad forms of calorie-rich edible grasses described by settlers as *Zea mays* or, more colloquially, as corn. The lead drawn from the Upper Mississippi River Valley would facilitate the necropolitical work of Indian removal, that is, of fabulism, murder, and genocide. In contrast, the regional corn monoculture inaugurated under the auspices of settler colonialism would be essential to the biopolitical imperatives of the capitalist mode of production, facilitating the formation and sustenance of an urban working class dedicated to nascent forms of industrial production as well as a slave-driven plantation monoculture predicated almost exclusively on the fabrication of the raw materials necessary for textile production. The history of corn within settler colonialism, I argue, embodies the literal and material, biological and geophysical metabolic of what Richard Slotkin has called "regeneration through violence." Whereas Slotkin was primarily interested in the mythology of the frontier as a site from which the cultural enactment of violence allowed the nation to renew its vitality and its purpose, I stake a claim to "regeneration through violence" as a process that draws together the violence of lead extraction and the forceful implementation of settler agriculture with the perpetual renewal of the laboring body and the body of the nation, with the physical vitality of the body and the nation maintained through the expropriation of Indigenous agriculture and associated ecologies of Indigenous sovereignties. A form of accumulation by dispossession, I am interested in the different scales at which these imbricated forms of primitive accumulation occur, that is, the ways in which processes of extraction unite the biomolecular and the nutrient, the soil and its produce, as well as its capacity to hold and sustain a variety of plant, animal, and human life, to say nothing of the infrastructural arrangements by which lead and land capture becomes extraction, and extraction becomes the mechanism of capacitation of labor and its reproduction. In addition to the local and the microbial, I am interested in primitive accumulation and agriculture as they assert themselves with respect to the transnational, global, and infrastructural mechanisms by which the obscenely realized nutrient densities become the matter of a commodity with a fully global itinerary. While I take corn as emblematic of the irreducibly complex interrelationship between Native peoples and settler cultures, I am less interested in corn in itself, than in corn as one among many nonhuman relatives that Indigenous and settler communities relate to as food. I am interested in the meaning of food as it relates to relations within and between communities, the role of food as a gift, or a weapon, as well as an elemental need that impels an ethical relationship to myriad others: the nonhuman relatives taken as food, the human relatives unable to secure a regular supply of food. Food, here, is a means to consider sociality through the guise of agriculture, and agriculture as a means of organizing the social meanings attached to and conveyed by consumption and conviviality.

A nonhuman relative wickedly objectified as a resource and made a commodity, I look at the produce of Indigenous agriculture as it is stolen and made part of the infrastructures of settler colonialism. I explore agrarian capitalism as composing a geophysical document, the ecological palimpsest of US counter-sovereignty. I am concerned with the ways in which "the prose of counter-sovereignty"—as a linguistic form that extends across written and spoken language—emerges to obscure and distort the imperial provenance of US nationality through the "deligitim[ization] [of] Indigenous modes of relationship" and the "solidif[ication] [of] a colonial sovereignty unmoored from them." In my reading, however, the prose of counter-sovereignty is a story told across the land and upon the land through forms of plant life, a story that attempts to efface the visual languages of Indigenous place but is nonetheless punctuated and punctured by its most indelible traces.[1] Like lead extraction, agricultural infrastructures compose a form of writing that imposes itself upon the land, shaping it to the image of capital and the desire to realize the self through capital. Indigenous plants, stolen from those people who shaped their histories and whose histories were shaped by them become unwitting collaborators in the history of primitive accumulation within settler colonialism and the structures of invasion.

Where nineteenth-century miners carved the history of lead extraction into the rock and soil and air of the Upper Mississippi region, the text of that history is largely illegible except for those who know where to look, what signs to read. An inscriptive ecology that shapes the geological, the sensible traces of this record have been all but erased: mines have been filled, shot towers have been knocked down, furnaces have been left to rot, slag piles have been washed away and turned into dangerously toxic levels of lead particulate that are carried along by the flow of the Mississippi. By contrast, in the Upper Mississippi River Valley, corn is unavoidable. Planted as part of a rectilinear Lockean theory of property and improvement, corn becomes domineering, so ubiquitous and so commanding as to acquire the invisibility of the obvious. Vertical in orientation, its general uniformity of height contributes to the illusion of an unvariegated terrain, flat and monotonous, just as the exacting rows in which it is planted create a sense of volume that allows for efficient calculability. The capitalist infrastructure of corn projects and legitimizes a settler conception of home and safety as defined by boundaries, separations, exclusions as well as by a kind of familiarity that traverses space through time. Corn is ever present within settler capitalism, a companion if not a relative. A comforting form, it is also vaguely menacing, a home to imagined threats, of beastly things lurking. Its tall stalks provide refuge and camouflage for escaped slaves, convicts, or bandits, relatively harmless game animals, or more vicious predatory species, and its infrastructure within agrarian capitalism composes a geography of flight and the ambivalence of freedom. Corn may write itself upon the land as a theory of property, its rows shaped to the uncanny rectilinear grid so studiously and laboriously maintained and asserted by the architects of the settler colonialism, it harbors and preserves the unwelcome sense of property as the result of a world undone, of places and people that were made to disappear, and of a past that agitates against the designs of colonial expropriation and racial capitalism. Corn inscribes a story about home, even as it harbors the memory of home and its production as the condition of something unmade, something waiting, an intimation of threat, of danger.

This chapter attends to the insistently and irreducibly local, the personal, and the everyday to illuminate the geopolitical and macroeconomic dimensions of primitive accumulation and property as elements of a regional, transnational agricultural economy. Although I am interested in the material infrastructures of that agricultural economy, as well as the ways in which commercial cereal production is implicated in the myriad networks of nutrient distribution that capacitate the laboring body, in what follows, I am concerned primarily with corn as food and as a technology of belonging, a source of sustenance, an occasion for conviviality and an expression of desire. One of the material bases for Indigenous sovereignty and self-determination, corn is also the material filament of a national and imperial geography running through millions of bodies, across space and time, constituting a global agricultural space, a story settlers tell among themselves about belonging, about property, and the nobility of their trespass on Indigenous land, knowledge, and place.

Among the early generations of settlers, the cultivation of corn was a means of survival, a technology of nutrient capture and transfer that fed and sustained life, allowing for settlers to live and make homes; but it was also a marker of foreignness and poverty as well as of the limits to their command of the environment, its human and nonhuman inhabitants, and the relations among them. One element within the ecological palimpsest of counter-sovereignty, corn preserves the precarity of home, the risks inherent to the settler colonial enterprise as well as the adjustment of rural agriculture to the dictates of an industrialized urban capitalism. In what follows, I look at the history of corn to elucidate the myriad stories it tells about home and the making of home; about intimacy as well as desire, need, hunger, and want. The history composed through corn, I argue, tells a story of interdependence, of the ways in which people are necessarily dependent upon one another, and how those interdependencies—their pleasures and their pains—are negotiated; how the necessarily painful need people have for one another is made into a source of delight, contentment, and joy. I take the transformation of the ambivalence of needing into the desire for belonging to be one of the dynamic elements of Indigenous sovereignty as a mode of organizing sociality, a means of negotiating the perils of intimacy through a conscientious recognition of the inherent fragility of life and the forms of extended mutualities—the ways of being together and being alone—that best serve to remediate its vulnerabilities. Beginning from an epigenetic history of the coevolution of Indigenous socialities and the cross-pollinated grasses that compose *Zea mays*, I read Black Hawk's account of corn and its braided social, political, economic, and cultural significance as an echo of the story traditions of the Corn Woman or Corn Mother common among many Native cultures. Drawing upon my reading of burial rituals from chapter 1, I look at corn as the nexus of materiality and metaphor within the maintenance and reproduction of Indigenous sovereignty, one that bears within it the history of kinship as a biochemical nutrient vitality. I look also to Black Hawk's descriptions of corn culture to think Sauk sovereignty and kin relations in relation to enlarged forms of kinship, the interlocking concentric circles drawing together nations and peoples, Natives and settlers, as well as Natives and arrivants, those whose transport to the Americas was neither volitional nor desired. I am most immediately provoked by corn as a site of entangled Indigenous and settler ecologies, an object through which to explore the parasitism of settler colonialism on Indigenous sovereignty; as well as the expression of a damaged, destructive intimacy, of kinship offered and refused. The history of corn within the culture of settler colonialism is the history of the dependency of settler lives upon Indigenous lifeways, agriculture, and hospitality. It is also the history of the exploitation of this hospitality as well as the pugnacious ambivalence, the outraged disdain, of those so dependent.

The history of this dependence unsettles the pretense of settler self-fashioning and bodily integrity asserted through the prose of counter-sovereignty. Literally consuming the remains of the Indigenous past—the nutrient densities of the Upper Mississippi River region and the Plains made possible by generations of Native agriculturalists, to say nothing of the decomposition of Native structures and Native bodies—the culture of US settler colonialism is built upon the genius of Indigenous peoples whose forms of agricultural husbandry, land tenure, and geophysical engineering gave rise to the material vitalities that continue to sustain forms of US agricultural capitalism. In this chapter, I explore this proposition through a consideration of testimonies recorded by settlers drawn to the Upper Mississippi River Valley in the immediate aftermath of the so-called Black Hawk War. The first testimony, from a 1919 manuscript composed by an elderly pioneer by the name of Isaac Kramer, looks to the history of settlement as one of hunger and perpetual deprivation, where food is a luxury and home is a bulwark demanding constant reinforcement. The second testimony expands upon the writing of Sarah Welch Nossaman; it relates the history of settlement as one of labor and bodily affliction, of the pain of growing, sustaining, processing, cooking, feeding. Nossaman's testimony is especially noteworthy as—among its many other attributes—it remains the only eyewitness account to the theft and dismemberment of Makataimeshekiakiak's remains. Throughout, I read the history of bodily need registered in these testimonies against more professional histories of the Black Hawk War that are taking their pains and their pleasures, their feelings of need, deprivation, and satisfaction as evidence of Indigenous presence, as marks of an Indigenous history denied, foreclosed, repressed. If histories of the Black Hawk War sought, among other considerations, to project an idealized national citizenry, an idealized national body—one constituted, in part, by rituals of bloodshed and the eternal recurrence of Indian war—these testimonies evoke myriad insecurities that belie the fictions of counter-sovereignty, exposing the relays tethering settler communities to Native peoples, and the forms of cannibalism by which settlers forged their homes, the ways in which they made their homes by overturning and exploiting the remains of their neighbors.

Maize and the Melancholy History of Settler Colonialism

Relationships between US settler colonialism, the extirpation of Indigenous land, and the emergence of commercial agriculture have been explored, generally, through studies of racial capitalism as a transatlantic formation—notably in histories relating the rise of the transatlantic textile economy to legacies of coercive and violent population transfer and the forcible extraction of labor. In this story, the theft of Indigenous land and the forced transfer of populations—that is, the violent displacement of ostensibly indolent Native peoples by planters and slaves conditioned by the appetites of the market—makes way for the expansion of cotton production in the southeast, on land long nurtured by the Cherokee and the Choctaw, the Seminole, the Chickasaw, and the Creek; the Trail of Tears makes way for the internal slave trade and the development of the cotton monoculture of the plantation South. Nonetheless, the biopolitical strategies that facilitated the flourishing of nineteenth-century Atlantic capitalism would have been unthinkable without complementary economies of food production and distribution. Much of this economy centered the commercial development of land seized from Native peoples along the riparian arteries of the Mississippi River and the attendant commodification of its variegated resources. Hewing close to the watercourses of the Mississippi and its tributaries, over the course of the nineteenth century, the North American Corn Belt—encompassing portions of present-day Illinois, Iowa, Ohio, Indiana, Michigan, Minnesota, Wisconsin, and Nebraska—produced twice the average yield of corn per acre than other land under cultivation through the United States, occasioning the rapid development of trade infrastructures that could make this surplus available for sale in eastern and southern markets.[2] Traveling by road, river, and rail, corn from the Old Northwest territory made its way east, stoking the fires of industry—first in Chicago, then in New York, Philadelphia, and Baltimore—while steamboats drove corn south, along the Mississippi, to Saint Louis and to New Orleans, historical sites of French colonial authority that by then had been incorporated within the body of the nation, as inaugurated under the protection of the state.

While the circumstances of the so-called Black Hawk War had opened the region to development within the terms of such geophysical and terrestrial capitalization, the formation as a regional economy around transcontinental, transatlantic agricultural production came about as part of what Jason W. Moore has identified as the global reorganization of cereal crop production and the associated demand for cheap food and cheap land. Confronted by the biopolitical exigencies of capital, expressed through a range of concerns touching upon the socioeconomic dynamics attendant the reproduction of labor and the sustenance of laboring bodies, the expansion of agricultural yields was necessary for the maintenance of laboring, urbanized proletarians to serve as vessels for the manifestation of surplus-value. Wedded to outmoded, feudal relations of production, the lords of European agriculture were incapable of meeting this demand. Coupled with the devastation suffered across Europe because of the inter-imperialist conflicts of the late eighteenth and early nineteenth centuries—the Seven Years' War and the Napoleonic Wars—the intransigence of the gentry pushed European agriculture into a steady political and economic decline, just as North American capital was identifying and colonizing new terrain for similiar exploitation. As a consequence, over the first decades of the nineteenth century, "the breadbasket of capitalism would migrate, from Europe to the United States," contributing to the dispossession of Native peoples and giving rise to a new market, a new mechanism for the regulation of labor, and a regional economy shaped by forms of commercial, industrial agriculture that bore less relation to the sustenance of local ecologies than to the extractive inducements of the market and new riparian and rail infrastructures.[3]

Corn was, of course, one of the instruments by which Europeans made their physical and material home in the Americas, as well as one of the ideological technologies by which Europeans made the Americas home. As Arturo Warman has indicated, the expropriation of Indigenous corn by European settlers was essential to the social and physical vitality of the colonial project, most especially among those British settlements in North America that would later compose the United States. A largely urban phenomenon, the religious dissenters who colonized New England were inexpert agriculturalists, and they were largely incapable of sustaining themselves without the support of Indigenous peoples. This was a hideous perversion of their sense of mission. Self-styled emissaries of a new covenant, this generation of settlers held fast to the pietistic dogma that they brought a figurative, spiritual salvation to the peoples of the New World, only to find themselves literally and materially saved by those Indigenous peoples whose knowledge, labor, and produce were their only weapons in the battle against starvation. In the United States, folklore and popular culture preserve something of the history of this dependency in the lore of the first Thanksgiving and through tales of the heroic figure of Tisquantum—one of the few survivors of the epidemic that wiped out the Patuxet nation—who enters the fairy story of American history as Squanto, the friendly Indian who taught the Pilgrims how to grow maize. As Warman observes, these romances, including the romance of corn as a gift—freely given, graciously received—obscures a more brutal record of coercion and capture, forced labor, and outright theft. When desperate, settlers did not necessarily hope for Native charity, but would steal food and grain outright, sometimes kidnapping individual Native people to serve as captive authorities on local vegetable and animal life and the best ways of coaxing food from the land. Over time, as the fear of starvation gave way to the motivations of avarice, settlers would lay claim to fields long cultivated by their Indigenous neighbors, while chopping down old-growth forest to make way for new fields that might serve a growing demand for American grain. While settlers consistently preferred and valued European wheat more highly than American corn, European cereals and farming techniques proved difficult to adapt to American ecologies; as such, even well after such foreign grains had become a staple of the American diet, corn continued to be planted, in abundance, as fodder for animals and a reliably hardy source of produce, especially in times of privation.[4]

The history of the capture of *Zea mays* and its transformation into a vector of colonial occupation composes an early moment in the history of its commodification and emergence as a global staple, while the subsequent rearrangement of trans-local agricultures—the adaptation of the plant to unlikely non-Native environments, people, and places as well as the adaptation of otherwise unsuitable ecologies to the needs of the plant—is only the most recent episode in the long epigenetic history of plant and animal, corn and culture. The forms of corn that are consumed by humans and animals are hybrids but not accidents. While genetic research on corn has demonstrated its origins in the cross-fertilization of teosinte and *Tripsacum* grass sometime in the past three millennia—with some countervailing theories positing the possible involvement of some extinct and unknown ancestor—it is unlikely that this process could not have occurred without some form of purposeful intervention. As the environmental anthropologist Jude Todd writes, "neither teosinte nor *Tripsacum* looks anything like corn. . . . Moreover, these ancient grasses are not different species of the same genus but members of different genera. Crossing *Tripsacum* with teosinte would be analogous to a human mating with a gorilla."[5] The resulting hybrid, Todd goes on to note, is incapable of regenerating itself without human intervention: covered by a husk, when the seeds fall to earth they are unlikely to germinate; and, if they do, the number of seeds on a single ear of corn is such that in their competition over soil-based nutrients, none would survive. Left untended, maize consumes itself, depleting its immediate environment of the resources necessary for other plant life to be sustained: it must be cared for to ensure its own well-being, as well as that of its companions and neighbors. As Todd suggests, the history of corn is not one of spontaneous cross-pollination or random mutation, but of coevolution with human communities, each developing "through an intimate dance of mutual interaction between [Native peoples] and [a variety of] ancient grasses."[6] For Todd, the record of these entwined histories are preserved in the genome of the *Zea mays* plant, as well as the multifarious varieties of corn nurtured by contemporary Native peoples, who have spared ancient varietals from later forms of intervention and exploitation predicated upon the commercialization of agriculture and the commodification of its produce.

Among Native peoples, these living, coevolutionary histories are themselves coextensive with the epigenetic literary traditions that concern the "arrival" of corn on earth, as well as its multifarious relationships to the formation and reproduction of Indigenous societies and cultures. Within these stories, these traditions—the genesis of Indigenous agriculture in general and corn culture specifically—are almost invariably traced to the figure of the Corn Maiden, or the Corn Mother, manifestations of the Corn Woman. An ethereal, superlunary figure who helps to sustain her terrestrial family by drawing vegetal life from the earth, the Corn Woman offers maize to their human children as a gift and a reward, a token offered in recognition of human generosity or rectitude. In tandem with beans, pumpkins, and game, the generosity of the Corn Woman serves to renew the earth and its produce, arranging vegetal and animal life to better sustain the lives of humans and human communities, while orienting the earth to the sky, the terrestrial to the otherworldly.[7] Although stories of the Corn Woman are preserved differently among different Indigenous nations, in their abundance and their variety, these stories convey much about the entanglements of Indigenous agricultural husbandry with nettlesome histories of habitation and competition over place, as well as histories that record the processes of becoming oriented toward a place, of becoming related to other people through the care shown in maintaining and shaping place through agriculture as a technology of geophysical secretion, a means of arranging growth and decay, sediment and nutrients, and their distribution across place and among peoples. Often concluding in her death and burial, and the subsequent transformation of the Corn Woman's body into a vessel of agricultural renewal, the story of the Corn Woman underscores the relationship between burial and the bounty of agricultural sociality as well as an attunement to specific places, that is, the notion of belonging to a place, to the body of the land, and the body that is the land. At the same time, to the extent that the Corn Women often meet their fate because of violence dealt them by their human children, stories of the Corn Women are also stories about the ambivalence of rootedness, about the anxieties that arise when humans accede to the necessary of their interdependence as well as their dependence upon beings who may appear only as distant, inscrutable others; beings both respirant and ethereal. Assuaging hunger, as food, corn fulfills an elemental need, while evoking desire and fear: the desire to eat and be satiated, to be at rest and at home, as well as the fear of complacency, of being exposed by staying in one place, building attachments to people and to place. Spread across the continent through Indigenous trade networks, the history of the ecology of maize was the history of this vulnerability, because it recorded the difficult and no doubt painful yet also likely joyous negotiations among nations seeking access to common resources of often limited amount or duration.

> I will here relate the manner in which corn first came. According to tradition, handed down to our people, a beautiful woman was seen to descend from the clouds, and alight upon the earth, by two of our ancestors, who had killed a deer, and were sitting by a fire, roasting a part of it to eat. They were astonished at seeing her, and concluded that she must be hungry, and had smelt the meat—and immediately went to her, taking with them a piece of the roasted venison. They presented it to her, and she [ate]—and told them to return to the spot where she was sitting, at the end of one year, and they would find a reward for their kindness and generosity. She then ascended to the clouds, and disappeared. The two men returned to their village, and explained to the nation what they had seen, done, and heard—but were laughed at by their people. When the period arrived, for them to visit this consecrated ground, where they were to find a reward for their attention to the beautiful woman of the clouds, they went away with a large party, and found, where her right hand had rested on the ground, *corn* growing—and where the left hand had rested, *beans*— and immediately where she had been seated, *tobacco.*[8]

While the tale of the Corn Woman as related by Black Hawk does not include reference to her death and burial—it preserves the image of corn as a gift from the extramundane, of the extramundane as flesh making fertile the earth—it is powerfully resonant with his account of the medicine feast that marks the beginning of spring, the burial of the winter's dead, and the prelude to spring planting. As noted, in Black Hawk's account, this spring medicine feast weaves together the social and communal life of the nation with that of the earth and its produce—its vegetable, animal, and human life—as well as its fertile, mineral components. At the end of the winter hunt, the remains of those who have died are returned home, physically, so they might be buried in the place that they knew as home, the place where their ancestors were buried, thus contributing to the composition of new strata of land, new elements of place. This is, I have suggested, a moment in which the history of the Sauk nation—the stories that bind the nation across time and shape its orientation to the present and future—are collected and seeded as part of the land, the bodies of the dead anchoring the history of the people to a specific place while contributing to the renewal of the soil as bearer of nutrient life. Corn, in Black Hawk's account, is emblematic of the substance of these relations, materializing the history of the people as a source of sustenance and composing the history of the people through the creation of new strata of soil. The nutrients of the dead support the crops that sustain the lives of both animals and humans; moreover, as they decay, the remains of those crops—the squash, beans, and maize common to Sauk agriculture—are enfolded within the earth, contributing another layer of matter to its surface. The relationship here between history and sustenance is one that also preserves the bitterness of death by evoking the body bent to the work of agricultural husbandry, the meticulous, tedious, and physically onerous work of tending corn to harvest. As in the Corn Mother stories, maize, for Black Hawk, is a gift, and as a gift, it demands reciprocity—in this instance, the pain of the body given over in supplication to the ground in which corn is planted. The blessings of the Corn Mother do not come without obligations, without torment; with pleasure, to be sure, but not without sorrow and grief.

In Black Hawk's account, the labor involved in planting corn is prelude to the obligations involved in making literal, lineal human kin: organizing intimate and emotional relationships within the nation through rituals of courtship and sponsoring the renewal of the nation through family and reproduction. "Our women plant the corn, and as soon as they get done, we make a feast, and dance the crane dance, in which they join us, dressed in their best, and decorated with feathers. At this feast our young braves select the young woman they wish to have for a wife." After arranging the match through the consent of the mothers of both parties, a young man "goes to the lodge [of the young woman] when all are asleep, (or pretend to be), lights his matches, which have been provided for the purpose, and soon finds where his intended sleeps. He then awakens her, and holds the light to his face that she may know him—after which he places the light close to her. If she blows it out, the ceremony is ended, and he appears in the lodge next morning, as one of the family."[9]

These relations, Black Hawk goes on, are intimate and full but not coercive. "During the first year they ascertain whether or not they can agree with each other, and can live happy—if not, they part, and each look out again. . . . No indiscretion can banish a woman from her parental lodge . . . the kettle is [always] over the fire to feed them."[10] Sex and marriage do not constitute the substance of kinship, Black Hawk tells us, but are merely one form of its expression. Kinship between people is sustained by a desire to remain within the terms of a kin relation, by a desire to share fire and what fire might feed them.

Albeit a seemingly conventional description of the rituals surrounding courtship and marriage, Black Hawk's account of these arrangements is nonetheless rife with curiosities that further elaborate the metaphorical and material relations among food, orality, corn, and consumption. Concluding with the image of the kettle over the fire and the infrangible ties among families, Black Hawk draws attention to the question of consumption and sustenance, of food and the preparation of food as expressions of fidelity among people. Refracted through the image of the match flame that passes between the suitor and his intended, fire manifests relations among kin, their ambivalence, and the expressions of desire that sustains kinship as a form of attachment. As a medium of food preparation—a means of finding pleasure, of taking and making pleasure in sustenance, a medium for the transformation of collectivity into conviviality—fire evokes the legacies of human relations with nature, of the transformation of nature as a means of sustaining multifarious forms of life through the secretion of nitrogen, potassium, phosphorus, carbon, and ash. In the form of the match flame, fire also serves as a token of desire, one that embodies the elusiveness of love and sex, the dangers of intimacy and their inscrutability. A prop dramatizing the matrilineal organization of kinship through the exchange of men among women, the ritual of the match undermines notions of biological reproductivity as the foundation of kinship by drawing attention to desire and sexuality as nonreproductive modes of intimacy. Inasmuch as the act of blowing out the flame serves to indicate assent to a marital arrangement, the ritual of the match forces an awareness of the relationship between orality and sex, and the matter of oral sex as nonreproductive form of copulation. Instead of forging the intimacies of nonlineal kinship through the creation of new life, through the creation of new people, intimacy with another is established through exhalation, through the expression of the breath; as well as through an act of consumption, of taking another person into your mouth and making them a part of yourself. Bypassing mundane expressions of genital sex and gender difference, in Black Hawk's account, kinship is forged through desire and the preservation of desire, illuminated, animated, and preserved through the geochemical mediation of flame.

More than simply facilitating the transit of desire between two lovers, the ritual of the match and the flame draws attention also to the obligations of kinship as they suture a more expansive sense of collectivity than those bound to lineal notions of decent and liberal nationhood. While the match and the flame materialize the forms of desire and reciprocity that sustain kinship, that materiality is routed through an object of conspicuously European manufacture, an object that is also an emblem of the material force of the rifle as a source of sovereignty and self-determination. Lucifer matches being largely unavailable for consumers until many years after Black Hawk's death, his description of the flame as sustained by a "match" would seem to indicate its affiliation with the matchlock and the matchlock rifle, an early form of musket in which the missile was propelled by a powder ignition caused by contact with a lit flame. As a matchlock, within the space of the courting ritual, the flame commands attention as an emblem of the rifle as well as of the hunt and hunting as part of the art of procuring sustenance as a means of sustaining home and sustaining the nation in its connection with place. The matchlock tethers this ritual scene of making kin not only to a mechanism of war and death-dealing but also to a history of manufacture and exchange and the obligations of kinship, a history that draws the aggressively other—the unruly, disrespectful other, the animal, as well as the human—toward a space of customary intimacy. "Match," in this sense, serves as a double entendre, naming the object of the matchlock as well as the figurative act of matching, of being paired with another, bound together, as a function of some abstruse likeness.[11] Like the burial objects interred with Makataimeshekiakiak's remains, as it sits at the center of the courtship ritual, the match is a peculiar artifact of the relationship of Native peoples to settler cultures, the ways in which Native and settler cultures impinged upon one another, as well as the ways in which Native peoples made space for the settler within the lattice of kinship that constituted their sense of themselves as a people, thus transforming objects of settler manufacture into emblems of a newfound intimacy.

The space instantiated by this ritual provides the metaphorical, physical, and emotional filament by which the abundance of the Corn Woman manifests itself upon, within, and through the body of the earth. Kinship, in this account, is the produce of corn, a form of association nurtured by the plant sprung from the seed that must be ruthlessly well tended and lovingly cared for, where care is understood as both solicitous and violent, part of a social ecology that recognizes the necessarily anxious work of making kin and sustaining kin relations. Corn, in Black Hawk's narrative, is both emblem and mechanism of these intimacies as they shape relations among Indigenous peoples and settlers. It is a vehicle through which to negotiate relations among peoples that also facilitates a debate over the arrangement of space and time, of gender, force, and value. This dimension of corn as a tether binding one people to another—as well as to the intimacies and violence that bind one to another—emerges, in Black Hawk, through his description of credit. "We next commence horse-racing, and continue our sport and feasting, until all the corn is secured. We then prepare to leave our village for our hunting grounds. The traders arrive, and give us credit for such articles as we want to clothe our families, and enable us to hunt."[12] Marking the end of the corn harvest and the beginning of the winter hunt, the arrival of the traders and the distribution of goods on credit was measured against the future payment in animal skins the men might negotiate with the traders, and secured by a payment of corn as collateral. "We . . . hold a council with them, to ascertain the price they will give us for our skins, and what they will charge us for goods. We inform them of where we intend hunting—and tell them where to build their houses. At this place, we deposit part of our corn, and leave our old people."[13] This exchange, both social and commercial, facilitated the movement of the year, the transposition of the produce of women's labor into that of men, and the disposition of people over space. "We disperse, in small parties, to make our hunt, and as soon as it is over, we return to our traders' establishment, with our skins, and remain feasting, playing cards and other pastimes, until near the close of the winter. . . . In this way, the year rolled around happily."[14]

Made into an object of exchange, in Black Hawk's account, corn becomes the medium by which Native peoples and settlers negotiate the "real history of our plural existence," as well as the obligations that plurality implies, even as the terms of that relationship were shifting from that of a gift economy to those of a more fully capitalized, more thoroughly commercialized form of exchange. Over the course of the early nineteenth century, the use of corn as collateral transformed the grain from a direct source of sustenance into a form of currency, its nutrient density overwhelmed by its utility as scrip. No longer a piece of an economy of reciprocity, corn was becoming part of an increasingly violent mechanism of dispossession and disorder, a vessel of capital and the process of its valorization, as well as a biopolitical agent of settler capacity and Native enervation. Brought under the managerial authority of the United States, this was most clearly signaled by the emergence of corn-based alcohols, beer and whiskey, and the widespread use of corn whiskey, among European settlers, as a means of settling debts while undermining the forms of physical, bodily discipline that composed a portion of Indigenous self-determination. "As the settlements progressed toward us, we became worse off, and more unhappy. Many of our people . . . would go near the settlements to hunt—and, instead of saving their skins to pay the trader for goods furnished them in the fall, would sell them to the settlers for whiskey! and return in the spring with their families, almost naked, and without the means of getting any thing for them."[15] While the use of maize as collateral had served to facilitate relations among settlers and Native peoples through a complementary exchange of equally useful objects, the distillation of corn as whiskey effected its transformation from a source of sustenance into a compulsively drinkable poison. Offered in exchange for game or skins—quickly, recklessly consumed—whiskey was of little profit for the buyer, transforming an economy of mutuality into one of desperation and dependency. Bereft of food and other provisions, those who traded away furs for alcohol put greater pressure on local game stocks, as they sought to make up their deficits, while the routinization of alcohol consumption put pressure on the social conventions and courtesies that allowed for both uneasy relations of coexistence among peoples and the cultural forms that contributed to the maintenance of equipoise within Indigenous nations.

The distillation of whiskey from corn, as well as its widespread use as an object of exchange, provides a ready image for the transformation of *Zea mays* from an emblem of conviviality—a vitality uniting the sacred and the profane; animal, human, plant, and mineral—into a banalized resource primed for commercial exploitation. With the arrival of American settlers and the steady growth and commercialization of US agriculture came new forms of competition between settlers and Indigenous peoples over both corn and land as increasingly valuable, yet invariably finite resources. The use of whiskey in trade was mirrored by the coercive enclosure of Indigenous land and the limitation of Sauk access to their own productive capacity. "During the winter I received information that three families of whites had arrived at our village and destroyed some of our lodges, and were making fences and dividing our corn-fields for their own use—*and were quarreling among themselves about their lines in the division!*"[16] Harbingers of enclosure and the irregular progress of US counter-sovereignty, the settlers who arrived at Saukenuk between 1829 and 1830 dispensed with the Sauk ambition of agriculture as a collective, social endeavor, carving property into the land by putting up fences and, Black Hawk feared, by "plough[ing] up the bones of our people."[17] Upon their return to Saukenuk following the winter hunt, in Black Hawk's account, the Sauk respected the divisions laid out by the interlopers; however, "in consequence of the improvements of the intruders on our fields, we found considerable difficulty to get ground to plant a little corn. . . . Our women had great difficulty climbing their fences, (being unaccustomed to the kind,) and were ill-treated if they left a rail down. . . . [O]ne of our young men was beat with clubs by two white men for opening a fence which crossed our road. . . . His shoulder blade was broken . . . he soon after died."[18] The seemingly anodyne technologies by which property is enforced and the affective dimensions of home engendered appear, in this instance, as the capacity to render pain ambient, a dimension of the landscape in which everyday interactions portend the rendering of the body, the unrelenting though mundane distress of a body in transit through an unfamiliar environment, and the recomposition of the body in relationship with those most insistent fractures.

In Black Hawk's account, the seizure of the cornfields was followed by a train of abuses that, in themselves, seem to have been driven less by necessity than by a sadistic desire, on the part of settlers, to humiliate local Native peoples. "One of my old friends thought he was safe. His corn-field was on a small island of Rock river. He planted his corn; it came up well— but the white man saw it!—he wanted the island, and took his teams over, ploughed up the corn, and re-planted it for himself! The old man shed tears; not for himself, but the distress his family would be in if they raised no corn. . . . [Another] time, a white man beat one of our women cruelly, for pulling a few suckers of corn out of his field, to suck, when hungry."[19] Not content with merely occupying Sauk land and harnessing its vitality, settlers looked for ways to hollow out the substance of Sauk sovereignty; to steal, cheat, and divest the Sauks of the capacity to sustain themselves through the nurturance of vegetal life, refusing access to corn except as an object of trade and then only in the form of whiskey or pork, a peck to the gallon, or a bushel to the hog.[20] This enforced debilitation, Black Hawk relates, was the condition of his hostility toward the settler community, the act that forced him to adopt a martial posture. "Our women had planted a few patches of corn, which was growing finely, and promised a subsistence for our children—but the *white people again commenced ploughing it up!* I now determined to put a stop to it, by clearing our country of the *intruders*."[21] Soon confronted by federal troops, on the direction of the Prophet, Black Hawk and his retinue attempted one last emissary to US agents and military leaders, dispatching "the daughter of Ma-ta-tas" to council with General Edmund Gaines. While hoping that the whites "would not be so unfriendly" as to take Sauk land, "if they were, she had one favor to ask . . . to be allowed to remain long enough to gather the provisions now growing in their fields; that she was a woman, and had worked hard to raise something to support her children! And, if we [were] driven from our village without being allowed to save our corn, many of our little children must perish with hunger!" According to Black Hawk's account of this affair, Gaines rejected her council out of hand, forcing her guard from the fort, before dismissing her with the salacious invitation that "she might remain if she wished."[22] Having ordered the warriors who accompanied her away from the fort, this remark is less an invitation or an example of martial chivalry than a lascivious rejoinder to an all too reasonable request, a dismissal and a rejection couched in a crass threat of sexual violation.

A portent of rape, Gaines's remark to Ma-ta-tas's daughter evokes the historical and material insinuation of the legacies of colonial expropriation, with myriad forms of sexual assault committed against Native women, as well as the relationship between settler attacks on Native agriculture and the erosion of the socioeconomic bases of women's autonomy within Native cultures. Historically, among the Sauk, women took charge of agricultural labor, and the corn they reaped was one of the primary mechanisms by which they wielded political power, providing a basis for their appreciation as political actors that was based not on ceremonial recognition but material relations. The theft of Sauk land and the destruction of their corn—the literal fruit of women's labor—undermined those relations, and thus, the forms of sociality that sprung from them. As Black Hawk notes, even among those Sauks who doubted his design to hold onto Sauk lands at Saukenuk, he retained outsized support among women. Describing his compatriots attempts at dissuading him of his plans, he wrote, "I had one consolation—for all the women were on my side, on account of their corn-fields."[23] Moreover, as the dialogue from Ma-ta-tas's daughter makes clear, the enclosure of the corn fields was not only an attack women's autonomy among the Sauk but also a threat to the survival of the nation. In throwing the Sauks off their land without allowing for a proper harvest—indeed, eventually burning crops and buildings rather than leaving behind any vegetable remains that the Sauks might return to collect—General Gaines was consigning the nation to near certain death, forcing them across the Mississippi to its over-crowded, over-hunted western bank, into more direct competition with other nations over game, and more coercive reliance on unscrupulous traders or Indian agents of the federal government.

The threat issued against Ma-ta-tas's daughter registers the historical transformation of a complicated, if mutually beneficial relationship, into one of casual, routine violence. Gesturing to an only lately acknowledged, still largely submerged history of sexual violence directed against Indigenous women, black women, and women of color, Gaines's remark evokes rape as another means of forging kin, of making kin through the act of taking, possessing, using, of making kin through assault and humiliation and force. Ostensibly directed at Ma-ta-tas's daughter, Gaines's remark was no doubt meant for his troops, a joke that forges community among himself and his men through the degradation of a Native woman, willingly exposed in all her vulnerability, before a company from whom she hopes to find some consolation. Kin, in this sense, refers less to the obligations that might obtain between Gaines and Ma-ta-tas's daughter than to the relationships his joke forges among the company of men, creating a homosocial bond between the men through the celebration of a cruel, heterosexual whiteness. Rejecting her emissary, in his verbal assault, Gaines foregoes any pretense of courtesy, treating her plea as evidence of her ready debasement, her willingness to make herself prone before the company as a sexual object as a means of gratifying her needs and those of her people, and through that plea making her into a laughingstock. If Black Hawk's account of the Corn Woman preserved some trace of a relationship between sexuality and sustenance, consumption and community, and the mutualities and indulgences necessary to sustain the inevitable losses and slights of kinship, in highlighting Gaines's cruel rejection of Ma-ta-tas's daughter, he draws attention to a moment in which mutuality and dependency—the texture of "the actual history of our plural existence"—gives way to rage and destructiveness, the refusal of the offer of kinship, of friendship, on the part of settlers and their agents.

A Howling of Wolves: Jacob Kramer Sows His Seed

Previous instances in the settler refusal of kinship and the denial of a common history comprised the refusal of a semiotic relationship, a common language built from a range of experiences of pain, pleasure, desire, need, want, horror, and curiosity. While the exchange of corn might be thought to constitute a similar language of mutuality, a similarly entangled and painful history, the semiotics of corn also concerned immediate, elemental needs and the capacity to fulfill those needs: a dependency bordering on the filial, a relationship based upon a forced reliance and maternal benevolence. In her appearance before the council of men who had come to destroy her village, Ma-ta-tas's daughter would have been received not as a woman, or as a representative of Indigenous women, but emblematic of a matriarchy realized through land and the production of food; an agent of the vegetal transformed and offered as sustenance; an instance of the primordial caregiver as manifest through the land and its tenure. Ma-ta-tas's daughter approaches Gaines as an emissary of her people's corn, here understood as an expression of the land and its history, shaped by the labor of women as agents of Indigenous self-determination. As Rogin has suggested, some elemental disdain for the mother as caregiver is at stake in the confrontation between settler and Native; yet here this disdain becomes an aspect of the land, its feminization as exploitable resource—as fertile and fecund—made into a source of rage over the land and its failure to yield its produce to best sustain the imperatives of labor as the conduit for the generation of surplus-value. In written testimonies from settlers, the rage of dependency and disavowal is often figured as a feature of the landscape, manifest as a rapacious hunger that stalks the horizon of their experience. Faced by wild beasts, recalcitrant grasses and watercourses, and illegible weather—a demanding, all-consuming nature—the appetite of the settler, his hunger and need, is transcribed upon a place shaped by generations of Indigenous stewardship, a place that refuses to bow or to break, that inhibits the satisfaction of his desire at every moment, with every part of its being. Indigenous sovereignty goes unrecognized, but Indian presence is everywhere, a vicious phantom waiting to strike, an absence that cannot be consoled. "Here we were in wild Indian country," Jacob Kramer wrote in his account of his family's 1839 settlement on Fox land in the newly created Iowa Territory. "Weird winds moaned and screeched, sweeping in cold waves over the seared earth. Wolves howled on the prairies and lynx screamed in the woods."[24] Abandoned to "weird winds" that moan and screech in chorus with the lynx or the wolf, "Indian country," in this account, is a ravenous beast that consumes. The howl of the wolf and the scream of the lynx become aural traces of an ever-present existential threat, remnants of images of jaws, teeth, and tearing flesh; of glowing eyes and long shadows stretched thin in the moonlit dark; of dangers seen and unseen, known and unknowable. Incapable of nurturing or sustaining, "Indian country," in this equation, is an unearthly scream from the woods, a terrible voice that conveys meaning without language, a portent of some unspeakably sadistic torture, the hungry beast lurking beyond every rock and every tree. The immediate antithesis of sustenance and the comforts of home, "Indian country" is "seared," but also cold; desolate and barren, eerie and hostile; a place to be disposed of, hated, broken.

In Kramer's account, this picture of insatiably cruel appetite is neither lyrical nor metaphorical. It conveys a very physical sense of vulnerability in the face of the blasted landscape.

At [the town of] Keokuk . . . some in our party walked [twelve] miles along the Mississippi to the head of the rapids. We who were unable to walk that distance rode on an open flatboat along with the boxed household goods. It was a cold, windy November day when horses, wading in the water, pulled this boat upstream. Arriving at Montrose we lodged overnight in the barrows of a long, log building. While awaiting a steamer from the north to come for us, we walked a way into the country. We found two graves that wolves had dug into trying to get at the bodies. Next day the steamer came and took us from Montrose to our landing place in the Iowa Territory.[25]

Rushing to make their claim before winter set in, Kramer and his family navigate the Mississippi northward against its flow, through the treacherous shallows of the Des Moines Rapids. One of two narrow passages on the Upper Mississippi River impeding steamboat traffic north from Saint Louis, the rapids forced riverboat passengers to take to the shore with their possessions, to walk or to mount ill-constructed keelboats that would then be hauled through the water, by horse or ox, while water rushed at the animals and their charges. Abandoned to the banks, settlers were alone with the wilderness and its many imaginable, uncertain threats. Left to the keel, struggling against the current of the indefatigable river, settlers risked themselves and their possessions being overwhelmed and submerged, their animals drowned, and their provisions lost. Mounting the rapids near the end of the fall, Kramer and his party risked frostbite, hypothermia, or death from exposure. In death, there were wolves, prowling, waiting, ready to devour whatever might remain. For settlers, the land was hungry, its every feature a trap laid for the capture of flesh. While Kramer does not dwell overlong on the overturned graves, in his account, they appear as a premonition of the inevitability of death—its unbearable proximity to the frontiers of colonial settlement—as well as a tale about deprivation and hunger, about the boundlessness of need. Digging after sustenance and gnawing on rotting flesh and calcified bone, the wolves embody a purity of need that is relentless, desperate, paying no heed to what limits might obtain between the human and the animal, the living and the dead. The embodiment of hunger, the wolves, for Kramer, are the face of the woods and the wilderness; yet they also serve as a presentiment of the declension of man into beast, the abandonment of all courtesies, all civilities, in the face of overwhelming, irrepressible craving.

Against these images of the irremediable curse of material and animal need, Kramer's account offering a description of his mother's facility

as a cook reinforces the work of settler colonialism as a struggle to subdue desire, to keep the wolves at bay by refusing to give into hunger. It is
a story about the maternal as the front of settler whiteness, as opposed to
desperation, dependency, and need. "To relieve our hunger, our parents
obtained a little flour that produced some of the best bread I ever ate.
Mother mixed the flour with river water and baked it on coals. We finally
succeeded in getting the boat off the [sandbar] after the men lightened it
by unloading the goods and provisions onto the bank."[26] A morsel created out of desperation, the bread she fashions from river water mixed
with flour she "obtained," "somehow," unleavened, unsalted, and baked
over coals, in this passage, evokes the narrative of the Exodus and the
bread of affliction, both as a token of bondage overcome—of freedom
obtained—and of the perils of the flight into freedom. "We were without
food, without money, and nine persons to feed. . . . Father somehow managed to trade household goods for corn or cornmeal. However, we often
had nothing to eat."[27] Here, Kramer's recourse to the conditional—
"somehow"—underscores ingenuity and luck as decisive elements of
their survival on the frontier, bestowing the continuity of their family line
and the relative success of the settler project with the imprimatur of Providence, the product of some superlunary dispensation. Just as his mother
had miraculously "obtained" some flour from which to bake bread, in
Kramer's account, his father—like the Corn Mother—magically appears
with corn. There are, of course, other people involved in this arrangement,
yet they go unrecognized and unnamed, as do the conditions and circumstances of the exchanges by which his parents made their acquisitions or
the obligations to which those exchanges gave rise. His father and mother,
instead, appear as the embodiment of genius, magnanimous spirits who,
fully self-possessed, procure the food to sustain their family and to maintain their independence. For Kramer, the possibility of his father or
mother having entered into a trade relation with a Native person—that
Native people could be the source of the benevolence that sustains his
family, or that they might even distantly be involved in the movement of
goods facilitating the distribution of produce—does not occur. If his parents have received, it is as a benevolent dispensation from some ethereal
source, manna gathered from the desert, to be mixed with river water,
and baked over coals, or pounded into meal, and baked into bread. The
remediation of hunger comes as neither an act of generosity nor of commerce but of a providentially ordained racial endowment for self-reliance,
ingenuity, and the capacity to defer appetite as a function of moral
fortitude.

Corn appears, throughout Kramer's narrative, in moments of absolute desperation, instances in which appetite and deprivation augur lupine discomposure. "Game was available but catching it required some skill in hunting and much ammunition. Ammunition was scarce and could not be had without money to buy it. . . . During that first winter there were no quail at all, and I heard of only one rabbit being found by all the men who made a business of hunting. . . . It was during this time, I believe, that Father obtained some corn."[28] The grain of affliction, tethered to memories of hardship and want, corn, in Kramer's account, is debased, less the ethereal substance of social relations described by Black Hawk than a tolerable means of sustenance, a form of food that is really no better than fodder. "Crops in the early years were mostly corn and wheat. Because markets were so far away, corn was not considered a cash crop. It sometimes brought only ten cents a bushel, and was costly to haul, but corn was considered a necessity. Corn furnished food for humans and all kinds of livestock. We depended on the wheat crop alone to bring in money."[29] Behind this convoluted celebration of wheat was an implicit statement of contempt with respect to corn, as well as a range of questions touching on nineteenth century standards of taste and class, the distinction of being able to afford flour as a staple, and the imputation of poverty connected to the "necessity" of maize within the household economy of settler colonialism. For early settlers, white bread was preferable to corn bread because it was made from grain that was literally more refined, but also because of its expense, the fact that wheat flour or wheat bread was more likely to be purchased than it was to be grown. Generally, one did not grow wheat to produce flour to make one's own bread but to offer it for sale or for trade. Moreover, bread made from refined wheat was white and finely textured, where pantry staples made from corn were of uneven coloration, and coarse in texture. Refinement as a figurative measure of class distinction is here literally manifest in the substance of bread and the aesthetic valuation of taste. As such, often, the settler relationship to corn was agonistic. In Kramer's telling, corn sustained settler farmers so they could produce wheat and it was wheat that made them money, while the acreage dedicated to corn diminished the space they could allot to the production of grain, thus decreasing what revenue they could draw from its exchange. "Not a cash crop," corn, like Native peoples, was both necessary to the elaboration and sustenance of the settler enterprise and hated as a condition of that necessity.

Pure instrumentalities for settlers, like corn, Native peoples were also necessary to the elaboration of the legal and ideological frameworks that underwrote the fictions of US counter-sovereignty as well as the forms of exchange that composed no small portion of the social fabric at the outposts of settler colonialism. While corn, for its part, comprised a significant portion of the diet for both humans and domestic livestock, among settlers, it also figured prominently as a vehicle of exchange, a medium through which to render the fungibility of commodities and to serve as collateral on loans extended by traders and factors who sought to draw Native peoples into the orbit of capital accumulation through labor exploitation. If, for Native peoples, corn had been at the center of an ecology of place and peoplehood—the material nexus of relations between human, animal, plant, earth, mineral, air, and sky—for settlers, corn was adjunct their terrestrial ambitions, a means to an end. As fodder, corn facilitated the reproduction of the means of production through the transfer of caloric energy and nutrient vitalities necessary to the renewal of muscle energy. As a function of the market, however, corn was of no value. Indeed, it was an expense, a loss, the time it took to sow, grow, and harvest placing a significant constraint upon the full potential of value that might be drawn from wheat. Anchoring production and accumulation to the earthly and the physical—to the limitations of bodies and ecologies, the question of ability, exhaustion, and the sociality of production— corn, for settlers, was an emblem of the limitations of their ambitions, a capitulation in the face of their own inflexible nature.

Attempting to overcome the limitations of their own fragile nature, settlers foisted their insatiable ambitions upon the physical geographies of the land they came to occupy. "Prairie was the chosen land for cultivation. However, it was covered by grass with a network of tough, fibrous roots. The roots were so thoroughly matted that breaking it required hitching three or four yokes of oxen to one plow." Describing the prairie grasses as a "network," Kramer inadvertently captures the ways in which the history of the prairie and its biodiversity was bound up in entangled histories of Indigenous sovereignties and ecologies, patterns and relations which the oxen and plow are present to overwrite. While absently gesturing toward the narrative of the Exodus through his description of prairie as the "chosen land," here too, the question of fodder is a preoccupation in Kramer's memory, as healthy oxen were the primary source for the muscle energy necessary to uproot the prairie. "Few settlers could do their own breaking. . . . The oxen had to make their own living by grazing at noon and during the nighttime. It was a manner of good policy to have a portion of prairie reserved to burn for late pasture. The new growth of grass that followed burning made good pasturage."[30] Using the commonplace "breaking" as a means of describing the process of uprooting the prairie, Kramer's discussion of this process incorporates a sense of the labor of cultivation not only as the physical overturning of the soil but also as taming—"breaking" the land like one might "break" a horse—as well as ruining or arresting, accelerating entropy within a complex system. Elsewhere, this appears as a kind of carving, a cutting that traces itself upon the surface of the earth: "It was best to have the plow shaped so that the sod would curl up into small peaks or cones. Thus turned up, the grass roots might dry out and die in the hot summer sun. The cones were easily harrowed down when thoroughly dried out, leaving the ground in good condition for putting in crops. It was remarkable how few weeds came up because none of the pests existed that now fill the soil."[31]

Overturning the prairie for acreage, the process of breaking described by Kramer transformed the historical density of root systems, legacies of animal presence, and generations of Indigenous cultivation into decaying matter that would feed new plants, new people, new forms of life and expressions of sociality. Left to rot, the root systems of prairie grasses became elements of a new topsoil, a new nutrient density that would sustain settler agriculture and, by extension, new forms of economic practice to which commercial Midwestern agriculture would give rise. Understood as a form of inscription, the breaking of the prairies was an attempt at overwriting the geophysical text of Indigenous sovereignty, imposing a new language, a new grammar, upon places that had been shaped, over generations, to the mutual advantage of the greatest number and to the myriad varieties of life those places sustained. The recomposition of these earlier geophysical narratives around principles of property—of fields and fences delineating ownership and rendering the juridical fictions of US counter-sovereignty as physical barriers, impediments to movement and to access—was necessary to the commercialization of regional agriculture and the commodification of its produce as well as to the overvaluation of wheat and depreciation of corn. This depreciation was coextensive with the elaboration of corn as a commodity and the commodity manifestation of corn as a grammar, a vocabulary, a set of rules for writing, reading, and composing the land. "Soil for corn was prepared by plowing and, if circumstances permitted, by harrowing," Kramer writes. "Then the soil was cross-furrowed with the broad shovel plow. The shovel plow could be pulled by one horse, releasing the second half of the team for other work." The prairie and its entangled forms of life having been uprooted, its nutrient vitality made over as the substance of commercial enterprise, here, the process of plowing, of harnessing animal muscle and human labor to the work of overturning the earth, etches the geography of settler colonialism and the history of commerce into the face of the earth, further altering its geophysical metabolic, drawing ecologies into the melancholy repetition of capital. The business of plowing was, of course, prelude to planting, which translated the horizontality of the terrestrial surface into the verticality of the plant. "Another person was the dropper. Guided by stakes, the man or boy dropped corn kernels in the furrows with one hand. The stakes were generally made of young wood with the bark peeled off at the top. Peeling made them more visible in marking the width of a row." Planted in rows, the language of corn as commodity became suitably visible, marking the strange pretensions of ownership, of property, and whiteness that came in the shape of neat, long rows, lending themselves to easy calculations of yield. "This was not a fast operation," Kramer tells his readers, "but an expert could drop six acres in a day. An experienced dropper who could keep up with the horse, dropped at least eight acres a day. Grown men received fifty cents per day; boys twenty-five cents. Corn was planted three and one-half feet apart and cultivated with the broad-shovel plow, two furrows to the row."[32]

Attending to the highly mechanical work of sowing the fields, Kramer's description of planting corn demonstrates not only the extent of its devaluation, but the relationship between its capture by settlers and the seizure of its sociolinguistic modes of signification. Once venerated as a gift from the relatives in the sky, in this account, corn has entered into a set of commercial relations, spaced and measured over distance and time as a means of calculating its value as a function of its yield. Allowing for ready calculations of likely volume, the social organization of the labor of planting under capital provided a means of predicting the future, while the rows and lines of the fields manifest the present as consecrated to inviolability of property, and the sovereign injunction of the state. Exploring the work of plowing the fields and sowing kernels as seed, Kramer's account illustrates the material labors that sustained the fictions of settler ownership, of property, and of law, while maintaining the integrity of the field and the farm against the reclamation of the prairie, or the woods. Routinely overturning the soil and planting it with corn—turning it over later for cattle, then for wheat—the insistent claim of the prairie, the river, and the woods is held in abeyance; postponed, though not denied. The material claims of counter-sovereignty here coincide with the geophysical metabolic introduced by the field and the fence as technologies of enclosure, while the ideological valence of corn as emblematic of place and nation is secured as a condition of time and time-discipline: "We always expected to have the corn laid by . . . the Fourth of July."[33] Plucked from the socio-symbolic networks that sustained relations of Indigenous sovereignty, corn here is acquainted, and equated, with rituals of US nationalism, the now routinized labor of its production sanctified in relation to the temporality of the nation and the rebirth of independence, made over as a token of the secular midsummer. Eclipsed by the pageantry of the Fourth of July, the significance of corn within the social and cultural lives of Indigenous sovereignties is transformed, its totemic value consumed by the fiery celebration of the federal union.

The eclipse of corn as a totemic figure occurred against the backdrop of its transformation into a commodity, itself coextensive with the juridical, military, and physical enclosure of Indigenous lands through the Upper Mississippi River Valley, and the subsequent recomposition of its underlying riparian-forest-prairie ecology as a substance for commercial agricultural extraction. For settlers, corn was largely a device for the transfer of nutrients, for the extraction of the vitality of the history of the land as well as the capture of the sky, of the water, wind, and sun. Seizing the inevitability of growth and change and harnessing them to the necessarily violent conversion of use- into exchange-value, settlers grew produce so the nutrient value of their land could be made to move, transported beyond the immediate circle of their acquaintances, and set into circulation among people, places, and markets far removed from their immediate concerns. One element, historically, of the elaborate plexiform infrastructure that sustains the global market in Cheap Food, the settler farm carried out the excavation and transformation of the geophysical remains of Native peoples lives and livelihoods, packaging the historical and material substance of Indigenous sovereignties as material for mass consumption. Among the Sauk, corn materialized history as a nutrient vitality, a means by which the living community of the nation might ingest the legacies of its forebears, converting ecologies sustained by death and decay into food as well as fable. Among settlers, the vital legacies of the Indigenous dead were nothing more than an opportunity to feed. Excised from the entanglement ecologies of Indigenous sovereignty, for settlers, land was not the dynamic terrain of history and memory but soil, a resource to be exploited. Valuable though inert, soil and its vitality were to be enclosed and consumed. For settlers, corn was part of the produce of this enclosure as well as its most inconspicuous moment, an everyday staple that entrapped the physical legacies and historical vitality of Indigenous peoples, their lives, and their sovereignties.

While it was not typically produced as a commodity for sale, corn nonetheless entered the bloodstream of the contemporary agricultural market by its transformation into a food that sustained the settler and his family as well as his livestock. A source of dense caloric energy, corn was

the vehicle by which the physical remains of the material decay of the Indigenous past—bone and sinew, skin and muscle, plant and mineral—
was transferred into the bodies of settlers, sustaining their social and
physical reproduction. Captured as a source of raw material, the transformation of corn into energy—the physical impetus to work, production,
and exchange—was facilitated by a variety of chemical processes through
which its nutrients were made ready, consumable, and nominally pleas-
ing to the palate. A carapace defending against the otherworldliness of
the unhappy frontier, the settler home was not merely a defensive edifice,
a repository of domestic order set against the uncanny dark; it was a manufactory, a furnace, a preposterously coarse mouth effecting the disappearance of corn as a raw material and facilitating its refinement as food.
These reversals—of home as the defense against all that which was not-
home, of home as the manufactory in which the not-home was rendered
homely—found expression through the relationship between fire and
the hearth, the cabin and the kitchen. In Kramer's account, the role of the
hearth, its material apparatus, echoes that which was assigned to the
smelter's furnace, in kind if not in function. Differently posed in relation
to the operations of the frontier economy and the elaboration of settler
colonialism and the infrastructures of racial capitalism, both furnace and
hearth are consecrated as altars to Lucifer, technologies for the maintenance and manipulation of flame. "The old-fashioned fireplace warmed
the home, cooked the food, and provided light," Kramer writes. "With a
pair of andirons supporting the ends, a blazing fire was kindled against
big back logs piled three high. . . . The hearth was made of flat stones, when
they could be had, laid flat on the ground. If such stones were not available, the ground made do for a hearth. The fireplace occupied space mostly
outside the cabin. The wall was cut out to make way for it. The outside
wall and two end walls . . . were built of stone to protect from fire." Rec-
ognizing the centrality of the hearth to the constitution of the domestic,
to the maintenance of the home as a technology of settler occupancy and
fortification, of inclusion and exclusion, Kramer goes on to offer a blueprint for his fabrication, one that implicitly recognizes the folly of keeping embers burning within makeshift, timber-built homes. "The stick
chimney, laid up like a bird trap . . . of split sticks, rose up against the outside wall and was plastered with mud on the inside. . . . The left-side jam
accommodated two firmly built iron eyelets. These supported an iron
crane that could swing back and forth over the fire." For the settler family,
the hazard of the stick chimney was worth the inevitability of chimney
fire, because flame was precious, necessary, and difficult to fabricate.
"I do not remember seeing a [Lucifer] match until about six years after

we came to Iowa. Father brought them from Saint Louis. They were made with cloth and saturated with oil. Not more than one in every twenty-five would strike a blaze." While so-called Lucifer matches would later become ubiquitous, allowing settlers easy command over flame as a technique of property formation as well as a weapon, well into the nineteenth century, the relative fragility of settler command over fire was a reminder of their dependence upon forces outside themselves, of the ethereal art and artifice of a world with its own unspoken priorities. "Pioneers had to obtain their fire from sun, wood, or flint . . . people kept fire overnight and even for a day or two by covering live coals with ashes. When the coals failed to keep the required time, 'borrowing' fire was common. For neighbors who lived two or three miles apart, borrowing was less satisfactory."[34]

A synecdoche of the frontier home, Kramer's description of the fireplace supplants a more thoroughgoing account of the process of cooking, presenting the fire as a chemical medium that saturates the lives of settlers, a source of light, heat, and cuisine. One of the eldest forms of media, as John Durham Peters has argued, fire is one of the most elemental mechanisms by which humans have inscribed their presence upon and through nature, a means of habituating life to place, of claiming a place through its chemical and material transformation, its illumination, and regeneration.[35] The primary source of light as well as heat, the hearth of the settler cabin provided a way of inhabiting the cold and the dark of an otherwise blasted, desolate landscape, transforming the illegible and un-homely into a space of comfort, if not joy. Just as the hearth preserved energy which converted raw produce into food, the hearth converted dark into light, night into day. Yet, behind Kramer's obsessive reconstruction of his family hearth, his exquisite attention to the details of its construction, his slightly paranoid account of building and maintaining a fire, is familiarity as well as fear, his memory of fire and its preservation conveying the anxiety of inversion, the dread inspired by the possibility that the hearth was not sufficient to contain the flame, that fire might spill out and consume all in its path. While noting the fear that one might lose flame and find oneself and one's family bereft of light and heat and food, Kramer's account betrays the fear that fire, more than simply animating the home, might destroy it and those it sheltered. Kramer's description of the chimney as a "bird trap" or birdcage materializes this fear within an image of the wild thing made domestic animal, the terror that the mechanics that enable the conversion of produce into food and the prairie into home are thus also technologies of its destruction, the forms by which cabin and field might be turned to ash and returned to prairie, the domestic and the domesticated undone. The hearth, in this sense, serves as a mechanism of enclosure, domesticating fire, while neutering the anxieties attendant flame as a mechanism of conflagration and a metaphor of mutinous desire.

Corn disappears from Kramer's account of the settler home, as does food, the labor of its preparation, and the benign pleasures of eating, of digestion, of waste. Transformed through the labor of cooking—the application of light, heat, and technique—corn, as food, is consumed, but the fact of its consumption is unacknowledged. Like the transformation and disappearance of resources fitted into the commodity chain, as food, corn is set into circulation and passes out of sight, forgotten, dispersed, unremembered.

Like the plow or the hearth, Kramer describes one of the mechanisms by which the process of this unremembering took place in penetratingly vivid detail; the unremembering of the earth or the flame now the unremembering of corn, of cooking.

> Our parents brought with them another utensil for baking—the Reflector. It had an iron frame about fifteen inches high on which pans of dough were set to bake. The pans were probably sheet iron. A top frame above was probably ten or twelve inches high in front and perhaps less than half that on the back. A sheet of tin covered this frame on top and extended down behind to the pan frame. Another tin plate underneath the bread pans slanted upward toward the back. The ends were closed up with the tin plate and the wide front left open. When the open side was set before the fire, the tin reflected heat from below and downward and over the bread, baking both sides quite evenly. However, the Reflector had baked better before a Pennsylvania grate coal fire than before the typical wood fire in Iowa. . . . We had no stoves in those days.[36]

Just as the furnace and the hearth secured flame as a tool of settler ingress, the apparatus of its capture describing a relationship to the terrestrial surface and its geophysicalities that was effectively inscriptive, here, the "Reflector" of Kramer's memory provides an apparatus for the capture and amplification of the sun as a source of sustenance, its energy focused and absorbed as food. Ruminating, at length, upon one of the many technologies of settler domesticity, Kramer demonstrates a general knowledge of the science of heat and baking; yet, he betrays no specific interest in or capacity for the art of cooking itself, much less the labor involved or the embodied forms of memory by which the art of that labor was preserved and transmitted. No one prepares the dough, no one bakes the bread; the mechanism alone is responsible for carrying out its purpose, and that mechanism operates primarily as a function of optics, chemistry, and convection—the transformation of matter into energy, the transmission of heat and exchange of caloric potential. While produce is grown as a function of labor, food merely appears, seemingly without effort. His mother, her body, her engagement with the materiality of place and the work of home, the work of sustaining, are obscured, as are the labor of homemaking and cultivating in their relationship to larger ecologies of economic extraction and capital formation. Kramer solves the problem of the vulnerability of the body, of the anxiety of bearing a body and being exposed to the fragility of the body, by making the body disappear entirely, surrounding it with a host of prosthetics that entirely alleviate its burdened physicality. The elision of cooking—of consumption, eating, enjoying, digesting, and defecating—effects the forgetting of bodily vulnerability, of the forms of dependency that are the necessary condition of the human, it effects its limitation as well as its horizon, fabricating independence from the denial of the body, its most irrepressible functions and needs.

The repression of the body, here, is the repression of corn as a bearer of a history of conviviality, of generations of work given to the social organization necessary to the alleviation of need and the care through which the human and the vegetal were entangled. It is the repression of the vulnerabilities of the settler home and the settler project and of the rage at its dependencies upon the scrutiny and guardianship of Indigenous peoples.

Mother Hides the Madman, or Sarah Nossaman Prepares a Meal

A melancholy repetition: Nossaman never forgot the night they came to clean the bones. "We knew the evening he went to steal the head and sat up to await his coming." Nursing James Turner's ailing sister-in-law, Nossaman's nocturnal devotions were prelude to a gruesome sacramental. "He got in with it at four o'clock in the morning and hid it till the afternoon of the same day, when he cooked the flesh off the skull."

Written in the sureness that she was near the end of her life—that, as she puts it, "time is not long for me even if I should live to be very old"—one might expect that Nossaman's account of the excarnation of Makataimeshekiakiak's remains would betray some element of remorse, some errant trace of sorrow. It does not. For all its obvious horror, Nossaman's confessional tells of no regret, no shame, but rather an unnervingly perverse sense of delight, the inadmissible pleasure of having witnessed something quite lurid and illicit, as well as the giddy excitement of divulging a long-kept secret. "So I can say that I am the only one now living that witnessed that sight, for it was surely a sight for me." Whatever else it might have meant to her, whatever impression the fact of Black Hawk's desiccated head stewing over the neighbors' hearth might have left upon her youthful constitution, in her narrative, the elder Nossaman conveys nothing less than an overwhelmingly impudent pleasure in witnessing, in seeing and being part of a scene. Instead of disgust or revulsion at what she has seen, or the memory of what she saw, Nossaman revels in having seen it, in having shared the fact of seeing it and being now alone in having seen. Not content being mere witness to this spectacle, in Nossaman's account, the excarnation of Black Hawk's skull is staged for her as an offering, a gift, "for surely it was a sight for me." Where James Turner had hoped to peddle the sight of Black Hawk's remains as debased popular entertainment, Nossaman claims it as the mark of her singularity, her uniqueness, her exceptionalism. Not merely witness to the act, Nossaman consumes it, absorbs it, makes it part of herself.

Composed a year before her death, in 1896, Nossaman's account of the theft and excarnation of Black Hawk's skull was merely one moment in a larger narrative, a brief sketch of the events of her life that she wrote as a bequest for her children, a hedge against the passing of her memory. "As I am now almost to my seventieth milestone, I will try to leave for my children a record of some of my 'ups and downs' in life that may be of interest for them to look over after I have crossed over to the other shore." Hoping to leave behind some trace of herself, in this moment of salutation, Nossaman establishes the basic outlines of the narcissistic fantasy which later emerges in her account of Black Hawk's excarnation; the singularity of her memory of Black Hawk made over, in this instance, as the singularity of the memory of her, objectified in writing, as an object to be "looked over," seen, consumed. Just as she encountered Black Hawk's remains as a gift, "a sight for her," so she gives the remains of her life to her children that they might be appreciated later, after her death. There is, behind this, an implicit rebuke, captured by the all too casual invocation of her death and its imminence, as well as the ambivalence she presumes with respect to her children and their concern for the details of her life. Seemingly nonchalant, the expression "may be of interest" bears a curious stress, an implication of their present and future negligence, while the indirect address renders her children passive, bystanders forced to watch their mother as she passes her final milestone and "cross[es] over to the other shore." While appearing to exonerate them from her imputation of neglect, with these opening gestures, Nossaman in fact demands their attention. She will not be overlooked; she will be "looked over." She will be seen.

This narcissistic, exhibitionist need was eventually met, well after Nossaman's death, when her narrative was printed in the journal of the State Historical Society of Iowa in 1922. Prepared for publication by her daughter and eldest child, Mary Nossaman Todd, the appearance of the narrative in the *Annals of Iowa* might have heralded the realization of Nossaman's long-held dream of recognition, but for her children, it was an act of renunciation, the transformation of a deeply cathected artifact of maternal filiation into an archival trace, a document among documents, speaking only to other documents. The exorcism of Nossaman and her memory from her children's lives is evoked in a postscript to the published text written by Mary Nossaman Todd. Taking note of the fragmentary nature of the text, Todd imposes herself upon it, completing the story her mother began by effectively writing her out of the picture. "Here my mother's narrative ends, much to our regret, and I will try to supply a few more reminiscences."[37] While confessing regret, Todd seems curiously incurious about her mother, extending Sarah Welch Nossaman's memories of pioneering by recounting the further history of Nossaman's life almost exclusively from the perspective of her husband—Todd's father—Wellington Nossaman. In recounting these memories, Todd mentions her mother twice: once as a shrewish harpy rebuking her husband by "flatly refusing" to live in a flood prone house in the bottomlands near Pella and once in connection with a long-forgotten skirmish between settlers over some fraudulent land deal. Nossaman, as she appears in these passages, is plainly monstrous. After describing her father's bloodthirsty initiative in the aforementioned conflict, his promise to deploy his scythe to "'mow' the heads off of any who dared try to capture him," Todd turns to the ways in which the circumstances of the conflict affected her mother, writing, "well do I remember the terror of my mother who sat up all night." Presenting the reader with a canny double entendre, this phrase folds back on itself to elaborate both Nossaman's experience of terror, and the experience of Nossaman as terror; she is the mother who is terrified, as the mother who terrifies. By offering her mother as mute witness to the circumstances of the immediate past, Todd unwittingly exposes Nossaman's violent intractability, her ironic absence within Todd's postscript covering over her otherwise viscerally traumatic presence in the lives of her children and family.

The sense of Nossaman as terror is borne out by the utter lack of sentimentality in the narrative itself, its absolute renunciation of anything nearing tenderness or affection or the consolations of human intimacy. Indeed, throughout the text, Nossaman makes few references to family or loved ones; and when she does, she does so only grudgingly, in passing. Other people appear, but they are generally inscrutable and indistinct, incorporeal beings that are nonetheless present as physical and emotional demands upon her, figures of need that leave Nossaman wasted, occupying her time and rending her body. Other people, for Nossaman, are not sources of companionship or outlets for compassion. They are variables within an economic relation that is ultimately exhausting, opportunities for labor that contribute to the depletion of her physical capacity as well as sources of revenue and material sustenance, though not of emotional satisfaction. This sense of calculation, of alienation from her fellows, emerges throughout the narrative, but never more clearly than when describing her work at the corn mill jointly operated by her father and her husband. "Often there would be fifteen to twenty men waiting their turn to get a bushel of meal to take to their hungry families. But it was hard for me for I baked for all of them, and most of the time some of the men that came to the mill would go hunting and kill some game, so that would make me more work to cook it . . . Your father used to say we could keep as many as there were puncheons in the floor, and I sometimes thought there were two to a puncheon." In this passage, the reference to the men as boarders, a group of figures distributed across the puncheons of the floor, evokes the overdetermination of intimacy by economy, the ordinarily intimate act of sharing sleeping quarters transformed by an immediately commercial necessity. Within the narrative, the human interactions between Nossaman and the men who come to have their corn ground into meal are entirely subordinated to the mindless labor of cooking and cleaning as elements of boarding. They are not part of the intimacy of homemaking; rather, they are different aspects of a labor of care maintained only as a function of money and its exchange. Sentimentality has no place in this relation; the only intimacy Nossaman has is with her own body, the amplification and alteration of its physicality through the "hardness" of her labors.

When looking at Nossaman's account from this perspective—the perspective of domestic labor and its unacknowledged affectivity, as well as the amplification of its physical toll through subsumption within a capitalist economy of scale—one might understand the terror Nossaman presented for her children as a condition of her remove from the emotional demands of the family relation, her reserve predicated upon the utter implausibility of maintaining a semblance of care in the face of the material cost suffered in sustaining their lives, the lives of their clients, and her own. Nossaman, in other words, becomes terrifying, for her children, only because she selfishly withdraws from them as a means of conserving some aspect of herself, some portion of herself that is not immediately given over to the labor of enabling consumption. The terror of her presence, for her children, is that she is mute, insensate, and absent. The desire that emerges elsewhere as the desire to be seen is, as such, cognate with a desire to have the otherwise unacknowledged labor of domesticity acknowledged as a contribution to the reproduction of the means of production, the sustenance of the social relations that obtain within her family and among her neighbors. Her posthumous address to her children thus appears as an injunction to memory, but not merely as the realization of some dour narcissistic wish. Nossaman wants to be seen not merely as herself but as an overlooked conduit for the labor necessary to the maintenance of the frontier community. She wants known the price she paid for pouring herself into the labor of caring and nursing, the desolation wrought by the work of making live.

Throughout the narrative, Nossaman seems quite openly dedicated to this purpose, though the effortlessness of her prose, its utter lack of pretension, militates against any sense of craft. Nonetheless, from its opening address—with its invocation of the passage of years and the imminence of death—the question of entropy, of decay and the passage of time, hangs over her recollections, threatening to transform every pleasure into pain, every joy into sorrow. Describing the circumstances surrounding her marriage, Nossaman writes, "In 1841 my father sold his claim and pottery shop and moved two miles east of Fairfield, Jefferson County, this state. There we took a claim and began anew. There we had it pretty hard again. . . . It was there I was married [on] March 17, 1842. I will now leave my father's house and tell you of your father's and my hardships." Laying emphasis on the specificity of place through the repetition of the word *there*, Nossaman draws attention to the history of her father's commercial embarrassment, his inability to support himself and his family as a farmer or in a trade, and the condition of finding herself as a bride, traded off as a means of relieving some measure of his patriarchal responsibilities. Marriage brings no relief of pleasure, only an attenuated sense of hardship as the condition of everyday life, and a relationship between father-in-law and son-in-law that might relieve both of their economic worries. For Nossaman, hardship provides a narrative framework, a figure through which to piece together the fragments of her life, providing them with some sense of design. This is made explicit later, when describing the first claim made by her husband and their family. Having believed themselves to be all but abandoned and alone in a great wilderness,

Nossaman and her sister-in-law soon discover that they are in the presence of other settlers. "To our great joy we soon found it to be a camp of white men, but no women with them. We were not long in getting acquainted and have remained warm friends ever since. But there are but three of us left to tell the tale of our hardships, and they are Robert Hamilton, Green Clark, and myself. The rest have gone to their reward, except George Hamilton who is in Australia."[38] As above, the pleasure of companionship is effaced by the fact of mortality, while the act of remembering becomes the act of recitation, the burden of enunciating the "ups and downs" of one's life, so that the outlines of that life, the space of its absence, might be preserved. In Nossaman's narrative, joy is irregular and extraordinary, while hardship is mundane. Every day is a trial, every moment an opportunity for some new affliction to present itself.

In Nossaman's account, the inescapable regularity of hardship as the inevitable condition of everyday life is figured through the labor of finding and preparing food, of cooking and the physical and emotional toll wrought by this most basic, this most necessary, element of social reproduction. The relationship between food and affliction, the mundane repetitive strain endured because of the labor of planting, harvesting, milling, and cooking, provides some measure of structure for her narrative, even as the monotony of that routine militates against any sense of direction or change. Sacrificing her physical vitality on the altar of domestic labor, Nossaman's relationship to food is one of ironic reversals and palpable distaste, both for the labor of cooking and the exaggerated pleasures of the frontier kitchen. While Kramer delights in the ingenious paste of flour and river water from which his mother fashions an improvised, unleavened bread, Nossaman entertains no such illusions about the food she is compelled to eat, steadfast in the conviction that, on the frontier, the fiendish demon of unalloyed, unbearable hunger can only be satiated by an equally debased cuisine of affliction. "My father brought property in Richmond, [Indiana] but when the Black Hawk . . . purchase was thrown open for settlement he sold it for half he gave for it for the sake of going to the new purchase. . . . When we got to the new purchase, the land of milk and honey, we were disappointed and homesick, but we were there and had to make the best of it."[39] Having abandoned their property in Indiana for the uncertain prospects of a homestead on public land that had been ceded to the US government under the coercive terms of the so-called Black Hawk Treaty, in this passage, Nossaman, her parents, and her siblings find themselves in the newly created Iowa territory with exaggerated expectations for all that they might accomplish at their new home. These hopes are almost immediately crushed, as the bare life necessity of food proves impossible to meet. The soil intransigent, the dream of unmitigated abundance dashed, in reporting to her children the circumstances of her early life in Iowa, Nossaman resorts to an acidic rejoinder, the "milk and honey" of the promised land presented as a barren cataract, its ostensibly inexhaustible plenty held up as a satire of frontier romance. "My father and mother went to work with a will to put some corn and potatoes in the ground that we might have something to live on the following winter, but it was so late in the season that our corn did not mature and we could not have it ground. It was badly frostbitten, so we had to live on frostbitten roasting ears for six weeks. I can't tell you just how good they were, for you must taste to know." A bitter inversion of the stories of covenantal purpose that had shaped earlier generations of settler colonial ambitions, Nossaman's derisive reference to the land of milk and honey throws the unyielding ground of the settler home into stark relief. The errand into the wilderness does not end with a triumphant passage into the land of Canaan or the land of Cockaigne nor with the abundance and the indolence born out of freedom from want but instead with exhaustion and illness; with rotten, frostbitten corn, and no way to cook it.

Nossaman's pugnacious relationship to the labor of cooking begins in this moment. Just six years old, when Nossaman and her family arrive at their "new purchase" in Iowa, she finds herself saddled with tasks generally assigned to someone far more senior, charged with nursing her ailing parents, cooling their fevers, and preparing their food. "By this time my father and mother were both down sick with bilious fever. I was the oldest child and I was expected to cook the corn and the best I could do was to wrap the husk close around the ear, and cover it in hot ashes, and heap coals of fire on it till it was done. . . . I can't describe the smell of it, but I will just say codfish is sweet by the side of a frostbitten roasting ear. But they sustained life and that was about all."[40] An untutored chef, forced to make do with unmilled corn, in an unfamiliar environment—a "purchase" without the comforts of home—six-year-old Nossaman is forced to invent a method of food preparation that will make her sad, rancid ears edible, dipping them into fire, coal, and ash as a means of breaking down the lignin which accumulated in the otherwise indigestible, inflexible cell wall. Contributing to the release of energy and the transfer of nutrients from the sun and the earth to the plant to the human, exposure to fire, no matter how inelegantly contrived, allowed for the corn to be accommodated to the relative weakness of human teeth; it allowed for the corn to be eaten, that is, if only as a means of recuperating the caloric energy necessary to sustain the barest forms of life. Nossaman's caustic description of her roasted, frostbitten corn, as well as her inexpert preparation as adequate only to the sustenance of life, evokes the declension of the art and aesthetic of cuisine, no matter how simple or rustic, from a matter informed by desire, taste, or pleasure to a mechanism for the circulation of caloric energy and mineral nutrients, a base but necessary form of consumption. Tending to her infirm parents, not yet capable of grasping the morbidity of their symptoms, the proximity of death and destitution, Nossaman learns to cook as a matter of biological urgency. Not merely a mechanism of nutrient transfer, Nossaman pours herself and her life, her vitality, into the work of cooking, so that the vigor of her person, her body, might be offered to and in sustenance of her infirm parents.

Nossaman's descriptions of food offer no sense of the joy of the table, the camaraderie of being together, sharing a meal; and no sense of the pleasure of taking part in the act of preparation. In her account, cooking and food become pure instrumentalities, just as corn becomes a banalized commodity, a resource necessary to the reproduction of social life within settler colonialism yet divorced from the semiotic frameworks that gave it meaning, for Native peoples, or the material relations that governed its production and circulation. Drained of any sense of art or design, cultivated as fodder, or as a hedge against the invariable, inexorable threat of famine, corn, as a commodity, is leeched of its relationship to ritual and pleasure and made over as a disposable triviality, the requisite material for the continuity of social reproduction conjured for its abstruse qualities as a vector of mortality. Food becomes solely a matter of sustaining life; but in sustaining life absent any consideration of savor or craving, it takes on the character of a devious venom, a slow acting poison that preserves life only as a hedge against the anticipation of death, that preserves life so that it might be consumed by death. The meals Nossaman prepared for her family were so consecrated, as their illness attests. An unwieldy, archaic designation for a range of liver inflammations that resulted in pronounced jaundice and severe fever, the "bilious fever" that felled Nossaman's parents was very likely a form of hepatitis contracted from contaminated food or water, a not uncommon circumstance among those settlers who placed themselves well beyond the reach of society, its economy, and its conventions. Just as earlier generations of settlers struggled to adapt to the unfamiliar conditions of the land—their agriculture inadequate in face of the conditions of the land and their capacities as stewards of agricultural necessity limited—Nossaman and her family encountered the terrain of the Black Hawk Purchase, the site of their "new purchase," as neophytes, subjected through a punishing dependency upon an unfamiliar, unyielding land; for her and her family,

THINGS SWEET TO TASTE / 159

the vicissitudes of self-possession, of self-reliance, could not be alleviated through recourse to family, friends, or the consolations of the market.

For Nossaman, the laboriousness of cooking, its affectivity, and its impact upon her physicality, her body, emerges as a technique by which to establish order against pandemonium and entropy; a way to ward against a premature, ungainly death, preserving life so that it might be depleted, and extinguished, only after its vitality has been thoroughly extracted. Cooking as art, as the improvisation of flavors for the satisfaction of appetite, is supplanted, within this calculus, by cooking as design, as architecture, a blueprint from which to mimic the form of the house as a container and a barrier to entry, to encounter. Just as the house is not a home or a provocation to a more expansive intimacy, an invitation to come inside, to partake of the shared pleasures of camaraderie and hospitality, cooking is not a means by which to manifest home as a sense of neighborliness but a means by which to fortify those whose bodies, whose sense of self-possession as subjects of property, were incessantly buffeted by the lupine peculiarity of the land to which they sought claim. The uncanniness of the land is held at bay, in Nossaman, by the work of cooking as a means of making the unfamiliar homely; but the homeliness derived from the work of cooking is one of mercenary exclusivity, a form of familiarity dependent upon tightly drawn boundaries, and systems through which to enact home as a structure, a sequence, a cycle, and a repetition. Improvisation is untenable, as is the emotional and physical vulnerability that it implies: the unknown must be smothered by routine. In Nossaman's account, routine is most powerfully manifest in her relationship to cooking as a regimen and a program, a set of recipes, or receipts.

> When we lived in the shanty and it rained we did not eat for I had to cook by a log fire, as it was before the days of cook stoves. It was [the] days of johnnycake boards, dutch ovens, skillets, and lids. But you may ask how can you bake bread on a board. I will try to tell you. Take a board eighteen inches long and eight inches wide, round the corners off and make the edges thinner than the middle, spread it with well-made corn dough, set it on the edge before a hot fire in a fireplace, and it will bake nice and brown, then turn and bake the other side the same way, then you have corn bread that no one will refuse. Set your johnnycake board in front of something that will keep it on the edge.
>
> I will stop giving receipts and talk about something else.[41]

Nossaman's description of the procedure for making johnnycakes absent skillet or stove echoes the description she offers of the procedure by which she roasted the rotting, frostbitten corn that she served her parents; yet, her account of the johnnycake board, of the preparation of the board as a technology of the hearth—a mechanism for the conversion of flame into a particular quantity of heat distributed across the surface of the board—is far more confident, far more precise, than the technique previously improvised by the young girl who was forced to cook so that she might support her family in their struggle against illness and death. Dry and dispassionate, Nossaman's recipe for johnnycakes does not convey a fear of sickness, of hunger, starvation, or death; illness and its familiars have been exorcised through the invocation of the recipe as a technology of the body. The recipe tells a story about food that is only nominally about flavor, but that guarantees the conservation of the body through the forms of its provision, its sustenance; moreover, it tells a story about pleasure that inheres within the capacity to repeat a given dish, to recreate a certain flavor profile, preserving the body, its physicality, and its affects, from the stimulations of novelty and the craving for difference.

In Nossaman's account, the recipe serves as a vector of story, a means of augmenting the health of the body as a vehicle for the expression of meaning through language and its purposeful arrangement, its manifestation as speech and inscription, as well as a means of drawing together, of telling stories as a means of conjuring sociality. "After we got our house built and new neighbors began to come in we began to feel like we could entertain all Iowa. Oh, how contented we were! . . . [T]he fall of 1844 found us with wheat and corn raised on our new home place, ripe and ready to grind."[42] Here, the material hardship associated with the labor of growing and cooking, harvesting and milling, is attenuated by its distribution among a community of people seeking assurance of their own physical health, as well as their relationship to one another, to the commonplace gestures of fellowship by which community was planted, nurtured, and sustained. Proprietors of an ox-powered corn mill that catered to the diffuse settler community near Pella, Iowa, Nossaman and her husband, Wellington, with her father, William McQueen Welch, offered a necessary service, one that drew people to them and that established relationships among those people, turning the fact of proximity into the possibility of neighborliness, and of friendship. Capable of processing only twenty-four quarts of grain per hour, it took an hour and a quarter to grind a bushel of corn; consequently, Nossaman and her family came to know their neighbors very well, and their neighbors came to know each other, as farmers congregated, waiting for their turn, for the oxen to recover their strength, and for the millstone to go on moving. "[It] ran day and night," Nossaman relates. "Often there would be from fifteen to twenty men waiting their turn to get a bushel of meal to take to their hungry families. But it was hard for me for I baked for all of them, and most of the time some of the men that came to the mill would go hunting and kill some game, so that would make me more work to cook it. But I did not think it hard."[43]

Rendered accidentally indolent by the necessarily tedious process of milling the corn, the men in Nossaman's account slip into an easy intimacy with one another, an unintentional camaraderie in which the tedium of waiting gives way to the vigor of hunting, where hunting appears less as a means of gathering food than an opportunity for sport, a form of play offering an appropriate occasion for masculine companionship. Nossaman does not describe the exchange of words among the men nor the stories they might have told about themselves, their families, their virility and their prowess, nor the circumstances that caused them to abandon society for the life of a pioneer, removed from the expectation of comfort for the certainty of inconvenience, and privation. Nevertheless, it is not difficult to imagine the circumstances in which they found themselves loitering as providing an opportunity to find company through commiseration. Of the men who offered their custom to the Nossaman-Welch concern, one of the more notorious was Nicholas Earp, father of Virgil, Warren, and Wyatt Earp, boys who—as men—would serve the cause of law in the West, even as they bent, broke, and discarded that law if it proved an impediment to their nefarious schemes for personal enrichment. An unforgiving and belligerent drunk, Nicholas Earp was a bully and a cheat, but his skullduggery no doubt offered ample opportunity for expressions of ridicule and contempt, for stories woven around tales of alcoholic stupors, and friendships forged through the exchange and telling of stories. Earp's sons, Wyatt especially, would go on to figure in the myriad stories that were told about the West, stories that the boys themselves told; stories that contributed to the romance of settler colonialism through the concoction of the frontier as a drinking story; stories that distracted from the banal violence of settler colonialism by highlighting violent encounters that involved the presence of a weapon, a knife, or a gun.

Largely fabricated from whole cloth, the fables the Earps embroidered were merely one part of an ecology of storytelling whereby settlers conjured the intimacies by which they might endow the lupine wilderness with a sense of familiarity, of homeliness. Waiting for their corn to be ground, spaces like those provided by the Nossaman-Welch mill afforded settlers with the opportunity to swap stories, and through the exchange, to find themselves in the company of others who shared their minds and their sentiments. The intimacy among the men who found themselves well back of the line for their turn at the mill is signaled, in Nossaman's account, by a joke that she relates, a satire on the sleeping arrangements by which the men pass the night that also provides an image of the fast, easy attachments that arose between them. Having established that the mill operates day and night, without cessation and only minimal rest, Nossaman describes the conditions under which her patrons found themselves boarding as well as the attention she was expected to pay them, cooking their bread and cleaning their game. "Your father used to say we could keep as many as there were puncheons in the floor, and I sometimes thought there were two of a puncheon."[44] With a description of the extraordinary number of her patrons and the tremendous volume of their corn, Nossaman provides an image of the intimacy among settlers that suggests the immediate proximity of one to another, of bodies arrayed in an orgy of indisposition, sharing the rough-hewn floor as a makeshift bed, unyielding and uncomfortable, composed of puncheons as soft as nails. Intimacy, in this instance, emerges from discomfort and is a source of discomfort. The need to rest—to neither stand nor sit but to lie, to relieve the body, muscles and bones, from the worst burdens of gravity, unequally distributed across its frame—forces recourse to the inconvenient, uncomfortable space of the mill and its floor. That discomfort becomes even more pronounced, ostensibly, as the men find themselves sleeping "two to a puncheon," forced to endure a relationship among bodies that flirts, however unwittingly, with the erotic, highlighting the elements of desire, the forms of homosocial conviviality, that compose some portion of the affective structure that sustains the reproduction of settler colonialism as a mode of enclosure and extraction.

This moment of social though not biologically reproductive intimacy is arranged, in no small part, by the enclosure and expropriation of corn as well as the crude mechanization of grinding, the transformation of the traditionally, isolated feminine work of the mortar and pestle into the ludic character of masculine homosociality—the indolence, the inadmissible desires—occasioned by the space of the water- or animal-driven mill. Breaking down the accumulated deposits of lignin—that form of the hard outer shell of the *Zea mays* kernel—so the nutrients it protects might be extracted as food and transferred to and absorbed within the body of the settler, the animals whose flesh might provide another source of caloric density, or those creatures (the oxen, the horses) whose musculature would be depleted in the service of the field and the plow, by expanding the scale upon which maize could be processed, the mill allowed for a more ambitious design for settler agriculture, enlarging the sphere of its commercial applications. The mill, in this sense, makes literal the figurative work done by the recipe and the story it tells about food and its replication, its design and utility as a mechanism of social reproduction. Taken as a set of directions for the transformation of dried corn meal into food, the recipe extends the literal transformation of the plant as a bearer of nutrients, the residue of the solar and the soil; but in both cases, the transformation is complicit within terms of its commodification and its alienation, the production and absorption of the object as something divorced from the erratic manifestations of desire and forced along paths congruent with those trails blazed by the architects of settler colonialism. Harnessing corn and its caloric density to the sustenance and reproduction of the body, the body finds itself harnessed to the reproduction of settler colonialism as a structure of invasion and extraction. Removed from itself and its affectivity, its sensuality, the desiring and suffering body is overwhelmed by the ideological body, by the body sacrificed—willingly and eagerly—to the imperatives of colonialism and enclosure, the reproduction of labor, the extraction of resources, and the accumulation of capital. The unspeakable, unrealized homosocial intimacies that contribute to the reproduction of patriarchy as the organizing framework for the realization of settler colonialism as a function of everyday life are here reflected in the asexual intimacies that produce corn as a commodity, as food, as fuel. As the lignin within the corn is broken, so is the body, rendered pliable in both the service of accumulation and the dream of capital as infinitely expansive.

As a story about the organization of the settler home, the recipe provided a vehicle whereby settlers came to coordinate their relationships to agriculture and to food, as well as the ways in which the work of planting, tending, harvesting, and cooking contributed to the formation of bonds among settlers, whether family, friends, foreigners, or strangers to Nossaman's community of fellow interlopers. Within the scope of her narrative, Nossaman's recipe for corn bread serves also, if only momentarily, to conjure the promise of the madeleine: it proffers a means by which to summon elements of memory long since relegated to the unconscious, exhuming images of the past through the provocation of the body and the stimulation of taste, calling to mind the ways in which food and the preparation of food served as a affectively laden mechanism for the organization of desire and the structure of familiarity. Within the settler community as described by Nossaman, prescribed by the recipe as an incitement to repetition, this structure of desire is effectively defensive, a means of conserving the vitality of the body and its affects, as well as the myriad insubordinate, unruly affects quickened through the proximity of bodies. The recipe, in this sense, appears as a prosthetic for the capacitation of the settler as a form of life, an inconspicuous mechanism of biopolitical administration that serves the reproduction of the settler as biological life while constraining the otherwise expansively plastic forms of life as a sociolinguistic formation, a way of being in the world shaped by utterance and inscription. Holding fast against the accelerated entropy of the body in flux, the manifestation of this compulsion—this resignation to given determinates of convention—appears in Nossaman's description of the work of cooking, cleaning, and preparing the game brought to her by the men who frequented her husband's mill: "It was hard for me. . . . But I did not think it hard." Bracketing her account of the collaborative work of the mill in providing for the material needs of the frontier community, these clauses evoke Nossaman's affected and excited body, only to effect its negation through the intervention of mind, the appearance of consciousness and ego as impediments to the imperatives of the physical frame. The "hardness" of her labors remains present as a feeling, but one that is insignificant and easily dismissed as a function of will. Nossaman is, in her record of this moment—in the moment she registers the record of this moment—wholly convinced of her self-possession, even as the terms in which she represents this moment betray the limitations of her will and its pretense of mastery.

As indicated in her recipes, this pretense of mastery extends itself over Nossaman's command of fire, her ability to negotiate the relationship between combustibles, flame, heat, and its radiation; the relationship between flame as a source of energy and the process of chemical transformation by which plant and animal matter are rendered edible as food, fit for mastication by human teeth, and readily digestible by an otherwise weak, monogastric stomach. Just as Nossaman, through the judicious application of her will, masters the affects of her body as it is effected by the performance of labor, peeling off an idealized, ideological body from her physical body, its agonies, and its pleasures, here, Nossaman masters the space of the mill and the components of her body as she learns to adjust herself to the mercurial temperament of flame, orienting herself and her implements such that heat is measured and contained, applied in such a manner as to avoid burning, and being burned. Adjusting the board on which she bakes her bread—"set . . . on the edge before a hot fire in a fireplace"—she recommends to her readers, her children, that they "set [their] johnnycake board in front of something that will keep it on the edge." More than a description of the placement of the johnnycake board in relationship to the hearth and the fire, in this moment, "on the edge" describes the evanescent boundary that divides browning from burning as well as the art and the technical expertise necessary to recognize the best moment to turn the board and the dough to achieve the most consistent, the most flavorsome results.

As a blueprint for self-possession—a formula by which to order the body, to dispense with its troublesome affects, and to become expert in the technologies of its sustenance, the techniques and the implements necessary to effect its reproduction—as Nossaman describes it, the recipe serves as an extension of the kitchen and the hearth. The recipe offers an image, in miniature, of the kitchen and the hearth as designations given to a set of oscillations that constitute the space of the home, the condensation and reification of spaces that serve to harness as well as to remove, to enclose, and exploit; to bring into conformity and to order processes of social reproduction abstracted from all of its otherwise ugly, awkward elements, its myriad biological necessities, chewing, swallowing, shitting, fucking. The ideological body projected through the recipe places what Siri Hustvedt has called the corporeal mess of the physical body under erasure, effectively rubbing out the fragility of the eminently permeable frame, the body as a sloppy, squishy mass of hard and soft tissues.[45] Difficult to bend, easy to break, the physical body here appears as an artifact of the primal scene, its bones and its fluids, its muscles and its fats a nominally less grotesque surrogate for the crass expressions of utilitarian genital sexuality that were the condition of its emanation. Less the elegant synthesis of a dialectic than the unfortunate product of traffic accident, the body here serves as the record of a collision between other bodies, other histories, and it tells of other ways of being in the world, of desires that do not fit within the convenient frame of the field, the kitchen, or the hearth; desires that find their closest relative through the contemplation of fire. The figures for the reification of the spaces of social reproduction, the kitchen and the hearth serve to sentimentalize sociality and reproduction, disconnecting both from the body and the erotic, the ways in which genital and nongenital expressions of intimacy knit incite the possibility of community, the ways in which those expressions of intimacy are never not more than ideological figures most congenial to the valorization of capital, its circulation, and its accumulation. Kitchen and hearth, recipe and food, are all stories about home; about home as the manufactory of homeliness, about home as a structure that attenuates the alien and the uncanny; that seeks to alleviate the unbearable, irresolvable anxieties of the unfamiliar and the unknowable, of the object that, against all reason, insists upon its inassimilable distinctiveness, its jagged edges, its sharp corners.

A means of circumscribing desire, the rhetorical figure of home emerges at the point where the material imperatives of social reproduction find themselves bent to the socioeconomic ambitions of settler colonialism and the continuities of racial capitalism. This notion of home is not only desperately, pathetically ideological, a means of cloaking the corporeal messiness of settler colonialism through the cunning arrangement of sentimentality and artifice; it is also woefully, violently exclusive, a barrier erected against the world, a means of narrowing of the scope of who might be counted as kin, who is allowed inside the house, who is invited to make themselves at home, and who is familiar enough to have been given a key. "Hospitality was the common denominator in pioneer communities, but raiders and horse thieves were the bane of early settlers. They were more to be feared than Indians or wolves. Even so, the latch string was always out."[46] Cataloging the architectural peculiarities of the settler home, in her description of the log house, Oneita Fisher fixates on the door and the latch as they mediate the relationship between inside and out, between the circle of the family and its patriarchal moralism, as well as among the miscreant elements that pose a threat to the home and its integrity. As for Kramer and for Nossaman, here again, the unflagging appetites of the Indian and the wolf, creatures ruled by irrepressibly sublime, sublunar forces, are invoked as agents of entropy and exhaustion, beings incapable of accommodating themselves to the squared logs and right angles, the adze cut timbers, that composed the intimate spaces of the settler home. Like the raider and the horse thief, the figurative Indian is denied entry, the latch string retracted, drawn into the cabin to prevent unbidden entry. "The latch was a wooden bar lifted by means of a leather thong run through a small hole above the bar. To 'lock' the door, one had only to pull the latch string inside."[47] Despite her assurances that the hospitality of the settler was so boundless that "the latch string was always out," Fisher resumes her description of the door with the wholly contrary assurance that the door can be barred and entry denied simply by means of removing the latch string as it toggles between inside and out, a statement of welcome and means of ingress that, absorbed within the space of the home, also conveys a bitter refusal, the purposeful fortification of the settler home, its transformation into a distinctively combative edifice.

This impoverished sense of hospitality—its self-congratulatory rhetoric of neighborliness countermanded by its seemingly unbearable fear of the lupine night revealed by the utter stinginess of its table—is to be contrasted to the forms of communion and kinship described by Black Hawk, the corn and the kettle, and the common fire against the domestic exclusivity of the hearth and the kitchen, the enclosure of food and the flame. The settler home, its adze squared logs, its door secured against the dark, compose a defense against the unbearable intimacies of the latter, of the proximity to the unknowable, inadmissible other, of the solicitations that undermine the necessary exclusivity of property as a measure of morality, accomplishment, and self-possession. Where corn, the kettle, and the common flame tell a story about "the actual history of our plural existence"—a story about pleasure, pain, and mutual distrust; about resentment, love, and the impossible though necessary attempt at finding ways of living together within the Lockean contrivances of the settler home—this history and its avatars can only assume the shape of monsters, unhappy phantoms seeking consolation in the ruin of the settler. Fire is the ideal emissary of this message and for the unbearable expressions of desire that emerge as a condition of the unmediated encounters that shape our plural existence. An irrepressibly erratic, respirant chemical process, as Bachelard has suggested, fire and flame are known but unknowable, pure surfaces, necessary surfaces, instances of media that reach out into and suture the world but that harbor no desire of their own, no form of wanting or need that is legible within the conventions of linguistics as a mechanism of exchange. The hearth, in this sense, serves not only to harness and preserve the radiant power of flame, to direct flame as a source of heat and illumination, but also as a means of protection, its enclosure as defensive as it is extractive. Enfolded within the circumscribed by the demands of social reproduction; to the production of food and the insulation of the body, the preservation of the body and its heat, as well as the integrity of the body through its relationship with its impossibly delicate, though largely insensitive, optic nerves. An expression of the ineluctably intransitive movement of desire, as contained within the appurtenance of the hearth, the appetite of flame is suppressed, as are its metaphorical effusions.

If flame was the avatar—the respirant surrogate for and representative expression of the myriad forms of desire that shaped and were shaped by the actual history of our plural existence—within the scope of Nossaman's story, Black Hawk appeared as the unavoidable instance of their embodiment. Taken as the incarnation of that history, those desires, the attention devoted to his frame and to his face, betrays the settler as prone to instances of uncertainty and longing. Looking at him, lingering over the contours of his form, evokes the effort of peeling away his surfaces and uncovering the meaning within, seeking to uncover the meaning of flame.

Often, in Nossaman's rendering, this meaning is made inextricable from all the ways in which the presumed depths of Black Hawk become an occasion for the unraveling of her story, a means of plumbing the depths of her person, collecting artifacts from her past from which to assemble an image of her life that might be conveyed to her children. "I was born in Wilkes County, North Carolina, February 26, 1825. When I was about six years old my father emigrated to Richmond, Indiana. We lived there one year. My father bought property in Richmond, but when the Black Hawk or Mackinaw purchase was thrown open for settlement he sold it for half he gave for it for the sake of going to the new purchase."[48] The first of four appearances Black Hawk makes in Nossaman's narrative, here, Black Hawk is manifest as a distant if inciting presence, a figure whose history provides the occasion for her own, an occasion for her father to exercise his capacity for self-possession, even while demonstrating his inconsistency and extravagance. The circumstances of the so-called Black Hawk War and the punitive cessions wrested from the Sauk and the Fox as recompense for their role in the conflict here appear as the condition of patriarchal ambition and property ownership, a moment roughly congruent with Nossaman's dawning awareness of a world beyond solipsism, a world in which the integrity of the self was bartered away in exchange for scraps of conversation and community; a world present to and preserved within the province of memory. Bound to her father as both the agent of her property and the terms of its development, Nossaman, in the narrative, inquires after recollection as a function of possession, aligning the capacity to remember with the irrepressibly Spartan aesthetic of the well-ordered household, its rhythms and routines carved upon the body as upon the land, a series of physical dispositions learned and retained through ignominious repetition. As the Black Hawk Purchase gives rise to property as a technology of self-possession, so does the occasion of Black Hawk as a dimly perceived figure of expectation and longing mark the emergence, for Nossaman, of memory as a dimension of a percipient relationship to the self, to one's body and one's persona, to what is hidden and what is displayed, to what resists all attempts at being known.

While tied to the realization of personal ambition and unaccounted desire through acquisition of property and its subsequent appurtenance, Nossaman's percipience is equally expressed in relation to the circuitous path to self-possession traveled by her father, the irregular trail he blazed leading hither and yon, backward and forward, and in multiple directions at once, regularly uprooting his family and bleeding money with every move, every new scheme to improve their condition, to make a new life. Confirmed in his role as paterfamilias, yet incapable of establishing his family in a home and a life with any degree of constancy, Nossaman's father is ineffective as a patriarch; her dawning awareness of self, memory, and history draws upon her frustration at this incapacity, a point registered by her ironic characterization of "the new purchase" as "the land of milk and honey," an unyielding land of disappointment and homesickness where her parents fall victim to "bilious fever," and she alone is left to care for them. Although Nossaman opens her written recollections with reference to her birth, her story begins only with Black Hawk and the purchase confirming the certainties of property, which are immediately undermined by fever as a physical manifestation of the hostility of the land as well as a hysterical symptom that registers her father's capricious volatility. An unconsciously cruel abdication of responsibility, this aspect of her father's variability is echoed, in Nossaman's account, by her decoherent chronology of those events she cites as being immediately relevant to the circumstances of her early life. Claiming the Black Hawk Purchase to be the occasion for her family's removal to Illinois, Wisconsin, and later Iowa Territory, as well as the moment of her dawning awareness of self and her relationship to the world, Nossaman nevertheless describes the Black Hawk War as having taken place only after her family set up housekeeping in Illinois, effectively substituting effect for cause. The six million acres of which the Sauk and Fox were dispossessed under the terms of the Black Hawk Purchase were acquired by the United States because of Black Hawk's rebellion against the US government; the purchase did not precipitate the war, it followed from it, an outcome, and a conclusion, one that justified and consolidated the extension of the legal and military infrastructures that underwrote the biopolitical elaboration of the settler state.

Nossaman's reversal of these events echoes the inversions that figure in much of the historiography of the Black Hawk War, confirming her and her family in their role as victims, vulnerable before and subjected to the predatory scrutiny of only dimly perceived, but most assuredly insensate, Native antagonists. Just as fever and famine serve to unsettle Nossaman's capacity to orient herself with respect to "the new purchase" as a space from which to derive a sense of home, to locate herself within a structure of belonging, the circumstances of the Black Hawk War arrive at her door—and in her narrative—as a wholly unbidden instance of trouble, a seemingly insensible, unarticulated challenge to the ideological, material, and physical structures that formed the bases of expropriation and enclosure as well as to the sentimentality which obfuscated the exquisitely violent instantiation of property through the institutions of the state. The proliferated, disseminating effusions of desire that accompany the actual history of our plural existence appear, in this instance, as a voracious sadism, one that is tempered, if not contained, by the identification of the settler with an originary masochism, a mode of relation to pain that is not so much solicitous as it is explanatory, enfolding the lupine intensity of the other through the punishing embrace of the erotic. Assuming the position of the masochistic subject, Nossaman's account of her relationship to Black Hawk and the Black Hawk War—as with the accounts offered by other settlers whose lives were upended by the circumstances of that conflict—eroticizes her condition as a form of subjection, implicating the violence of the Native antagonist as part of a dyadic structure organizing the circulation of pleasure and pain. Sadism, in this sense, becomes an explanatory framework, one that effectively neutralizes the existential threat of unfocused, unknowable desire through its enclosure within a set of racialized tropes concerning Native sexuality and its relationship to the manifestation of violence within and among Indigenous nations.

Black Hawk's later appearances in Nossaman's narrative extend and amplify this mechanism of enclosure, embellishing his person through the imputation of uncommon intimacies as established in moments of charmed felicity between Black Hawk and settlers, moments in which the settler routinely figures as the broker of a characteristically buoyant chivalry, his grace in victory as boundless as the Indian's forbearance in defeat. At first only an ethereal presence, an inciting phantom, as the narrative continues, Black Hawk is drawn into the orbit of the settler home. Disarmed and disarming, he is invited into the settler home and objectified through the extension of genially phlegmatic expressions of camaraderie. "In 1835 my father moved to what is now Iowa. . . . We settled one mile below where Bonaparte now is, in Van Buren County. . . . It was here we had for neighbors Black Hawk, Keokuk, Wapello, Hard Fish, Kishkakosh, Naseaskuk and a score of others of the Sac and Fox Indians. Here we had hard times and were often hungry. . . . While we lived there Black Hawk and his son were frequent visitors and often partook of my father's hospitality."[49] Thrust into proximity of one another as a function of US expansion west of the Mississippi River into territories acquired, coercively, as reparation for Black Hawk's rebellion against the United States, Nossaman cloaks the knotted history of relations between settlers and Native peoples—the legacies of anxiety and pleasure, the pains and joys and unalloyed weariness that attends the history of our plural existence—in a costume of uncommonly generous friendship, a sense of guarded neighborliness derived from the transmutation of enmity into affection. Within the terms of this relation, hospitality is the exclusive province of the settler: Black Hawk and his fellow warriors "partake" of Nossaman's father's hospitality, but they do not extend themselves in return. Heedlessly abandoning the conventions of reciprocity and the ethics of kinship, in partaking of the hospitality of settlers, the Sauks revel in taking, exposing the profound stinginess of their demeanor, as they exploit the witless benevolence of their neighbors. A premonition of later, exceedingly racist descriptions of Native peoples and their willfully cultivated dependency, Black Hawk comes into focus, here, as someone always on the scrounge, a figure of extraordinary appetite who is nonetheless prone to dearth and dissipation. Incapable of sustaining himself, Black Hawk reaches for that which belongs to others; and, in so doing, exposes himself to enclosure within and subjection to the biopolitical liberality of the settler state.

While much of the earliest historiography of the Black Hawk War treats settler colonialism as the catalyst for an effervescent vitality, a means by which to renew the land and its life through the elaboration of property as protected by the custodianship of the state, in Nossaman's rendering, the land is stingy, almost barren, yielding rot and decay, and leaving settlers vulnerable to an unrelenting hunger, exhaustion, illness, and death. Black Hawk appears as the demonic emissary of this chronically punishing asthenia, a vampiric wraith of insatiable appetite, a creature who survives only by leeching the material resources that are meant to sustain the lives and livelihoods of its pretended neighbors and friends. Where settlers labor, Black Hawk reclines, his indolence a prelude to the grim occasion of a cannibal feast, the willing submission of the settler before the desperation of his craving, his need. This, too, represents a delicate instance of translation and inversion, a casual disentangling of the plural histories wrought by the imposition of settler colonial relations upon already existing frameworks for the expression of Indigenous sovereignties that begets the elaboration of a conveniently Manichean cosmology, a vision of the world in which good and evil, giving and taking, generosity and greed are woven into the fabricated substance of racialized social antagonism. In fact, the question of who was consuming and what was being consumed was both far more gruesome and far less ambiguous, even as the menu did not entertain the aesthetic preferences or flatter the epicurean vanities of the settler at his table.

"Black Hawk's burial place was near old Iowaville, on the north side of the Des Moines River, under a big sugar tree. It was there Dr. Turner severed the head from the body. . . . We knew the evening he went to steal the head and sat up to await his coming. He got in with it at four o'clock in the morning and hid it till the afternoon of the same day, when he cooked the flesh off the skull. . . . I can say that I am the only one now living that witnessed that sight, for it was surely a sight for me."[50]

Nossaman's description of the theft and excarnation of Black Hawk's remains does not take the form of a recipe, but it partakes of the rhetorical gestures that often accompany descriptions of home and the labor of homemaking, here rendered most gruesomely through reference to cooking, flesh, and food. Where historians of the Black Hawk War described the forms of everyday, capillary violence that emanated from the bloody heart of the conflict as part of a grim sacramental, a forbidding inversion of the Eucharist, here, the figurative sketch of the cannibal feast is made literal as Black Hawk's head is cooked, its decaying flesh, cartilage, and muscle leeched from its bones.

Conclusion

Under conditions of settler colonialism, the cost of independence is a melancholy attachment to a repetitive cycle of destruction, to the mitigation of self, and annihilation of others. Sewn into the wearisome cycles of agricultural production, settler colonialism is both constant anxiety and unbroken tension as well as uncomfortable stretches of insipid repose, extended periods of watching, of waiting, a wasting away in anticipation of an event that will never arrive, an end that is never end enough. The agriculture of settler colonialism provides for the sustenance of the world, for the biopolitical maintenance of life and labor, while providing a model for agriculture as a surplus-driven enterprise, less an art or a way of life than a vocation attuned by the profit motive. Eating to live, living to work, working to eat, to live, to work: the unrelenting circuits of everyday life make the substance of life go sour, mixed with acid and curdled into melancholy. The bread of life is the bread of affliction and mother stands for pain.

5 / They Prove in Digestion Sour: Medicine, an Obstinacy of Organs, and the Appointments of the Body

The previous chapter addressed the material history of corn and consumption—from the history of maize as a product of Native ingenuity, to the circumstances of its capture by settlers and promulgation as a staple of colonial projects globally, to its commodification, that is, its presence as a cipher of capital and its relationship with the exploitation of land—as a way to approach food and agriculture as mechanisms by which to explore the social organization of kinship and belonging. Attending to the seemingly inconsequential rituals by which the flavor and texture of social relations are sustained, it sought to elaborate the sedimentation of these histories, of the everyday, the local, and the global. One aspect of the biopolitical structures that perpetuate the impoverished solidarities and punitive exclusions endemic to the capitalist mode of production, much of what has been written about agriculture as a dimension of racial capitalism in the United States has touched upon the formation of a transnational market in cotton and the production of the raw materials necessary to the maintenance of industrial textile production. Within this literature, the expropriation of Native land throughout the southeastern United States is understood to have been carried out as a means of expanding the ambit of cotton production to better service the seemingly insatiable demand of textile markets in Liverpool and Manchester as well as the emerging markets of Massachusetts, New Hampshire, and Connecticut. Carried out on the backs of slaves, the expropriation of Native land and the development of a regional cotton monoculture gave rise to a corresponding demand for inexpensive means of provision, what Jason W. Moore has called cheap food.[1] Part of an increasingly proletarianized global capitalist workforce, slaves—forced to work the formerly Native-held land of the Southeast—were themselves sustained, in no small part, by the expansion of commercial grain and cereal production through the Old Northwest, those states of the present-day Midwest immediately adjacent to the Mississippi River and its major tributaries, the Wisconsin, Ohio, and Missouri Rivers. Moreover, chapter 4 addresses these questions through a consideration of consumption under settler colonialism as a nexus of the literal and the figurative, looking at the cannibal rites involved in consuming Black Hawk's body by tracing them to the deeply submerged affective lives of the settler home. It sought to tell a story about the social rituals of conviviality and love within the everyday spaces of settler life, as these enfold less savory, if no less elemental, questions touching upon the distribution of misery, destruction and hate.

This chapter begins by telling another story about consumption, love, and destructiveness. Unlike the previous chapter, however, which looks at the necessity of food, from the ways in which that necessity—that uncanny combination of hunger and appetite, need and desire—was shaped in relation to the most highly variable conditions of scarcity and plenitude, this chapter moves from the question of planting, growing, harvesting, cooking, and eating to consider matters less elevated, less conspicuously festooned in the garlands of romance, the sentimentality of family and motherhood. In this story, I look at food not as a form of sustenance—that is, a contribution to expressions of conviviality and the aestheticization of social conventions or to the obfuscation of globalizing processes of commodification—but as an opportunity to interrogate processes of mastication and insalivation, deglutition and digestion; to consider hunger and appetite, need and desire as elements necessary to the health of the living, wanting body which are nonetheless occluded through the observation and analysis of these processes: the processes that, through their interaction, constitute the involuntary elements of digestion.

While the study of digestion might at first seem an unlikely guide to the analysis of settler colonialism, the prose of counter-sovereignty, and the literatures of the so-called Black Hawk War, insofar as the circumstances of the Black Hawk War contributed to the transformation of the Upper Mississippi River Valley into a hub of global cereal and staple crop production, the conflict had a very dramatic impact upon questions of diet and digestion, and the general health of populations. Shaped by a rising demand for cheap food, conditioned by the nutritional requisites necessary to the sustenance and reproduction of the transnational working class, over the course of the nineteenth and twentieth centuries, the agriculture of the Upper Mississippi lead region would come to shape the lives and livelihood of working peoples throughout the world as a function of their role as consumers of agricultural commodities. The rise of Midwestern agriculture transformed diets, integrating new forms of produce into well-established food cultures, and giving rise to anxieties concerning abundance as opposed to scarcity. Since the beginnings of regular transatlantic contact between Europe and the Americas in the sixteenth century, trade networks, forged by colonization and warfare, had given rise to new types of cuisine, new patterns of consumption that touched peoples around the world, and the possibility that surplus, not lack, might shape human diet. The amplification of extractive processes under the demands of capitalist enterprise, as well as the introduction of canning as a means of preservation, served only to concentrate and reinforce these changes. Waged in defense of the settler annexation of the Upper Mississippi River Valley and the consequent transformation of Indigenous land adjacent to the river and its tributaries into spaces consecrated to agrarian capitalism, the military incursion that accompanied the so-called Black Hawk War served not only to consolidate US control over the region and its resources, it also positioned the region to take up a commanding role within emerging networks of global trade, giving rise to new patterns of consumption, new ways of eating, new symptoms of food-borne distress.

I raise the matter of digestion as a means to highlight the problem of the body in settler colonialism; to approach the body and its medicalization from an oblique angle; to consider the body and its relationship to medicine, capital, and the state as well as to the capillary networks of power that find a welcoming home within bodies and that, through bodies, pursue a relationship to the land that is possessive, jealous, and destructive. While the ritual consumption of Black Hawk's corpse draws attention to the relationships between food and the ostensibly social processes of production and distribution, approaching the respiring body through digestion offers a means by which to approach consumption and circulation—and the global processes to which they contribute and upon which they depend—as elements of a generally opaque interiority, a realm of processes and movements largely unwilled and generally inaccessible to all but the most privileged observers. The history of digestion within capitalism, I suggest, offers an uncommonly rich means to explore the problem of the body as a form dressed in language, clothed in desire; the body as a figure whose needs, whose hungers, are cloaked in appetite, in wanting, in wanting something, in wanting something else, in wanting something more. This is the problem of the body as a gross physicality but also the problem of the body as an inexpressibly radiant metaphor, the problem of metaphor as an irrepressible exuberance that is, nonetheless, the only means by which one might relate to and inhabit the body. It is, moreover, a problem that evokes a story about the body as a site of biopolitical administration, a story about medicine and the biopolitics of alienation, of the management of alienation and the biopolitical negotiation of the body as an unbearable other, an ugly excrescence somehow separate from and unequal to the effervescent brilliance of the mind, of the possibilities inherent in language and thought unburdened by gross limitations of speech, of words and sounds and gestures and vocalizations. The story of digestion also gives rise to another, perhaps just as uncanny story about the question of time, about the management of time and time as something consumed, used up, scarce; just as the body can be exhausted, used up, spent.

The story of digestion, as recounted in this chapter, is a story about the history of medicine. In particular, it is a story about the history of medicine as a profession, the history of its professionalization, its moving away from a ludic addiction to the gruesome and toward an ostensibly more elevated sense of itself and its method. This is the history of medicine in capitalism, which is also a particular history of the body in capitalism, a history of the administration of the body as a resource to be consumed, to be cannibalized. The second story this chapter tells is also a story about medicine, but a story that does not address itself to medicine as a profession, medicine as part of the grim day-to-day of settler culture, or medicine as the quack pharmacology so common to the nineteenth-century frontier. This second story looks at medicine as a sensual aspect of Native lives and Native sovereignties; to the question of medicine not as a technique for the administration of the body as a component within systems of power, economy, and extraction but as a name assigned to Indigenous practices that touch upon the health of the body, its preservation, and its restoration; the body as the physical manifestation of the ineffable networks of care that sustained dynamic expressions of kinship; the body as a node within the circulatory structure traced by kin relations, sutured and maintained through obligation as a form of recognition. Within the exuberant traditions of Native medicine, the effectiveness of medicine is not measured in relation to the time necessary for the restoration of health, nor is health conceived exclusively as a condition of the body reduced to its physicality and its capacity as labor. Rather, Indigenous expressions of medicine rest upon an understanding of time as allowance, a definite quantity that will expire, and of health as the expression of the time that is necessary for healing, where health is understood not as a quantity but as a quality, one that touches upon the capacity to live in common, to live with others and among others, to love and to celebrate, to work and to eat, to live with oneself, to wear the body as the uncanny double of the self. Where the history of medicine in capitalism is oriented by the question of what the complaint was or whether the wound has closed; within the tradition of Native medicine, the question of whether the wound has closed is closely followed by the question of whether it has left a scar, what the scar might tell us about the wound, and what the wound is trying to tell us about the spirit. The body, here, is not a cipher for the operations of power within the mechanics of production or the circulation of value, but for the manifestation of the ineffable, the invisible, the illnesses of our unloved, unacknowledged relatives.

In developing these stories, I explore two texts that emerge from the circumstances of the Black Hawk War and the settler colonization of the Upper Mississippi River Valley. The first of these is by a doctor named William Beaumont, the army surgeon stationed at Fort Crawford, Prairie du Chien, Wisconsin Territory, during the Black Hawk War. First published in 1833, Beaumont's *Experiments and Observations on the Gastric Juice and the Physiology of Digestion* is an early text in the study of gastroenterology and one that is now considered foundational to the field. Based on experiments he conducted over an eight-year period, from 1825 to 1833, Beaumont's writings on the subject of gastroenterology were based, in large part, upon his work with Alexis St. Martin, a French-Canadian voyageur and employee of the American Fur Company. Beaumont first attended St. Martin in 1822, while he was assigned to Fort Mackinac in Michigan. Within the field of gastroenterology, the specifics of St. Martin's case are generally well known. While hunting on Mackinac Island in June of that year, St. Martin was accidently shot, from behind and at close range, in the stomach with buckshot. Appealing to the local US army post for surgical attention, he encountered Beaumont, who proceeded to treat the wound over the course of the next year. According to Beaumont's notes from the early days of that treatment, when he first met the patient, St. Martin's lung and stomach were exposed to view, and his stomach was perforated in such a way that food would simply "pour out" of the aperture. In addition to removing damaged tissues from the site of the wound, Beaumont made sure St. Martin remained nourished by administering anal feedings, before attempting to close the wound by means of a poultice.[2] Fully expecting St. Martin to die, Beaumont was delighted and amazed when his patient not only lived after a year of treatment but that the wound he sustained had healed, even though it never fully closed. He was even more pleased to realize that, through the wound, he could see

into St. Martin's stomach and observe the workings of his digestive processes, offering Beaumont a privilege vantage on a never-before-seen living digestive system.

While Beaumont's observations on St. Martin's digestion are often fas-
cinating (and sometimes hilarious), I am most compelled by his text not
for what it tells us about the stomach or about deglutition but for providing a suspiciously quiet theory of history, time, and labor. Considered not
as a historical document but a chronicle, a story about digestion told by
one with a particular sense of the dynamics of history, Beaumont's study—
with its pretense to the romantic and the affective and narrative as a device for the instantiation of the nation as a felt collectivity—sits at some
odds with the conventions of liberal nationalist historiography discussed
in previous chapters. It is, however, perfectly at ease in relationship to another, concurrent tradition of liberal, statist history, in which history becomes a matter of record keeping, time management, and a general
disinterest in affect outside biopolitical matrices of self-discipline and social control. This is the history that would seem to belong to the figure of
the state and to capital; the history that regards time as something that is
consumed, spent, and—if not carefully guarded—will be wasted. Indeed,
Beaumont's attention to St. Martin as body, when brought into consideration with his brief and largely indirect references to St. Martin as
labor—particularly his description of that labor as characterized by "all
the duties of a *common* servant"—draw attention to the ways in which
the text, in abiding interest in the body and digestion, perform an intervention that is as much managerial as medical, insisting on a particular
diet, taking care to observe both the process of digestion as well as its duration, and creating a set of standards for best eating practices to opti-
mize the process of digestion so to minimize the physical distress of digestive processes. Behind whatever concern for the physical health of the
body, the implication here is also that digestive health is directly linked
to the prevention of disease; and to prevent disease is to save time, to keep
the body—a well-oiled machine, primed to enter into service wherever it
needs be put—in motion. Beaumont's work, in this sense, sits within a
perhaps unlikely genre of the prose of counter-sovereignty configured to
a sense of the state as machine; it is also one that reads the body and the
time of the body as something to be preserved so it can be exploited and
drained as a laboring body, a resource materiality within the capitalist
mode of production. Extending life only for the purposes of exhausting
it is a work of capitalist melancholy in which life and the body are experienced only through endless circuits of repetition, in which the body and
its myriad capacities are reduced to the smallest possible instances of feel-

ing. Cast as labor, the body is robbed of the plenitude of its affects. Those it is allowed are impoverished, stripped of meaning, and made hollow.

Whereas Beaumont's work is shaped by an unexpressed, though not wholly inarticulate understanding of the relationship between history, time, and the body, the second story explores the question of time as it relates to forms of Native medicine as they relate to histories of encounter, kinship, and the obligations that enfold the body. It draws upon the text of the *Life of Black Hawk*. Of these works, the first treats medicine as a component of settler coloniality, the state, and the repressive, repetitive circuits of capitalist melancholia; the second considers medicine in relation to Indigenous sovereignty and its vibrancy, its vitality, its endurance. Composed at a moment in which Native peoples were marked for extinction, the *Life of Black Hawk* advances this intuition of Native survivance by collecting history as medicine; by telling a story about the lives of his people that weaves together the long past, the near past, and the present as well as relationships among different peoples, different ways of life, and different forms of life, including different forms of relations among the seen and the unseen, the human, the geophysical, the animal, and the ethereal. The story presses all that is speakable and not into the form of writing. Where histories compiled by settlers marshaled affect to affirm the material force of those forms of writing through which the expropriation of Indigenous land was encoded and confirmed in law, in its appropriation of history and writing as medicine, the narrative attributed to Black Hawk rewrites both history and treaty; appropriating paper, pen, and print; stealing the secret of their necromancy, their capacity to endow the otherwise inert, dead letter with material life.

In what follows, I read the *Life of Black Hawk* for the contradictory temporal and narrative frameworks that occur throughout the text. Reading the narrative in relation to the history of the book as a technology of liberalism and the attendant emergence of insidiously capitalist modes of temporality and state formation, I explore the text and its introductory matter as a means to discuss the ways in which its translator and editor sought to fit Black Hawk's discourse within conventional narrative frameworks, those predicated on the capacity to adjudicate rationality and truth, oriented by the fables of nation and state. I consider these effectively liberal modes of narrative in relation to the *Life of Black Hawk* as a record of the so-called Black Hawk War, an effectively partial recounting of the conflict told within the conventions of a linear historiography resonant with settler descriptions of invasion and repulsion, injury and triumph. Against this, I return to the beginnings of the text to consider the ways in which Black Hawk's voice emerges through discussions of dreaming, blacking, and medicine. Where settler historiography presumes to assert control over time, as well as the ability to press time and history into a conveniently useable shape, Black Hawk's account of dreaming and blacking evokes humility in the face of time, a refusal to commodify or calculate and to encounter instead the ambiguity of each moment as a record of the past and a window on the future.

In the Pit of the Stomach

As indicated, the study of digestion may seem an unlikely place from which to approach the materiality of settler colonialism and its history, but the foundational literature of the field offers a useful framework through which to think the material enclosures that were visited upon the land were expressed, also, as a set of expropriative claims upon the physicality of the body, claims that reconstituted the figure of the body and its physicality as a matter of its historicity. William Beaumont's intervention takes place at a moment of transition within the field of medicine, one in which a more rigorously documentary style of study and analysis, of experimentation and hypothesis, is becoming institutionalized and generalized, even as other, less credible, less salutary medical practices continue to hold sway. While the distinction between these traditions should not be overdrawn, the medicine Beaumont practiced was of more immediately practical, more professionalized bent and oriented—however crudely—to healing and care. As a technology of the body under capitalism, however, this tradition of medicine, while ostensibly devoted to the alleviation of suffering, is shaped by a much narrower ambit: less an offering of care or concern than a means by which to intervene upon the body, to identify and treat the symptoms of disease as a means of restoring the body to health. In this formulation, under the terms of this imperative, the clearest measure of health is not the absence of pain or the conciliation of anxiety but the capacity of the body to be adapted to and to assume a role within the apparatus of the state, the means of production, and the reproduction of the means of production. From this angle, medicine serves a diagnostic, a disciplinary, and a pedagogical function, instructing the body and the subject of the body in how to properly comport themselves to their role as both instrument and instrumentalist within the bitterly atonal symphony of production, while at the same time sounding the often discordant notes that accompany the physical reproduction of the body, and of bodies, as elements within the multifarious networks that constitute the social order under the hegemony of capital. Circumscribed by the imperatives of capital, the forms of medicine that took shape in the early nineteenth century presume health as a general index of value, and they value a scale of legibility whereby the body is rendered meaningful and worthy only insofar as it is judged capable of carrying out certain functions; of integrating an otherwise unruly collection of voluntary and involuntary processes—organs and limbs, gestures and reflexes, ticks and needs—and rendering them quiescent and obedient to the sadistic impulses that seek to inhabit and to constitute the body of the well-tempered subject.

In Beaumont's work, however, the temperament of the subject, the tempering of the subject, is tempered by a morose relationship to the material, mercurial temporalities of desire; and to the body as a vessel for the expression, and reception, of enjoyment, of pleasure. His system expresses a particular variety of capitalist melancholia, one that resolves the unbearable weight of desire, the infuriating senseless, aimless perambulations of desire, by resolving the affective physicality of the body into the purposefully catatonic activities that constitute the general principle of capital, its production, valorization, and reproduction. While Beaumont's system is fundamentally caught up in the utilitarian currents of early nineteenth-century science and the imperative to remake those aspects of human nature least convenient to social order—to the reproduction and maintenance of order and the long-term expansion and accumulation of capital—behind the utilitarian concern with time and time-discipline is a much thornier question about the confrontation with the body as a vessel for longing, craving, and wanting. Reading Beaumont, the body appears as that which must be explored through the measure of science and the scientific method, as a means to discipline both the body and the self who would study it; to channel a prurient hunger—an uncanny, unwanted, and impossible need for the body—into a discretely scrupulous course of inquiry. Like the digestive processes that Beaumont anatomizes so thoroughly as to strip all meaning or pleasure beyond utilitarian constructions of health as a measure of value, scientific inquiry, in this sense, becomes another site for the expression of capitalist melancholia, for the expression of life and its processes reduced to a joyless pursuit without object or end and leaning forever into interminability. The enclosure of the body in Beaumont's system, in other words, is about both time-discipline and the attenuation of desire, not through its sublimation but through its instrumentalization, through its melancholy application to the purposes of its own exploitation.

In Beaumont's writing, the entanglement of these processes—one largely explicit, the other almost entirely unconscious—is manifest throughout, but it first appears in language touching upon the operations of the visual. "I had opportunities for the examination of the interior of the stomach, and its secretions, which has never been so fully offered to any one. This most important organ, its secretions and its operations, have been submitted to my observation in a very extraordinary manner, in a state of perfect health, and for years in succession. I have availed myself of the opportunity afforded by a concurrence of circumstances which probably can never again occur."[3] Making a claim for the originality of his experiments, Beaumont highlights the singularity of his research as a function of the circumstances that made it possible while allowing that other researchers might reach similar conclusions if his experiments could be repeated, which is unlikely to come about. In establishing the validity of that claim, he cites privileged, visual access to the stomach as the seat of digestive processes; his observations were elevated by exclusivity of access, a condition he enjoyed largely as an accident—a "concurrence of circumstances"—when St. Martin appeared before him, his stomach exposed, presenting itself for inspection by the most zealous student, who was ready to look, see, and record; ready to enclose the stomach and its secretions through the knowing attention of the informed eye.

Rendered transparent as a condition of its laceration, the stomach here appears as a piece in a puzzle and Beaumont appears as a fully embodied, imperious eye, a spy with unusually privileged access to the interior of a living, healthy body; a body still in motion; a body secreting, operating, housing organs as if a machine waiting to be taken apart, disassembled, studied. "I saw him in twenty-five or thirty minutes after the accident occurred, and, on examination, found a portion of the lung, as large as a Turkey's egg, protruding through the external wound, lacerated and burnt: and immediately below this, another protrusion, which, on further examination, proved to be a portion of the stomach, lacerated through all its coats, and pouring out the food he had taken for his breakfast, through an orifice large enough to admit the forefinger."[4] Describing the pathology of the wound, Beaumont traces its shape with his eye, that shape, that description; all except rendered into language by his voice, by his hand. Beaumont appears here as St. Thomas and St. Martin as an unlikely Christ, with Beaumont claiming the prerogative of doubt as the foundation of the scientific method, a prerogative that eventually founds something near to a truth. Moreover, the engagement between eye and stomach, made between hand and voice, forms a copula, a point of articulation, one that establishes the dominance of the organ of sight—as well as the volitional organs of movement and vocalization—over the organ of digestion, the organs of secretion, and elimination. Food pours forth from the open wound, involuntarily spilling from the body that is

meant to enclose it, the body it is meant to nourish; Beaumont's eye captures it, his pen records it, the record itself a story about the superiority
of some over others, about voluntarism and will over secretion and process, about the opening that secretes and the finger that penetrates.

While given only as a unit of measurement, Beaumont's description
of the size of the wound as "large enough to admit the forefinger" lends a
concrete, physical sensuousness to the less conspicuously material presence of the eye and the gaze, gesturing toward the destructively erotic
character of Beaumont's relation to St. Martin and the experiments he
performed upon his person. The body deracinated is, here, the body that
can be penetrated, stimulated, fed, probed. "On the fifth day a partial
sloughing of the integuments and muscles took place. [Eventually what
was] left [was] a perforation into the stomach, plainly to be seen, large
enough to admit the whole length of my fore-finger." As more and more
tissue is sloughed off, the patient is no longer able to retain food or fluids;
as such, Beaumont resorts to anal feeding. "For seventeen days, all that
entered his stomach by the oesophagus soon passed out of the wound;
and the only way of sustaining him was by means of nutritious injections
per anus, until compresses and adhesive straps could be applied, so as to
retain his food."[5] Within days of this procedure, "the bowels became grad-
ually excited," and following a series of cathartic injections, "a very hard,
black, foetid stool was procured, followed by several similar ones; after
which the bowels became quite regular, and continued so."[6]

Following upon his insistent discussion of the "sloughing" of the
integuments—the progressive shedding of skin, muscle, and surrounding ligatures such that Beaumont can penetrate St. Martin's body—these
entirely clinical references to anal feeding, excited bowels, the injection
of cathartic fluids, and anal discharge seem the fulfillment of a very queer
set of intimacies. The body penetrated, initially, by cataclysmic exposure
to buckshot—propelled violently from the barrel of a gun—the resulting
injury, as Beaumont describes it, produces an aperture, surrounded by a
corona of dead tissue. As the healthy body sheds itself of this necrotic
matter, the "sloughing" of the "integuments," the remedied wound is exposed as an orifice, a point of routine contact between the body and the
world, between inside and out. Perforation gives way to penetration, leading to excitation and discharge. "The usual method of extracting the gastric juice, for experiment, is by placing the subject on his right side,
depressing the valve within the aperture, introducing a gum-elastic tube,
of the size of a large quill, five or six inches into the stomach, and then
turning him on the left side, until the orifice becomes dependent."[7] Inserting his finger, inserting tubes, inserting food to be consumed so that

he might observe the gastric juices of St. Martin's stomach, Beaumont carries out, under the guise of experimentation, a strange and sadistic ritual of control and dominance, his position as superior, as intellect, as eye, realized in the moment of holding St. Martin down and extracting his fluids. "Its extraction is generally attended by that peculiar sensation at the pit of the stomach, termed sinking, with some degree of faintness, which renders it necessary to stop the operation."[8] Pleased by the excretion of feces, Beaumont's investment in the anus is transferred to the stomach, to feeding as the preliminary of evacuation. A living body, Beaumont is not particularly interested in St. Martin's affects, just his discomfort; not his pains, but the quiet agonies of overeating, of light starvation, of having foreign objects inserted into your body against your will. St. Martin becomes, in this tableau, little more than an infant, and Beaumont its mother, taking pleasure in watching and feeding, in serving the obnoxious vulnerability of the creature before him, and in serving that vulnerability, exacting some portion of revenge.

Whatever pleasures Beaumont might have extracted from his interaction with St. Martin, as it emerges in the text, the carnality of their exchange, the blandly sadistic control Beaumont exercises over St. Martin's body, over his person, appears as a substitute for his lubricious entanglements with other men. "TO JOSEPH LOVELL, M.D., Surgeon General of the United States' Army. . . . Whose merit justly entitles him to the rank which he holds, and whose zeal in the cause of Medical Science is equaled only by his ability to promote it. As a tribute of respect for his public and private virtues, and as a feeble tribute for a long tried and unvarying friendship, this work is respectfully dedicated by the author."[9] Beaumont's dedication to Joseph Lovell, the first surgeon general of the United States, provokes a range of questions touching upon the moment in which the homosocial dimensions of mentorship under patriarchy meet the carnivalesque unfurling of homoerotic longing, the longing for a teacher, giving way to the longing for a father, and the longing for a lover. Without conceding the metaphorical character of this relationship, much of what seems wanting, much of what Beaumont's dedication seems implicitly to request, is recognition and love. Offering his triumphant opus to his senior officer and teacher, Beaumont asks only to be seen, that his "feeble tribute" might be acceptable to this demiurge. Making his book into a body, an offering, Beaumont disassembles St. Martin's organs, his secretions, and then puts them back together in the shape of a codex, here taken as both a book, and a collection of medical knowledge, a compendium of bound pages, vellum scraped from St. Martin's skin.

As the dedication suggests, the erotic dimensions of Beaumont's admiration for Lovell are largely submerged, inverted, turned inside out. Just as Beaumont literally disassembles St. Martin's body so that it might be reconstructed in the shape of his book, the text figuratively dismantles the homoerotic attachments among junior and superior officers, among men of different intellectual gifts and outlooks, and reconstitutes them in the shape of friendship. A supposedly elevated relationship among men, friendship does not describe an institutionalized relationship, or a clear set of power dynamics, but rather sentimentalizes the homosocial relationships among men that constitute the substance of patriarchy. "To Professors SILLMAN, KNIGHT, IVES, and HUBBARD, of Yale College, DUNGLINSON, of the Virginia University, and SEWALL, JONES, HUNDERSON and HALL, of Columbian College, for the unsolicited friendship; for the interest which they have taken in the experiments."[10] Staking a claim to friendship with Lovell, Beaumont goes on to extend his thanks and dedication to other teachers and erstwhile collaborators, contemporaries of far greater influence and status, thereby leveraging his research as his assertion of membership in a powerful club, an association among white men of a certain class, of a certain status, who claim the authority to shape certain aspects of social life.

The class dimensions of these relationships are revealed in the depths of Beaumont's disdain for St. Martin. "He now entered my service, and I commenced another set of experiments on the stomach and gastric fluids. . . . During this time, in the intervals of experimenting, he performed all the duties of a common servant, chopping wood, carrying burthens &c. with little or no suffering or inconvenience from his wound. . . . He subsisted on crude food, in abundant quantities, except when on a prescribed diet . . . under special observance."[11] Fawning over men of superior position, rhetorically negating their elevation through an aspirational claim to friendship, Beaumont seeks access to their circle, but not one of their orifices. St. Martin, meanwhile, is all orifice, secretions, breath, sweat, discharge, and shit. Prone before Beaumont's forefinger, the bony forceps asserting itself, wrenching apart his flesh to exposing his stomach before Beaumont's omniscient eye, St. Martin is forced to abase himself, again, as Beaumont's servant. He is crude, he is gross, he eats too much unless Beaumont is watching. A creature of unbound appetites, Beaumont takes his disgust for St. Martin and secretes it away, its juices hidden among the anemic language of the clinician. The negative image of Lovell and his fellows, St. Martin is offered no laurels. His contribution to the experiments goes unremarked. He is the body, Beaumont the mind. Beaumont houses him, feeds him, and gives him injections. Beaumont penetrates him, stimulates him, and takes his fluids. Beaumont tears away his flesh, looks inside, and quietly builds his book.

Bound together, Moebius fashion, the surgeon general and the university deans face the image of St. Martin—one the portrait of nobility, the other a face drawn in mud. Between the two, Beaumont is twisted, the torsions of his desire bending him between one and the other, from the need for elevation and the pleasures of intellectual life to the dark secretions of the body and the pleasures of its pains. The sublation of the erotic in his relationship with Lovell recurs in his relationship to St. Martin, the refinement of friendship, of relations with a master whose rank has placed in abeyance, supplanted by the fetishization of mastery, the identification with the master as the source of all pleasure, the master as the finger that stimulates and takes pleasure in causing pleasure and pain and observing the proofs of his power: the gastric juices, the chyme, the blood, the shit, the feeling in the pit of the stomach that is called sinking. Between the image of the deans (holy) and the image of St. Martin (prone), Beaumont's text unspools the filaments of his desire, the scope of his unspoken, inarticulate longing so much greater than him, so much greater than his inadequacy. He turns and turns, spinning in all directions, the character of friendship exposed, not as the name of an institutionalized relationship but as the designation given to an unknown and unknowable quantity, a duration. A friendship is not given by marriage or by birth, nor is it conveyed by membership in the military or the state. It comes as a measure of time, but what measure of time is impossible to say. One hour, two days, five months, ten years? How long does it take to become a friend? How does one recognize a friendship? Much the same could be said of experimentation, of the relationship between the clinician and the subject, the study of the body, of nature, an unending abyss leading toward nothing but expanding to encompass the impossibility of the subject, the plenitude of the world.

The problem of desire in Beaumont is specifically a problem of time, of time as a plenitude that cannot be filled and that obeys no law. In Beaumont's observations on digestion, that problem is resolved through Beaumont's very carefully noted references to time as a structure; to the days, later months, then years during which St. Martin is convalescing, then the years of his experiments, the months and years—so very carefully preserved in his case study—where St. Martin is absent, the time when he has left Beaumont, the laboratory, and their experiments. Beaumont abases himself and his desire before the time of the state, of the calculation, of capital, bending the bodily processes of direction in that terribly melancholy direction. The queer time of their relation is not so much foreclosed as it is displaced. Taking as its object the narrative figures of day, month, and year—the socially agreed upon standards by which time is registered as moving, flowing, passing away—what was foreshortened, twisted, and tangled is elongated, straightened, and given direction and duration.[12] The reconstitution of time and desire around a specifically uniform, singular direction is reflected in the preface to the study, where Beaumont makes his earliest references to the ways in which time figures as a variable in his studies. Having spent "years in succession" studying St. Martin under a "concurrence of circumstances" not likely to be repeated, Beaumont claims authority over the scene of the laboratory as over his conclusions, aligning himself with the sphere of institutionalized knowledge production, while moving away from the clinic as the scene of murkier predilections. Here, the health of the moving, living body—as well as the physical and moral health of the examining physician—is measured with and through the time of the experiments themselves, which are dutifully recorded, sequential, yet somehow singular, an exception that describes an event. The evocation of an event, "concurrence of circumstances" suggests the explosive possibilities of pleasure and desire, whereas "years in succession" suggests, as much as anything, an experience of time as passage, which is drudgery, tedious, deadly, and, for St. Martin, likely torturous. Falling into the text through these narrative figures, "concurrence" and "succession" evoke a reified sense of both the markers of temporal motion and those that mark instances of great moment, holidays that fall regularly on the calendar during the course of the year. Beaumont's "concurrence of events," in this sense, captures something of the way in which instances of great moment capture the contradictions inherent to the carnivalesque, the dialectical tension between transformative possibility and the maintenance of social order through preordained celebrations of disorder.

This tension finds a means of resolution as the text moves from experiment and observation to analysis and prescription. "With respect to the agent of chymification, that principle of life which converts the crude aliment into chyme, and renders it fit for the action of the hephatic and pancreatic fluids, and final assimilation and conversion into the fluids, and the various tissues of the animal organism—no part of physiology has, perhaps, so much engaged the attention of mankind, and exercised the ingenuity of physiologists."[13] Discussing the "gastric juice" as carrying out an effectively chemical process, Beaumont touches upon the importance of aliment and deglutition, of chewing and the formation of a bolus. Dwelling on the role played by "gastric juice" in the dissolution of

food and the formation of chyme, as well as the circulation of chyme
through the lymphatic system, Beaumont finds a story about movement
and direction, taking a set of organic processes and analyzing them as
moments in a sequence, parts in a machine. Ignoring all the myriad ways
in which the organic components of the human body are unavoidably,
unpredictably misintegrated, like a hearty pioneer, Beaumont blazes a
trail from the mouth to the stomach to the lymphatic centers and the
secretion of waste and the promotion of immunity. This movement
through the body describes a trajectory through space; it is also a route
through time, a way of organizing time, of narrating temporality, through
a consideration of the process by which food is made to decompose, to
dissolve, moving from a recognizable consumable to generalized aliment,
chyme, lymph, and blood.

Taking the organic processes of digestion as a model, Beaumont charts
an idealized movement through conveniently integrated bodily systems,
a movement that allows for him to map a course through his desire, chan-
neling the depth of its reservoir onto a course bound for meaningful
application. Winding his way through the digestive tract, Beaumont's
analysis of St. Martin's secretions offers a conceptual framework through
which to project the social and cultural components necessary for the op-
timization of digestion as an integrated, organic process, shaping the
different aspects of that process into an unperturbed flow, much as contemporary engineers might have reshaped the erratic pools of an ersatz
river into a mighty stream. "Attention must be paid to preliminary
processes . . . [to] thorough mastication and moderate or slow deglutition. These are indispensible [sic] to the due and natural supply of the
stomach; for if food be swallowed to [sic] fast, and pass into the stomach
imperfectly masticated, too much is received in a short time, and in too
imperfect a state of preparation, to be disposed of by the gastric juice."[14]
Extrapolating from his observations of the stomach to consider the importance of chewing, and swallowing, Beaumont's account of digestion
extends the process in multiple directions, across multiple spaces, forward
and backward in time. Connecting the stomach with the lymphatic system and bodily immunity, to the intestine, the colon, and the elimination of waste, he begins the process from the mouth, from the speed with
which one eats, the time one devotes to chewing and the formation of aliment, and the passage of aliment from the mouth through the esophagus to the stomach.

Behind this simple projection is a movement in time as well as space,
but also a prescription for behavior imagined through the fabrication of
a spatial-temporal axis; a prescription for the modification of habit to

approximate a better model for thinking about the table, for the manners surrounding food and consumption, as those serve the health of the body, not just some antiquated sense of social propriety. Just as food is converted into aliment—and aliment to chyme through the cooperative interaction of the mouth, the esophagus, and the stomach—so too are the habits of the well-tempered subject stripped away through the repetitive practice of proper eating, leaving behind the most well-balanced, the most health-ful routine. "There appears to be a sense of perfect intelligence conveyed from the stomach to the encephalic centre, which, in health, invariably dictates what quantity of aliment . . . is naturally required for the purposes of life; and which, if noticed, and properly attended to, would prove the most salutary monitor of health, and effectual preventative of, and restor-ative from, disease."[15] Describing the relationship between stomach and mouth as one that seeks only that quantity of food necessary to the proper functioning of the body, Beaumont warns against the translation of hun-ger and need into want, the passage of want into a morbid indulgence of Epicurean pleasure. "In the present state of civilized society, with the provocations of the culinary art, and the incentives of high seasoned food, brandy, and wines, the temptations to excess in the indulgences of the table are rather too strong to be resisted by poor human nature."[16] Con-fronted by the plenitude of the table, by the mysteries of the culinary arts, one must exercise caution in monitoring the shape of one's wants so as not to pass beyond the equivalence of want and need to a parody of sat-isfaction, to recreation and play masquerading as necessity and nutriment. The fallibility of human nature comes into conflict with the arts of civi-lization, which lead into temptation, to eating beyond what is necessary, or "eating too much at once for the wants of economy . . . distending the muscular fibres beyond the point so admirably fixed . . . for agreeable sensations."[17]

Beaumont counsels his readers not to overeat, and not to eat too quickly, not to over-extend the chemical properties of the gastric juices. "If food be swallowed too fast, and pass into the stomach imperfectly masticated, too much is received in a short time, and in too imperfect a state of prep-aration, to be disposed of by the gastric juice."[18] Measuring time by tempo, the speed with which one eats measured by metronome, the pace at which one indulges is at least as important as what one consumes. Insofar as mastication converts food into aliment, indistinguishable pieces of nu-trient prepared to meet their end, to undergo another transformation through exposure to motion of the gastric bath. To overeat is to tax the capacities of the gastric system, to inhibit the proper functioning of the gastric acid, to hyperextend the muscles of the stomach to a degree that the organs and processes within the digestive network become misaligned, malfunctioning. To under-eat, however, does not invite any such concern. "The male semen is constantly being secreted, and deposited in its proper seminal valves, ready to be ejected during the venerial [sic] orgasm; and yet how many men live for years or perhaps for a whole life, who have no intercourse with the other sex. What becomes of the semen under those circumstances? Taken up, unquestionably, by the absorbing vessels, as the gastric juice of the stomach is."[19] Likening the digestive process and the production of gastric acid to the production of semen in the testicles, Beaumont indulges a metaphorical association between fluids that finds their unique characteristics converging, overlapping, the tension between the corrosive and the catalytic left unresolved except with respect to the rhetorical enclosure of the body, the transformation of the body through the application of language, the transformation of language through the penetration of the body.

Designed as a system for the management of desire, of manifesting that which is unspeakable in desire, through the regulation of the body, Beaumont's study of gastric juice and its place within the ecology of digestive processes prompts a metaphorical exuberance that manifests an impossible connection among organically unrelated organs, between the stomach and the testes, the acid and the semen. Describing the ostensibly post-Malthusian problem of deprivation, Beaumont turns, ineluctably, toward the problem of population, reproduction, and sex. Here, the problem of desire as the intolerable conceals itself as a problem of sex and reproduction, of the denial of sexual contact and the regulation of birthrates, of the relationship between the injunction to reproduce and the obligation to feed. "Man is a creature of habit and circumstance, carrying about him the effects of a primeval disobedience, destined not only to earn his food by his own exertions, but to partake of such as the climate in which he resides may supply him."[20] A hopelessly fatalistic portrait of the human as chained to his most animalistic instincts, to those aspects of his nature which are most thoroughly carnal, this assessment of human nature draws together the need for food, for alimentary nourishment, and the obligation to labor, the need to work to produce that which will satisfy need and sustain life. Placed in correspondence with a "primeval disobedience" and its enduring impact, the metaphorical flourish by which the stomach is placed in conversation with the testes is filled by the disseminations of Eden, of Genesis and the Creation, and the theological mythos of original sin. Having eaten of the fruit of the tree of knowledge, Adam and Eve and their progeny are forever condemned to wander, toil, and reproduce. A primordial gluttony begets hunger and labor—both the labor of everyday life, of scratching a living from the earth, and the labor of childbirth and reproduction, the work of bearing a life and feeding it, caring for it, ensuring that it find a place in a world shaped by the imperative to wander, to never be at home, to eat but always to want for more. Beaumont thus returns to the question of the sexual economy implicit within his system; the system as a theory of sexual regulation, the regulation of bodily impulses and of their tendency to express themselves in excess.

For Beaumont, the regulation of the digestion is a means of resolving the tensions of desire. What he presents is not a map back to the Garden, but a way to atone for the sin of having once partaken in too great a share of its delights, in enjoying the good things just a little too much. This excess of enjoyment and pleasure accounts for some portion of Beaumont's clinical recommendations as to proper diet and mastication, which reveal themselves as particular measures in time—a specific, defined portion, a duration—toward which otherwise pleasurable activities should be directed. The systemization of medicine as a science—a justifiably reasonable adherence to the principles of hypothesis, experiment, observation, and analysis—appears here as a set of anxieties of appetite. It is about the problem of the management of the body as a function of time, the problem of how to regulate the time of labor so as not to exhaust the body but to maximize the potential inherent to the body as a system of contradictory energies, while not fully exhausting the system, allowing enough time for their recovery. Beaumont's system is, in this sense, about the enclosure of the body within a system of labor discipline that is, if not punitive, repetitive and dreary, likely unending, and almost certainly injurious if not ultimately murderous. It draws upon and epitomizes the time of capitalist melancholy: a condition of desire absent any particular object, any specific destination, endless chasing itself around in circles in an attempt at getting somewhere without knowing where, safely ensconced in the little joys of repetition, vaguely moving toward some satisfaction, knowing that nothing which satisfies will ever satiate. It is the melancholy as the face of the clock, the leaves in a calendar, the passing of years; the pulling of levers and toting of bales, the tilling of fields, the planting of crops, the cooking of meals, the obligatory compliment, the peck on the cheek, the once a week obligatory missionary sex. It is the time of settler colonialism and the stories it tells: the compensatory romance of the score to be found in the new territory, the land that will yield more fruitfully just over the next hill, the satisfaction that will come after one more harvest. It is the time of endurance waiting until exhaustion.

Dreaming and Mourning and the Blackening of Faces

While there has been no dearth of scholarly engagement with Black Hawk's narrative, much of it—including much of what is included in this book—has taken Black Hawk as a Native informant, an autoethnographer leaving behind traces of a lost world. Approaching the *Life of Black Hawk* as an unwriting of the strategies of counter-sovereignty requires examining the text from a slightly oblique angle, one that reads the text less as source than as story. Once erroneously considered the first autobiographical text composed by a Native person, the narrative has circulated in countless editions since its publication in 1833; it has been widely anthologized and extensively scrutinized by professional and amateur critics alike. As Kendall Johnson has pointed out, the initial reviews of the published text were concerned largely with its "authenticity"—that is, the extent to which it was a true reflection of Black Hawk's voice, or a fabrication designed to play upon Black Hawk's celebrity. The question of authenticity also touched upon Black Hawk's relationship to the "truth" of Indian character and mores. On this point, Johnson cites William Joseph Snelling's review of the *Life of Black Hawk*, which contains an ardent dismissal of William Apess and his *Son of the Forest*—a work that predated Black Hawk's by at least two years.[21] For Snelling, Apess's work could only be described as "non-Indian," as Apess's "taste, feelings, and ideas were derived from the whites and [he is] in all essentials a civilized man." Black Hawk, in contrast, was a "wild, unadulterated savage, [with] gall yet fermenting in his veins,"[22] a representative of all that was properly noble, sublime, and terrible in the life of Native peoples.

None of this is to ignore the many voices that speak through the text. As a collaboration among a settler merchant, a French-Pottawatami trader, and a Sauk warrior, purpose and desire are especially difficult to divine, and the inherent multivocality of the text is amplified by the multiplicity of interests seeking to express themselves through it. Though questions concerning the authenticity of the text as an honest representation of Black Hawk's voice have lingered, most scholars now agree that *Life of Black Hawk* was a genuine coproduction of Black Hawk, translator Antoine LeClaire, and editor and amanuensis J. B. Patterson; and that, even though Patterson would amend the text to his liking in editions published in the years after Black Hawk's death, at the time of its initial composition, Black Hawk was clearly in command of the dialogue and its transcription. Relieved of this burden of proof, more recent commentary has explored the text as an instance of the elegiac mode in Native poetics, understanding the elegiac as a service to the survival and continuity

of the Sauk nation. For Laura Mielke, the text sits uneasily within a tradition of nineteenth-century sentimental literature, borrowing, bending,
and shaping the conventions of the genre.[23] Frank Kelderman has exam-
ined the text in relationship to forms of Indigenous writing and oral
performance—most notably that of Black Hawk's rival, Keokuk—to identify the rhetorical strategies Native leaders employed in their attempts at
negotiating relations with empire.[24] Reading the text for Black Hawk's
commentary on peace medals and metal money, Kendall Johnson identifies the ironic in Black Hawk's voice, as he offers a furtive critique of
the value of promises made by the United States, and a presentiment of
the 1837 financial crisis inaugurated by Andrew Jackson's land and mon-
etary policies.

Within the scope of these readings, the Life of Black Hawk preserves
not just the memory of one person but the remnants of a conversation
that encodes a history of the Sauk and the Fox and the region they called
home, as well as long legacies of entanglement with imperial power and
with other Indigenous nations; it captures the legacies of ceremony,
mourning, suffering, and joy as well as something of the meaningful
substance of the Indigenous community; and by describing "the actual
history of our plural existence," it maps the coordinates of Sauk self-
determination and sovereignty, the processes that sought to sponsor
their erosion, as well as their continuities and their irrepressible, inextin-
guishable vitality. The Life of Black Hawk, in other words, is a work dedicated to the expression of survivance: a set of reflections from the present
on the past designed to maintain and guarantee Indigenous futures.
While these critical positions are fundamentally sound, each of these
scholars analyzes the Life of Black Hawk as if its meaning is broadly and
patently literal; and as if that literalism is the mode through which Black
Hawk chose to convey his disdain for settler culture as well as his defense
of Indigenous sovereignty and self-determination. This is not a wholly in-
appropriate way of approaching the text: at the beginning and at the end
of the narrative, Black Hawk states his hope that, through his discourse,
he might "contradict the story of some of the village criers [newspaper and
magazine publishers]," by offering his own "statement of truth," something that could "satisfy [and convince] the white people among whom I
have been travelling" of the nobility of his intentions and the character
of his people.[25]

The book in its modern incarnation has been—sometimes purposefully, often incidentally—a contributor to the life of the nation-state, as
well as the organization of the elements of desire, the forms of affect, that
sustain social reproduction. By the very history of the circumstances of

its preparation, the *Life of Black Hawk* critiques—without overturning—these arrangements. Just as Makataimeshekiakiak's remains should not be mistaken as merely a body, the narrative should not be mistaken as merely a book. Composed in cooperation with a white settler publisher, J. B. Patterson, and Black Hawk's translator, a French-Pottawatomie métis trader named Antoine LeClair, *Life of Black Hawk* reflects something of the social conventions that governed life in the Upper Mississippi River Valley in the decades before the US colonial project began to take shape with its emphasis on a far more dogmatic, militarized approach to regional governance. The negotiation that shaped the text—the movement between Black Hawk as narrator, LeClair as translator, and Patterson as scribe—suggests something of this history, while their collaborative work tracks that history in the movement across communities, languages, techniques of inscription, modes of production, and avenues of dissemination. If every instance of translation is necessarily an act of recomposition, and every instance of transcription another step removed from the original utterance, the circumstances of the production of Black Hawk's narrative themselves betray a fissure at the heart of the text; a crack that does not so much put into question the text and its authenticity, as put into question the authority imagined as a component of all such texts. Such negotiations suddenly are no longer binding but open to renegotiation, reinterpretation, revision, or abandonment.

To take note of these formal characteristics of the text—its relationship to the braided histories of empire and Indigeneity, as well as the immaterial yet necessarily unavoidable dimensions of language and its instability—is to draw attention to the status of the narrative as story which is less an authoritative account than a provisional, if socially effective, fiction. The story Black Hawk tells may be a piece of the fictions of social and political power among the Sauk; yet the language it speaks, the mode of its telling, bears no resemblance to the voice of counter-insurgency and the signature of the state. This element of their exchange is largely lost on Patterson and LeClair, for whom the narrative does not speak to the social mediations of sovereignty among the Sauk but to forms of address that are both entertaining and informative. "It is presumed no apology will be required for presenting to the public, the life of a Hero who has lately taken such high rank among the distinguished individuals of America. In the following pages he will be seen in the characters of a Warrior, a Patriot and a State-prisoner . . . [as well as] the Chief of his Band, asserting their rights with dignity, firmness, and courage."[26] Prelude to Patterson's 1834 "Advertisement" for the book, here, Patterson fashions Black Hawk as a classical stage performer, a mummer donning masks for his audience and their amusement. Black Hawk's tale is presented as a story, but one that follows all too predictable, well-trod paths of narrative gratification. For his part, LeClair was far more direct, emphasizing not the dramatic, but the contractual. "I do hereby certify, the Ma-ka-tai-me-she-kia-kiak, or Black Hawk, did call upon me to have a History of his life written and published. . . . I acted as Interpreter; and was particularly cautious, to understand distinctly the narrative of Black Hawk throughout. . . . [I] have no hesitation in pronouncing it strictly correct, in all its particulars."[27]

Echoing the language of jurisprudence, the rhetorical device of testimony, in his prologue to Black Hawk's narrative, LeClair does not hesitate to declare his translation of Black Hawk's discourse complete and accurate, abjuring the possibility of linguistic incompatibilities that might lead to misinterpretation or misunderstanding. The text is the text, and it is the record of a discourse in which a history was faithfully recorded, straightforward and truthfully. Opening with "I do hereby certify" and closing with "given under my hand," LeClair appends the title "U.S. Interpreter for the Sacs and Foxes" to his signature, casting himself as a bureaucrat in the service of the state and, thus, a person whose authority as memoirist and scribe was effectively beyond question. Offering implicit assurance to a would-be reader concerning the precision of the state and its discourse, especially as concerns its relations with Native peoples, LeClair's testimony as to the veracity of his translation seals the narrative as a document, official and officious—a statement of truth that, while not necessarily factual, serves as evidence of the condition and capacity of one Native person, marking something of the perpetual adolescence of Native peoples. His testimony, in this sense, is its own secondary instance of translation, a means of transposing Black Hawk's words, no matter how faithfully rendered, into the discourse of the state.

Tracing the signature of the state, LeClair's testimony follows his work in another coproduction, the 1832 treaty that ended the so-called Black Hawk War, forcing the Sauks and Foxes into extensive land cessions for the audacity they displayed in defending their sovereignty. "WHEREAS, under certain lawless and desperate leaders, a formidable band, constituting a large portion of the Sac and Fox nation, left their country in April last, and, in violation of treaties, commenced an unprovoked war upon unsuspecting and defenceless citizens of the United States, sparing neither age nor sex . . . the said States . . . demand of said tribes . . . a cession of a tract of the Sac and Fox country."[28] Prelude to the articles of cession— including a special grant to LeClair made at the request of the confederated nations—this officious statement etches a vernacular history of something that would come to be called the Black Hawk War into the archive of the state and, ever so delicately, into the written history of the nation and the state. In the testimony that precedes Black Hawk's narrative, LeClair stages a similar attempt at reifying not just the translation of the narrative but the narrative and its relationship to other instances of historiographic fabulation, including the ongoing effort to retrofit the circumstances of the conflict among the Rock River Sauk, settlers, and the United States military into a clearly delineated story of invasion and warfare, aggressor and aggrieved, victor and vanquished.

This voice, speaking in this register, in the *Life of Black Hawk* conveys the history of the so-called Black Hawk War. "During the night, I thought over every thing Ne-a-pope had told me, and was pleased to think that, by a little exertion on my part, I could accomplish the object of all my wishes. I determined to follow the advice of the prophet, and sent word by Ne-a-pope, that I would get all my braves together, explain every thing that I had heard to them; and recruit as many as I could from the different villages."[29] Attributed, of course, to Black Hawk, this passage is one among many that conveys a subtle transposition into narrative linearity and a focus on events as components of a sequence, of information, contemplation, decision, and movement, the passage from aspiration to action. Having received intelligence from Ne-a-pope concerning the designs of the Prophet, Black Hawk spends a night deliberating over the course of his efforts on behalf of his people, before coming to the conclusion that he will assemble his forces and to recruit those who might be willing to follow him. Similar chronologies recur throughout the text and its description of unfolding of the Black Hawk War. "My party having all come in and got ready, we commenced our march up the Mississippi—our women and children in canoes, carrying such provisions as we had . . . and my braves and warriors on horseback, armed and equipped for defense. The prophet came down and joined us below Rock river, having called at Rock Island on his way down, to consult the [American] war chief, agent, and trader."[30] As above, there is a confident projection of sequence, of events piled one upon another, evoking the irrepressible flow of the river itself. In this instance, that sequence is further reified by its entanglement with space and trajectory, of movement "up" the Mississippi and "down" the Rock. There is also a sense of spatial confusion, of the Sauk party moving against the flow of the Mississippi, just as they would violate the direction of the Rock. This literal movement suggests a figurative passage into the past, a presentiment of decline and disappearance that echoed those found in most settler accounts of Native futurity. Preceded by the verb *commenced*, however, the passage offers a clear sense of a beginning and a movement that echoed settler historiography and its insistent promulgation of Sauk incursion and attack. Taking invasion as the initial moment of injury, the moment the Black Hawk War began, settler historiography exonerated itself of culpability in the events of the conflict. These passages in the *Life of Black Hawk* confirm that sense of innocence, telling a story about Black Hawk as the architect of a war that, while sympathetic to the cause of the Sauks, confirms the prejudicial narrative of Indigenous rapine.

Although it is difficult to distinguish among the cacophony of voices that are preserved within the *Life of Black Hawk*, this linear presentation of the circumstances of the conflict seems most likely attributable to Patterson and LeClair, for whom the text was less an act of preservation and survivance than a commercial opportunity, a commodity within the expansive culture of Blackhawkiana. Linearity echoed the logic of the commodity as a consumable, disposable thing, while the evanescence of the commodity captured the inevitable decline and disappearance of Native peoples. As seen in his preface to the text, for Patterson, this meant casting Black Hawk in the role of the Hero, with the fate of the Hero always to be fated for death. For LeClair, it meant a turn toward the law and the discourse of treaty as the preserve of history, as treaty renders history and projects it into the domain of the law. In contrast, Black Hawk's preface to the narrative militates against these acts of legalistic—liberal and linear—transposition, bringing into question both Patterson's description of its contents as the journey of a hero, a singular individual striving to preserve his people and their rights, as well as LeClair's insistence on treaty as the language through which history speaks to the future. Couched as a dedication to Brigadier General Henry Atkinson, commander of the Sixth Infantry at the Battle of Bad Axe, Black Hawk opens his statement by emphasizing circumstance and contingency, citing the "changes of fortune" and the "vicissitudes of war" that "made [Atkinson his] conqueror."[31] Refuting any notion of military or civilizational superiority, Black Hawk's address to Atkinson insists upon a kind of social and temporal parity between himself and his antagonist, refusing the narrative pieties of the state and its puerile recourse to the rhetoric of warfare as structured around beginning and end, invasion and expulsion, attack and defeat. Black Hawk is clear: he was not defeated, but "conquered," and only after his "last resources were exhausted" did he consent to "yield" and "[become] your prisoner." Without making any overtly hostile overtures, this insistence on the coeval suggests that, for Black Hawk, the conflict among these parties is not over; it is suspended, momentarily put into abeyance. Implicitly rejecting counter-sovereign appeals to injury and victory as mechanisms for the legal and material dispossession of Sauk and Fox lands, Black Hawk's dedication further obscures clear delineations between aggressor and aggrieved, conjuring "the actual history of our plural existence" as one that braided the inevitability of conflict as much as the possibility of friendship and care. "The story of my life is told in the following pages; it is intimately connected, and in some measure, identified with a part of the history of your own: I have, therefore, dedicated it to you."[32] Claiming a sort of broken fraternity with Atkinson, Black Hawk's dedication solicits fidelity to the ethics of kinship without promising it. Neither precluding violence nor inviting it, the dedication leaves open a space of mutuality and negotiation, quietly asserting the ongoing purchase of Sauk sovereignty as a means of configuring coexistence upon the land while leaving intact the fiction of Sauk quiescence.

Black Hawk's dedication to Atkinson prefigures something of the voice that will continue throughout the narrative, as well as its ambiguities, underscored by his stated purpose of "[vindicating] my character from misinterpretation." This phrase is echoed in the final paragraphs of the narrative, where, insisting that he never participated in the murder of "women and children among the whites," Black Hawk declares, "I make this statement of truth, to satisfy the white people among whom I have been traveling . . . that when they shook me by the hand so cordially, they did not shake the hand that had ever been raised any but warriors."[33] Without abandoning the kindliness of this rhetorical gesture toward his "conquerors," it is difficult to peer into the narrative—its sharp critiques of settler vigilantism, its passionate assessments of the bankruptcy of the American character—without seeing in this statement the sort of ironic voice identified by Johnson: it is equally difficult to see Black Hawk much troubled about "vindicating" anything he had done, much less to white people, especially as settlers were clear aggressors in the campaign to rout him and his people. Instead of reading these statements as ironic, however, I propose that we read them as statements of ambiguity of the text, and regarding the book as commodity, statements about the desire to put himself into circulation, even if it means availing himself of the most devilish technology as printed text. "How smooth must be the language of whites, when they can make right look wrong, and wrong right."[34] Describing conditions prevailing in the years between 1830 and 1831, Black Hawk's statement echoes an earlier critique of textuality and its use in the dispossession of Native lands and Native lives. "For the first time, I touched goose quill to treaty—not knowing, however, that, by that act, I consented to give away my village. Had that been explained to me, I should never have opposed it, and never would have signed their treaty. . . . What do we know of the laws and customs of white people? They might buy our bodies for dissection, and we would touch the goose quill to confirm it, without knowing what we are doing."[35]

Intuiting the emerging culture of Blackhawkiana, Black Hawk's statements on the dark magic of written language offers a critique of the reduction of himself and his people to curiosities, commodities to be traded among white people; even as his willingness to submit to the language of settler culture offers a suggestion of his purpose less interested in the "vindication" of his character among settlers, and in the preservation and proliferation of his story. In this instance the preservation of his story brings into focus the significance of medicine as it is collected within the sacred medicine bag. "On my arrival . . . I . . . took my *medicine bag*, and addressed the chief. I told him that it was 'the soul of the Sac nation—that it had never been dishonored in any battle—take it, as it is my life—dearer than life—and give it to the American chief! He said he would keep it . . . and if I was suffered to live, he would send it to me."[36] Drawn from Black Hawk's recollection of his surrender to the US garrison at Prairie du Chien, the delegation of the Sauk medicine bag to the Ho-Chunk chief—and through him to the Americans—represented a profound and unusual degree of trust, one explained only by Black Hawk's fear that he might be killed upon his surrender and the bag would be lost. The hope that it might be protected was not misguided, but it was unfortunate: as the narrative comes to a close the whereabouts of the medicine bag remain in question. Upon returning to Detroit after the conclusion of his captivity in the east, Black Hawk makes an inquiry to General Joseph M. Street as to the disposition of the medicine bag. "I told him I left my great medicine bag with his chiefs before I gave myself up; and now, that I was to enjoy my liberty again, I was anxious to get it, that I might hand it down to my nation unsullied." Street's reply is less than palliative. "He said that it was safe; he had heard his chiefs speak of it, and would send it to me. I hope he will not forget his promise, as the whites generally do."[37]

Hoping to pass the medicine bag on to his people, Black Hawk implicitly signals his loss of status among the Sauks, his being "now an obscure member of [my] nation" and therefore being unfit to retain possession of the bag.[38] At the same time, he makes clear the relationship between the medicine bag and the negotiation of leadership, as well as their connection to a temporality less linear than enduring and perpetual; not a record of the past, but a living remnant of it. First presented to his great-grandfather, Nanamake, by Mukataquet, the one-time principal chief of the Sauk nation, according to Black Hawk's account, the medicine bag signified the rights and privileges of leadership in war, the right to determine the necessity of going to war, and the right to direct the conduct of a war. Having been bested in battle, Black Hawk implies that the medicine bag, both as a repository of the nation and its history and as a totem of leadership, must pass to another custodian.

This implicit digression on the place of the medicine bag within his life and the life of the Sauks draws a clear line between Black Hawk's life, the bag as the soul and life of the Sauk nation, and the narrative as a technology for collecting all that has been lost in the delegation of the medicine bag to US or American-allied forces. The narrative is composed as a supplement for the missing medicine bag; but it is a poor and incommensurable supplement, one that again highlights the power and poverty of written language over the generations spent in the composition of a sacred artifact. The medicine bag was a sacred artifact that was always a work in progress, that could lend itself to no literal, legalistic creed, and that tethered sovereignty to the memory of the past and the certainty of the future. Black Hawk's narrative, by contrast, preserves the memory of the Sauks over a limited period of time, set down in the language of the conquerors and marred by their insistence on literal meaning. Uninterested in vindicating his character among settlers, Black Hawk leaves the narrative as a vindication of his character among his people. It is a way to remember themselves under conditions of harsh dispossession and deprivation; yet as a memento it is necessarily fraught, bound to an irremediable loss that the dark magic of white writing just cannot fill.

While an impoverished substitute for the medicine bag, Black Hawk fills his narrative with such detail as necessary to preserve the Sauks in the memory of their past and to insist upon the continuity of their sovereignty, even under conditions of dislocation and division. Couched in the imperfect yet arrogantly certain language of the whites, Black Hawk goes to great pains to convey the social and cultural negotiations that preserve the adaptability of sovereignty in the context of multiple, overlapping claims upon land. This includes the living relations that thrive upon that land, and that preserve multifarious forms of human, plant, and animal life. Hardly a testimony to peace among Indigenous nations, the narrative does offer many examples of the negotiations that allowed for their coexistence under the conditions of manufactured scarcity introduced by capital and empire. Taking pride in these negotiations and the variability it preserves, the narrative extends its critique of countersovereignty through its presentation of Sauk history and Sauk lifeways, as forged over two centuries of colonial encounters.

The occasions where the text dwells upon the representation of medicine are implicitly bound up in the ways by which it conveys an external struggle over a sense of time and its registration, a sense of what the text is doing, and how it relates to contemporaneous accounts of Black Hawk and the so-called Black Hawk War. Evidence of this struggle within the *Life of Black Hawk* appears from its very beginning. "I was born at the Sac Village, on Rock river, in the year 1767, and am now in my 67th year." Couched in one of the most pietistic conventions of autobiography, this preliminary statement of natal origin was almost certainly an invention coaxed or created by LeClair and Patterson, a means of grounding Black Hawk and his narrative in a place and time, one that situated his life in proximity to relevant events in an evolving narrative of US history. This collapse of Black Hawk's personal history into the history of the settler nation is almost immediately countered, as the text moves from the autobiographical conceit to the figure of Nanamake, Black Hawk's great-grandfather, who served as the Sauks' first emissary to the French colonial enterprise in the Greater Lakes region. "My great grandfather, Na-na-ma-kee, or Thunder, (according to the tradition given to me by my father, Py-e-sa,) was born in the vicinity of Montreal, where the Great Spirit first placed the Sac Nation."[39]

A statement of origin that slips the yoke of autobiography, recourse to the history of Nanamake—a history conveyed to Black Hawk by his father—provides a window onto a past that offers a very different sense of self—as well as the relationship between the self and time—than the liberal conceit of self-generation so celebrated by the architects of American self-regard. As in the example of the medicine bag, time here does not so much pass as accumulate, forming a collection that is always and ever present. Black Hawk's precis of Nanamake's history goes on to further challenge the fictions of liberal self-fashioning, both of self and of collectivity, the fictions of contract or of possession so necessary to the fabrication of settler colonialism as a benign project of improvement through transformation. "[The Great Spirit] inspired him with a belief that, at the end of four years, he should see a white man, who would be to him a father. Consequently, he blacked his face, and eat [*sic*] but once a day . . . for three years, and continued dreaming throughout all this time . . . when the Great Spirit again appeared to him, and told him, that, at the end of one year more, he should meet his father."[40] Here, blacking is less a form of mourning than an act of prayer, a state of contemplation, one that removes the supplicant from the conventional and the everyday and announces a suspension of one's obligations to self and social reproduction as well as to the forms of temporal organization to which both contribute. Moreover, the time of blacking, in this account, is closely associated with dreaming, which—as well as a domain of inspiration and vision—is also a time of suspension; a realm in which the most elaborate, the most extensive, the most boundless eventualities might occur; a realm that is both never and now.

If liberal forms of association and self-hood make their claims for political legitimacy from such gross materialities as contract or possession, what appears in this early passage of Black Hawk's narrative is a distinctly ineffable, if still material, account of the ways in which kinship is forged and association negotiated. It is also a powerful indictment of the acquisitive vision of selfhood that traffics between liberalism as a political logic and capitalism as a social imperative, as well as the implicit notions of temporality and temporal motion present within and for both. Foregrounding dreams and blackening, fasting and deprivation, Black Hawk's account of Nanamake's first encounter with the French takes the shape of a story about survivance that foregrounds sacrifice and mourning, dreaming and prayer, as aspects of a relationship to time that is neither acquisitive nor anxious. Where Lockean notions of property presume an equation between sacrifice and labor, the expenditure of self through time and toil as a means of proving the righteousness of one's claims upon property and self-possession, Black Hawk's account of Nanamake's sacrifice describes a relationship to place and to people, a form of association, that emerges from a time outside of time, from a virtual space inaccessible to history as measured in relation to accounts of labor, surplus, or accumulation. Nanamake's ceremonial practice evokes this other time—this other space—as that which prepares the earth for new life and new shapes of association, new relationships, as well as the possibility of carrying the past into the present as a means of preserving the future.

Much of what follows this passage concerns Nanamake's journey to his first meeting with the French, including a gift of medals and a discussion about their relative meanings, their corresponding ranks. Presented with a medal by the French journeyer, Nanamake proffers it to his brother Namah, only to be corrected. "[The journeyer] told [Nanamake] that he had done wrong—he should wear that medal himself, as he had others for his brethren: That which he had given him was a type of the ran he should hold in the nation: That his brothers could only rank as *civil* chiefs,—and their duties should consist of taking care of the village." Having installed Namah and their brother Paujahummawa in their new positions as guardians of civil peace, the journeyer goes on to explain to Nanamake the obligations attached to the medal that was gifted him. "If the nation gets into any difficulty with another, then his puc-co-ha-wa-ma, or sovereign decree, must be obeyed. If he declared war, he must lead them on to battle: That the Great Spirit had made him a great and brave general, and had sent him here to give him that medal, and make presents to him for his people."[41]

This passage speaks to the deep ambiguities in the negotiation of co-existence among peoples in the context of European colonialism as well as the social and material consequences for relations within and among Indigenous nations through the introduction of new forms of abundance and scarcity. While the ceremonial presentation of the medals echoes the rituals by which the European colonial powers in North America had made cause with Native peoples, securing their fidelity by presents of "guns, powder, and lead, spears and lances," as well as "various kinds of cooking utensils," the introduction of new forms of rank—consolidated by the same guns, power, and lead, as well as access to credit and trade networks—illustrates the ways in which those relations left indelible marks upon Native societies. Access occasioned a range of asymmetries among people and nations. Firearms made those asymmetries virtually unassailable. Moreover, as has been noted, the application of guns to hunting and the transformation of hunting in relation to the fur trade would begin to eat away at ecosystems; it also exacerbated the forms of material scarcity that occasioned intensified conflict among nations. At the same time, it is the word *sovereign* that speaks to perhaps the most insidious European import. The name for a power that is absolute and unyielding, restrained by nothing but its own conscience, the application of European legal norms concerning sovereignty would have long-lasting consequences for Indigenous nations; yet here it is qualified, if not explicitly challenged, by the use of the ostensibly Sauk word *puc-co-ha-wa-ma*, a figure that leaves its imprint in the text, spoken if not understood.

This is a curious moment in the text. Drawing attention, again, to the immediate, intimate social dynamics of the conversation taking place among Black Hawk, LeClair, and Patterson, it also suggests the ways in which that conversation is implicated in the forms of power that inhere within the traffic among languages as well as the social and political implications of the story they are weaving. The impossible time of the blacking and the dream goes missing, dropping here into a more conventionally liberal, linear mode of the passage into history as part of the record of imperial practice. One of a few instances in which an Indigenous word is found inserted in the text of the narrative, the immediate movement between *puc-co-ha-wa-ma* and *sovereign* evokes the declension, suggesting an equivalence between an Indigenous concept of governance and the legal construction of sovereignty current among Euro-American nations. Disregarding the linguistic complexity of the Indigenous original for an entirely legalistic notion of authority, of the eminence that stands outside the civil and legal order and pronounces upon it, in this instance, the text allows for the sovereignty of the Sauks as a means of establishing the nation as compeers with their Euro-American counterparts. Here, the use of "sovereign" is clearly meant to devolve all responsibility for the 1832 conflict upon Black Hawk while, through him, implicating the whole of the Sauk nation as conscripts. Rather than pronouncing on those who chose to follow him into battle, *sovereign* follows the legal framework of the Treaty of 1832, in which the whole of the confederated Sauk and Fox nations were saddled with the burden of restitution. Moreover, the implication that the Sauk and Fox and the United States share a framework for understanding war and civil order as ineluctably separate conditions further pronounces upon the legitimacy of the Treaty of 1832. *Sovereign*, in this sense, appears as a trace of the prose of counter-sovereignty, stabilizing the linguistic framework through which the social will be narrated. Insisting upon the primacy of US law as a framework for the organization of social relations, *sovereign* expands the power of the United States over the forms of association through which Native peoples enact their relationships, taking authority over the names by which they choose to organize social and political power, imposing the temporality of US law and European liberalism upon time-space of Indigenous life and association.

The anecdotes preserved in this passage suggest a contest over meaning inherent to the materiality of translation and transcription, the circulation of words among languages and media. This language mimics that of a liberal conception of time, space, and social order, of sovereignty as spatialized; a form of rule that is realized in and through history and in which war appears as a temporal abnormality. Indeed, the form of power ascribed to Nanamake calls attention to its identity with European notions of sovereignty, where the sovereign is the person who pronounces upon the limits of civil order and the movement between civil peace and warfare. Moreover, the language in which these anecdotes are couched makes explicit a connection between the exercise of this form of authority and "invasion," the violation of a boundary that inheres among and divides peoples. War occurs along this boundary as a condition of its violation, just as the boundary designates the space covered by the architects of civil peace. As we have seen, among Native peoples, warfare was not an exceptional activity but rather part of the texture of everyday life; less an event than a practice, one bound up in forms of sociality and economy as well as forms of personal and collective discipline and the calculation of rank and social hierarchies. To ascribe Nanamake command over war as an exceptional sphere, an event that establishes an exception within history—one that emerges only in response to invasion—was to translate the ambit of his authority and its exercise from that of a Sauk warrior to that of a European prince, a person endowed with a variety of powers that nonetheless culminated in this ultimate authority over the historical continuity of social order.

While the translation of "pu-co-ha-wa-ma" as "sovereign" may have been yet one more attempt at stabilizing—of appropriating—the meaning of Black Hawk's narrative by forcing it into a settler colonial framework, the history that follows immediately from this passage offers a sketch of the term and its meaning, one that contravenes the effort to evacuate its nuance, relating it to the temporal register of medicine and the significance of the medicine bag. Continuing the history of Nanamake and his brothers, the next section of the narrative describes events that follow the return to their village, the transfer of power between generations, and the narrative fictions by which authority was sanctioned and secured. "The three newly-made chiefs returned to their village, and explained to Muk-a-ta-quet, their father . . . [and] the principle chief of the nation, what had been said and done. The old chief had some dogs killed, and made a feast, preparatory to resigning his scepter, to which all the nation were invited."[42] Confronted by the vicissitudes of time, the sacred, and the material consequences of his sons' newfound relationship with the French, Muk-a-ta-quet consents to surrender his position, declaring to the assembled members of the nation that "the Great Spirit had directed that these, his three children, should take the rank and power that had been his,—and that he yielded these honors and duties willingly to them,—because it was the wish of the Great Spirit, and he could never consent to make him angry!"[43] Presenting the Sauk medicine bag to Nanamake, Muk-a-ta-quet continues, "[I] cheerfully [resign] it to him—it is the soul of our nation—it has never yet been disgraced—and I will expect you to keep it unsullied!"[44]

The question of medicine and the medicine bag as a manifestation of Sauk sovereignty and leadership—and their relationship to a time outside of the impoverished domain of history—continues, as the text goes on to record the story of Nanamake's attempt at establishing his authority among those who challenged him. "Some dissension arose among [the people] in consequence of so much power being given to . . . so young a man. To quiet this, Nanamake, during a violent *thunder storm*, told them that he had *caused* it! and that it was an exemplification of the name the

Great Spirit had given him. During this storm, the *lightning* struck, and set for to a tree, close by; (a sight they had never witnessed before). . . . He went to [the fire and with it] made a fire in the lodge, and seated his brothers thereby."[45] A literal, physical manifestation of power, the fire set by the lightning becomes a figurative symbol of Nanamake's authority, as he takes it as the source of light in his lodge, placing his brother in relation to it and making it a totem of his charge. As the remainder of a meteorological phenomenon, the material trace of an otherwise evanescent atmospheric event, the fire also carries with it the substance of a temporality outside of history, an eventuality known but impossible to know or to capture. This, moreover, is reflected in Nanamake's command to preserve the fire, to keep it burning at all costs. "You have all witnessed the power which has been given to me by the Great Spirit, in making that fire—and all that I now ask is, that these, my two chiefs, may never let it go out: That they may preserve peace among you, and administer to the wants of the needy: And, should an enemy invade our country, I will then, but not until then, assume command, and go forth with my band of brave warriors, and endeavor to chastise them!"[46]

Within the text, this account of Nanamake's election serves as prelude to a story of Black Hawk's birth and early life, one that echoes the autobiographical narrative laid out in the first paragraph of the narrative, but with a difference. Eschewing the liberal, linear conceits of autobiography through the evocation of his ancestor, the second account of Black Hawk's birth and early life evoke the temporality of blacking and the dream. Just as the invocation of lighting and thunder served to figuratively substantiate Nanamake's claim to power, his invocation of the fire—the literal trace of the atmospheric event—and the imperative to keep it burning serves, in the *Life of Black Hawk*, as a directive toward the manifestation of future generations. Fire and its continuity become the metaphorical and material instrument of power as bound to its passage over generations. "At this village [Saukenuk] I was born, being a regular descendant of the first chief, Na-na-ma-kee, or Thunder. Few, if any, events of note, transpired within my recollection, until about my fifteenth year. I was not allowed to paint, or wear feathers; but distinguished myself, at that early age, by wounding an enemy; consequently, I was placed in the rank of the Braves!"[47] Drawing social reproduction in relation to the reproduction of life and lives, as a trace of the impossible eventuality, the no-time of blacking or dreaming, the invocation of the fire as both totem and ancestor elaborates upon the relationship that obtains among generations, coalescent insofar as each occupies this same temporal orientation, each generation carrying its own trace of the dream, the thunder, and the fire.

The question of the relationship among generations, of the belonging of generations as stitched through a time inaccessible to linear, liberal history, is further elucidated in Black Hawk's account of the relationship between birth and death—between his coming into the world, and his father's remove. Describing the circumstances following upon Black Hawk's father's death in battle, the text relates in Black Hawk's voice, "I now fell heir to the great medicine bag of my forefathers, which had belonged to my father. I took it, buried our dead, and returned with my party, all sad and sorrowful, to our village, in consequence of the loss of my father. Owing to this misfortune, I blacked my face, fasted, and prayed to the Great Spirit for five years—during which time I remained in a civil capacity, hunting and fishing."[48] Echoing its earlier account of Nanamake's inspiration by the Great Spirit, in this instance, the text describes blacking in relationship to fasting and prayer, less an act of mourning than of contemplation and remove, a passage into a time and space outside of time or space, a time of waiting defined by no imperative to overcome. Fasting and prayer, here, appear as manifestations of this temporality, its exuberant difference with respect to the conventions of liberal historiography as the order of service that orients the prose of counter-sovereignty and the discourse of law. Uncoupled from Protestant fealty to ideologies of labor and profit, in this instance, fasting and prayer appear as moments of deprivation that, from the perspective of capital, exist only as wastes of time, means of turning time into waste. Each of these, moreover, find their expression in the appearance of the medicine bag, here a repository of the past as accumulation, a vehicle for the expression of history not as series or concatenation but as entanglement, as embeddedness, as relation.

With respect to the history of blacking, this sense of entanglement, of a life lived outside the pretense of linear history, at times resembles the assumption of personal life as death, as a sharing in death with those who had passed on: "About this time my eldest son was taken sick and died. . . . Soon after, my youngest daughter, an interesting and affectionate child, died also. This was a hard stroke, because I loved my children. In my distress I left the noise of the village, and built my lodge on a mound in my corn-field, and enclosed it with a fence, around which I planted corn and beans. Here I was with my family alone. I gave every thing I had away, and reduced myself to poverty. The only covering I retained was a buffalo robe. I resolved on blacking my face and fasting, for two years . . . drinking only of water in the middle of the day, and eating sparingly of boiled corn at sunset. I fulfilled my promise, hoping that the Great Spirit would take pity on me."[49] Fencing his lodge, here, Black Hawk makes

literal the figurative distinction between himself and his village community while evoking the barrier that separates life from death, even as his
plants, fruits, and vegetables suggest the eventual effacement of that bor-
der; the eventual passage of all through it and their return, ultimately, as
new life, new vitalities and pleasures.

Within the *Life of Black Hawk*, at other moments, blacking appears
not so much as the suspension of linear time as a function of narrative,
but of the linearity of colonialism as a sociohistorical process, one shaped
through narrative but ultimately wrought through violence. Where the
death of Black Hawk's children appears as the intervention of disease and
its irregular temporalities upon the everyday life of the community and
its entanglements, elsewhere, death appears as part of a social and temporal logic, an acceleration of the decimation of Indigenous life for no
purpose other than manifesting the prophecy of Indian decline. Following the War of 1812, when a party of Pottawattomies encounter American farmers, they are met with immediate violence; even after presenting
their guns to the Americans as a gesture of peace, the Americans fire upon
them. Relaying a story told to him by his friend, the chief Gomo, Black
Hawk reports that their friend Ma-ta-tah fell, "covered with blood from
his wounds . . . almost instantly expired."[50] "The remainder of the night,"
Gomo continues, "was spent in lamenting for the death of our friends.
At daylight, I blacked my face, and started to the fort to see the war chief.
I met him at the gate, and told him what had happened. His countenance
changed; I could see sorrow depicted in it for the death of my people."[51]
Here, what might at first appear as a conventional instance of mourning
also marks an interruption in the symbolic and material violence presented by the fort, a moment in which the networks constituting the
emerging infrastructure of US colonialism are placed in abeyance; a moment in which Native peoples refuse to "come inside" but insist upon occupying the threshold, of holding onto and insisting upon the threshold
as the space of an otherwise unobscured by the institutions and proposi-
tions of counter-sovereignty.

A similar dynamic appears in accounts of Black Hawk's dreams. Describing a campaign during the War of 1812, Black Hawk relates, "I was
very tired, and soon went to sleep. The Great Spirit, during my slumber,
told me to go down the bluff to a creek—that I would there find a hollow
tree cut down; to look into the top of it, and I would see a large *snake*—to
observe the direction he was looking, and I would see the enemy close
by, and unarmed."[52] The next day, Black Hawk relates to his fellow warriors what he was told in his dream; they follow the directions of the Great
Spirit and discover the hollowed tree and the snake, and they discover

"two war chiefs walking arm-in-arm, without guns." An echo of Nana-make's dream of the French, the uncanny element of Nanamake's dream is here preserved as well, as the circumstances of the dream pass into the course of waking life, as illustrated by the two war chiefs walking "arm-in-arm," connected like the eternal nether world of sleep and the motion of the world. As with Gomo's story of the blacking that suspends the time and space of the colonial infrastructure, however, in this moment, the uncanny relationship between sleep and waking disrupts the pretense of colonial design, those designs being put into abeyance by the ingenuity of the unconscious mind deployed against its enemies.

In yet other circumstances, Black Hawk's dreams are not so immediately predictive; they rather move in more elliptically symbolic directions. After an 1832 feast during which Black Hawk unveils the medicine bag and enjoins his warriors to give themselves over to his defense, he proceeds on a course west with his warriors; dreaming, eventually, of an elaborate feast. "I directed my course toward sunset, and dreamed, the second night after we started, that there was a great feast for us after one day's travel! I told my warriors my dream in the morning, and we all started for Mos-co-ho-co-y-nak. When we arrived in the vicinity of a fort the white people had built there we saw four men on horseback. One of my braves fired and wounded a man, when the others set up a yell, as a large force were near and ready to come against us."[53] Deciding eventually that the force garrisoned at the fort is too numerous to be overcome or destroyed without burning their barracks, Black Hawk and his men avail themselves of the fort's stores, drawing out and fulfilling a literal interpretation of the dream; but one that impoverishes the far more figurative rendering of the dream as a reference to the men they would find and the feast they would encounter in the banquet of combatants. The living, waking feast of the medicine bags here becomes the cannibal feast to their honor, the one passing into the other in a spiral, a streamer, an exuberant hoop.

Conclusion: The Afterlives
of the Black Hawk War

We remember most vividly the things we have forgotten. We no longer know their names, but they never leave us, these tireless ghosts, these palinopsia, these echoes. They float across the surface of our eyes. They busy themselves in dreams. The image of the Black Hawk War presses itself against the eye and leaves a stain, a shimmering along surfaces, light refracted in the deeps. We tell the story of the Black Hawk War so we might forget the way it bends the light, the penumbra of light and dark, a space of uncertainty, the place where the world and its words are haunted by their emptiness, their awkwardness, their inadequacy.

The title of this book invokes afterlives. This also is a misnomer. A literary convenience, "afterlives" summons an opulent tradition of words dedicated to the explication, the animation, of a stupid theological contrivance: another world, a better world, a world less corrupted, a world where reward and punishment are meted out, a world in which such things are merited. The afterlife commends the precision of justice, of judgment, the clarity of a sovereign who brooks neither nuance nor equivocation, the glassy-eyed appraisal of the effulgent sun the morning after an opiate delirium. "Afterlives" evokes the afterlife and its disseminations, the myriad "afters" conjured by the faithful, the unseen worlds to which they relate, to which they steer their broken barques. The afterlives of this book are less thoroughly anthropomorphized, less terrestrially limited, less imperiously certain of goodness, mercy, righteousness, and damnation. The afterlives of this book are perhaps better understood as after-images, as the indefinite traces of a history or story, as the visual remainder, the echo, the feeling in the bones of that which has been but has been lost;

of that which is remembered but remembered in the body, the symptom of an unremarkable hysteria, commonly known, commonly held. Stare at the object, close your eyes; see the negative image float away, as unsubstantial as the light at the bottom of a still clear pond. Follow the shadow as well as the light. Look for objects buried in the sand. Their story is the story of what has been lost—the remains of what has been forgotten; of the forgotten, what remains.

This book has tried to think the history of settler colonialism as a history of disavowal, of renunciation and destructiveness; a history about the incubation of a gnashing, grinding hatred, born from the bosom of an intimacy that was rich and difficult—labored and impossible—but often sustaining. In the United States, the legal provisions that substantiate the fictions of property are dependent upon the discourse of treaty and cession, the expropriation of Indigenous land through the agency of the state obscured by notions of title, contract, and sale. This legal dependency reflects a longer history of social dependencies, of mutualities, whereby settlers were necessarily beholden to the hospitality of their Indigenous benefactors. Over time, they came to chafe at this hospitality. They needed the meal, but they hated the food, and they were no longer interested in the conversation. So they upended the table and burned down the cornfields. They dammed the rivers and stifled the fish; they killed all the game. They saved the best seed for themselves. They collected the animals and put them in pens. They ripped up the prairie and stole its carbon; they released its carbon into the world, into its waters. They built an infrastructure of purposeless destruction, of floods and floodplains, and dislocated top soils; the mouths of rivers choked with silt, flows arrested, levies busted, cities broke by floods. They killed the beavers to make their hats, to line their coats against the cold, another weapon in their imperious war against the weather. For this, for their incomprehensible vision of gentleman's dress, the Mississippi became necrotic, became seductively undead, languid, and murderous.

The Black Hawk War was both a symptom of this disavowal and a mechanism. Less an event than an archipelagic relation among disparate, if familiar circumstances, the story of the Black Hawk War was a coral, a reef, a rhizomorphic assemblage of tissues, of numerous conjoined lives, treated as a substance, a resource, mined for its calcium and alkaline. Employed in building and in farming, the residues of the story of the war, like the mineralized traces of coral, do not betray their original appearance. They do not call attention to themselves. They are unobtrusive, absorbed: the cement in the foundation, the lime in the garden, the stuff that holds the world together. They stabilize the building, they correct for the acid in the soil. The story of the Black Hawk War prepares the ground for the ongoing reproduction of settler colonialism as the structure of invasion. It grounds that which is ungroundable. It breaks up the world and rebuilds it in the image of its refusal, the negative image of all it rejects. It burns the corn so that it might own the fields. It bakes the coral so that the world might be made ugly, so that the value of the beautiful does not compromise the unspeakable loathsomeness of capital, of the value of money as the standard of all that is good and true and aesthetically, affectively delicious; the measure of all that delights, and delights in common, without being desirous for recognition or remuneration. It hides the blood and the pores.

This is a story about disavowal, about what is gained and what is lost, about the cost. It is about settler colonialism as the architectural form bearing the encrustations of whiteness, a hideous baroque monstrosity that hosts the parties where the patriarchy meets and where capital hides the receipts. The Black Hawk War was the name given to something less immediately tangible, less immediately intrusive than a war, a name by which to explain the course of human affairs without reference to the slow violence that ate away—that still eats away—at the obligations of kinship, at the accommodations made among peoples as a way to negotiate the possibility of living and living together, even in those instances when togetherness was grudging at best. The story of the Black Hawk War is part of the masonry of nationalism and empire, of settler colonialism and capital accumulation. The story obscures the slow violence of invasion and expropriation, presenting instead a tale of victims and heroes, of sacrifice and honor, of a cataclysmic event that brought momentous change. It is a story about disavowal as an event that begins and ends. It trades in the spectacle of war so that we might ignore all the ways in which the disavowal of Indigenous sovereignties must be continually reproduced, reenacted. It allows us to ignore all the ways in which Indigenous sovereignty continues to assert itself as a physically present, politically meaningful dimension of social life. It allows us to believe in a past that is past, a transient instance of calamity through which we endured; a moment that is over, a tragedy transcended.

The Black Hawk War knows neither beginning nor end, but you could be forgiven for thinking otherwise. It started much earlier than you might have guessed. It is still ongoing. It is biding its time in the corner of the room. The Black Hawk War did not happen. The Black Hawk War is happening. It is yet to happen. It looks for sticks; it looks for the matches. Quietly, it starts to build a fire.

ACKNOWLEDGMENTS

I began writing this book in Brooklyn. Later, it would travel with me to Algeria, then to Beirut. I finished writing it in Lebanon, in the midst of a pandemic, in the month after the devastating, horrifying explosion at the port. Along the way, it collected a legion of friends and more than a few enemies. For my part, in this time, I assumed a mountain of debts. The relationships that shaped and sustained me during the writing of this book were in no way transactional. Nonetheless, I owe a great deal to a great many people, many of whom I might not have known as well as others that I have sadly forgotten. To the unnamed, know that I remember you and that you are present in these pages, even if I do not remember what I know of you.

Here are the names of some of the people I still remember; the people I can never forget.

First, I must thank the dancers and their supporters at the 1998 American Indian Movement Sundance at the Sacred Pipestone Quarries in Pipestone, Minnesota. I thank the Proud Indigenous Peoples for Education (PIPE) at Macalester College for their work in the anti-mascot movement, and making Indigenous activism a central part of my education. I hope I have done justice to their teachings.

My colleagues in the Department of English at the American University of Beirut, as well as fellow travelers in the Center for American Studies and Research, the Center for Arab and Middle East Studies, the Department of Sociology, Anthropology, and Media Studies, and the Department of Fine Arts and Art History. Most particularly, I am indebted to Ira Allen, Lisa Armstrong, Lisa Arnold, Heather O'Brien, Greg Burris,

Josh Carney, David Currell, Omar Dewachi, May Farah, Nate George, Dalia Gubara, Lisa Hajjar, Esmat El-Halaby, Sirene Harb, Waleed Hazbun, Hatim El-Hibri, Jim Hodapp, Syrine Hout, Rana Issa, Susann Kassem, Roseanne Khalaf, Marwan Kraidy, David Landes, Alex Lubin, Patrick McGreevy, Karim Makdisi, Rania Masri, Kathryn Maude, Tariq Mehmoud, Sonja Mejcher-Atassi, Sara Mourad, Robert Myers, Jennifer Nish, Vijay Prashad, Jasbir Puar, Steven Salaita, Nadya Sbaiti, Kassem Shaaban, Samhita Sunya, Jonathan Takahasi, Michael Vermy, Ali Wick, and David Wrisley.

The debt I owe Anjali Nath and Kouross Esmaeli cannot be repaid. I love you both.

Doyle Avant has sustained me and saved me, on more than one occasion. I cannot express how much I care for him, and how glad I am that he is part of my life, my platonic partner in the pandemic, in the pandemonium of Beirut.

Likewise, I am deeply moved by the support Richard Morrison gave me in the earlier stages of this project, and the tolerance and encouragement he showed near the end. I doubt I would have been able to finish writing without his guidance.

Marie Curie is the devil himself.

Other Beirut friends who have sustained me: Marj Henningsen, Ibrahim Jamal, Mary Henningsen, Vicky Enea, Tracey Mansell, Brighid Webster, Karen Matta, Ali Nasrallah, and Elwood Blues.

The book was shaped through conversations with Jasbir Puar and Omar Dewachi. The rough ideas that emerged from those conversations were further developed in a workshop with Vijay Prashad, Lisa Armstrong, Alex Lubin, and Patrick McGreevy. An afternoon with Vanessa Redgrave brought things into focus.

Undying gratitude and love to friends and colleagues at New York University: Aliyya Abdur-Rahman, Rich Blint, Andre Carrington, Cristian Ayn Crouch, Betsy Esch, Ifeona Fulani, Alyosha Goldstein, Miles Grier, Madala Hilaire, Peter James Hudson, Rana Jaleel, Manu Karuka, Carmelo Larose, Seth Markle, Jasmine Mir, Dacia Mitchell, Njoroge Njoroge, Sobukwe Odinga, Milo Obourn, Kimani Paul-Emile, Dawn Peterson, Khary Polk, Dan Rood, Ted Sammons, Hillina Seife, Emily Thuma, and Carisa Worden.

Walter Johnson commands my deepest respect and my greatest thanks for all he has done for me over many years. The friends and mentors who have encouraged my work are too numerous to mention, but these are the people who have been with me through the long haul: Duchess Harris, Linnea Stenson, Peter Rachleff, Beth Cleary, David Roediger, Ruthie Wilson Gilmore, Laleh Khalili, Alex Lubin, Eric Lott, Cindi Katz, Brian Edwards, David Kazanjian, Josie Saldana. The late Amy Kaplan was gracious and encouraging even after I offered a cutting, if clumsy, critique of her work during a walk down Bliss Street under a cold winter rain.

My thanks to the many other New Yorkers with whom I shared the adventure of the city; the people that allowed me to crash on their couches after I made the unfortunate mistake of leaving. They include Peter Hudson, Najla Said, Mariam Said, Hannah Emmerich, James Mumm, Leo Mumm, Finn Mumm, Alison Emmerich, Tony Emmerich, Dania Rajendra, Ajay Singh Chaudhary, Ifeona Fulani, Emily Arsenault, Mae Anderson, Alison Altschuler, Erica Pearson, Edward Schneider, Elise and Emilia Pearson-Schneider, Michael Givens, Kennard Jones, Matthew Smith, Roberto Lynch Steed, Caipirinha, Feijoada, and Yussuf Rezk, my beautiful refugee boy, who gave a pound of flesh to this effort.

Much gratitude also to Kathy and John, Mom and Dad, Sister Jill and Harley. How could I have done this without you?

Shukran

Notes

Introduction

1. Sarah Welch Nossaman, "Pioneering at Bonaparte and Near Pella," *Annals of Iowa* 13, no. 6 (1922): 443.

2. See Robert J. Swan, "Prelude and Aftermath of the Doctors' Riot of 1788: A Religious Interpretation of White and Black Reactions to Grave Robbing," *New York History* 81, no. 4 (2000): 417–456.

3. On celebrity, its history, and emergence in late eighteenth and early nineteenth century, see Fred Inglis, *A Short History of Celebrity* (Princeton, NJ: Princeton University Press, 2010).

4. Laura L. Mielke, "'native to the question': William Apess, Black Hawk, and the Sentimental Context of Early Native American Autobiography," *American Indian Quarterly* 26, no. 2 (Spring 2002): 258.

5. See Joanne Barker, *Critically Sovereign: Indigenous Gender, Sexuality, and Feminist Studies* (Durham, NC, and London: Duke University Press, 2017); see also Leanne Betasamosake Simpson, *As We Have Ever Done: Indigenous Freedom through Radical Resistance* (Minneapolis: University of Minnesota Press, 2017).

6. Taiaiake Alfred, "Sovereignty," in *Sovereignty Matters: Locations of Contestation and Possibility in Indigenous Struggles for Self-Determination*, ed. Joanne Barker (Lincoln: University of Nebraska Press, 2005), 33.

7. Manu Karuka, "Counter-Sovereignty," *J19: The Journal of Nineteenth Century Americanists* 2, no. 1 (Spring 2014): 142–144.

8. Elizabeth Povinelli, *Geontologies: A Requiem to Late Liberalism* (Durham, NC, and London: Duke University Press, 2016).

9. Sigmund Freud, *The Joke and Its Relation to the Unconscious*, trans. Joyce Crick (New York: Penguin Classics, 2002).

10. Jamieson Webster, *Conversion Disorder: Listening to the Body in Psychoanalysis* (New York: Columbia University Press, 2019); Josef Breuer and Sigmund Freud, *Studies in Hysteria*, trans. Nicola Luckhurst (New York: Penguin Classics, 2004).

1 / The Indifferent Children of the Earth: Lead, Enclosure, and the
Nocturnal Occupations of the Mineral Undead

1. On entanglement of multifarious forms of life, see Anna Lowenhaupt Tsing, *The Mushroom at the End of the World: On the Possibility of Life in Capitalist Ruins* (Princeton, NJ: Princeton University Press, 2015); see also Elizabeth Povinelli, *Economies of Abandonment: Social Belonging and Endurance in Late Liberalism* (Durham, NC: Duke University Press, 2011); Joppe van Driel and Lissa Roberts, "Circulating Salts: Chemical Governance and the Bifurcation of 'Nature' and 'Society,'" *Eighteenth-Century Studies* 49, no. 2 (Winter 2016): 233–263; and Tanya Richardson and Gisa Weszkalnys, "Resource Materialities," *Anthropological Quarterly* 87, no. 1 (2014): 5–30. The literature on enclosure and extraction is voluminous, beginning with Karl Marx, but it has been very profitably employed by Indigenous scholars thinking about the question of resource capture and theft of the substance of Indigenous lifeways by settlers. Nick Estes's recent work on Standing Rock, the Dakota Access Pipeline, and the inevitability of the poisoning of Indigenous communities—as well as outright violations of Indigenous sovereignties—is exemplary in this regard. See Nick Estes, *Our History Is the Future* (New York: Verso, 2019).

2. I draw the concept of "slow violence" from the work of Rob Nixon, whose writing offers a model for negotiating fissures between American Studies and postcolonial studies as both are implicated in the study of literature and the manifestation of literary merit. For Nixon, violence is generally figured as powerfully immediate, and immediately affective, explosive. The concept of slow violence forces a confrontation with the ways in which violence unfolds in the everyday, across days, insidious, undetectable, and accumulative. An example might be drawn from the work of Omar Dewachi, who writes of the toxicity of everyday survival in Iraq to describe the long-term effects of depleted uranium with respect to the health of the body politic. The US war in Iraq was not a nuclear war in the conventional sense; yet the war was nuclear, in that the use of depleted uranium irradiated the landscape in ways that will be felt for untold generations to come. Elizabeth Povinelli has written about this phenomenon as one of the signal characteristics of what she calls "late liberalism," the condition of the ongoing deferral of social and environmental reckonings through the unremarkable violence of the liberal state. See Rob Nixon, *Slow Violence and the Environmentalism of the Poor* (Cambridge, MA: Harvard University Press, 2011). See also Omar Dewachi, "The Toxicity of Everyday Survival in Iraq," Jadaliyya.com, August 13, 2013; and Elizabeth Povinelli, *Empire of Love: Toward a Theory of Intimacy, Genealogy, and Carnality* (Durham, NC: Duke University Press, 2006).

3. Frederic Lordon, *Willing Slaves of Capital: Spinoza and Marx on Desire* (London and New York: Verso, 2014).

4. On the history of mining in the early republic, see John C. Greene and John G. Burke, "The Science of Minerals in the Age of Jefferson," *Transactions of the American Philosophical Society* 68, no. 4 (1978): 1–113. See also Roger Burt, "The Transformation of the Non-Ferrous Metals Industry in the Seventeenth and Eighteenth Centuries," *Economic History Review* 48, no. 1 (February 1995): 23–45; and Scott Frickle and William R. Freudenburg, "Mining the Past: Historical Context and the Changing Consequences of Natural Resource Extraction," *Social Problems* 43,

no. 4 (November 1996): 444–466. On the political economy and aesthetics of resource extraction, see Macarena Gomez-Barris, *The Extractive Zone: Social Ecologies and Decolonial Perspectives* (Durham, NC: Duke University Press, 2017); and Gaston Gordillo, *Rubble: The Afterlife of Destruction* (Durham, NC: Duke University Press, 2014).

5. Weber, Max. *The Protestant Ethic and the Spirit of Capitalism* (Mineola, NY: Dover Publications, 2003).

6. Manu Karuka, *Empire's Tracks: Indigenous Nations, Chinese Workers, and the Transcontinental Railroad* (Oakland, CA: University of California Press, 2019).

7. For a more contemporary take on this question with respect to Native relations among themselves and in relation to the state, see Joy H. Greenberg and Gregory Greenberg, "Native American Narratives as Ecoethical Discourse in Land-Use Consultations," *Wicazo sa Review* 28, no. 2 (Fall 2013): 30–59.

8. See Matt Cohen, *The Networked Wilderness: Communicating in Early New England* (Minneapolis: University of Minnesota Press, 2009); and Matt Cohen and Jeffrey Glover, eds., *Colonial Mediascapes* (Lincoln: University of Nebraska Press, 2014). See also Birgit Brander Rasmussen, *Queequeg's Coffin: Indigenous Literacies and Early American Literature* (Durham, NC, and London: Duke University Press, 2012).

9. My approach to questions of infrastructure have been informed by many scholars, touching on the analysis of physical infrastructures as well as less immediately sensate forms of capital, labor, race, and gender as logistical puzzles. See John Durham Peters, "Infrastructuralism: Media as Traffic between Nature and Culture," in *Traffic: Media as Infrastructures and Cultural Practices*, ed. Marian Naser-Lather and Christoph Neubert (London: Brill, 2015); Deborah Cohen, *The Deadly Life of Logistics: Mapping Violence in Global Trade* (Minneapolis: University of Minnesota Press, 2014); Laleh Khalili, *Sinews of War and Trade: Shipping and Capitalism in the Arabian Peninsula* (London: Verso, 2020); and Hatim El-Hibri, *Visions of Beirut: The Urban Life of Media Infrastructure* (Durham, NC: Duke University Press 2021).

10. Andrew Jackson, "Message to Congress on Indian Removal" (1830).

11. Susan A. Miller, "Native America Writes Back: The Origin of the Indigenous Paradigm in Historiography," *Wicazo sa Review* 23, no. 2 (Fall 2008): 9–28.

12. Dana Luciano, *Arranging Grief: Sacred Time and the Body in Nineteenth-Century America* (New York: New York University Press, 2007), 1–24.

13. Lewis Cass, *A Discourse Pronounced at the Capitol of the United States in the Hall of Representatives, before the American Historical Society*, January 30, 1836 (Washington, DC: P. Thompson, 1836).

14. Tony C. Brown, "The Barrows of History," *Studies in Eighteenth-Century Culture* 37 (2008): 41–58.

15. Charles Whittlesey, *Description of Ancient Works in Ohio* (Washington, DC: Smithsonian Institution, 1850), 10.

16. Whittlesey, 13.

17. Patricia Givens Johnson, *William Preston and the Allegheny Patriots* (Blacksburg, VA: Walpa Publishing, 1992), 12.

18. J. D. Whitney, *Report of a Geological Survey of the Upper Mississippi Lead Region: Made by the Authority of the Legislature of Wisconsin, Under a Contract with Professor James Hall, Principal of the Geological Commission of the State, 1859–1860* (Albany, NY: n.p., 1862), 81.

19. Allen V. Heyl, Allen F. Agnew, Erwin J. Lyons, and Charles H. Behre Jr., "The Geology of the Upper Mississippi Valley Zinc-Lead District," *Geological Survey Professional Paper* 309 (Washington: US Government Printing Office, 1959), 68–69.

20. Anonymous, "Galena and its Mines," *Harper's Monthly* 32, no. 192 (1866): 681–696.

21. T. A. Rickard, *A History of American Mining* (New York: McGraw-Hill, 1932), 152f.; quoted in M. C. McGill, "The Diffusion of Ore-Heath Smelting Techniques from Yorkshire to the Upper Mississippi Lead Region," *British Mining* 43 (1991): 122.

22. Heyl, et al., "Geology," 70.

23. Carl Parcher Russell, *Guns on the Early Frontiers: A History of Firearms from Colonial Times through the Years of the Western Fur Trade* (Berkeley: University of California Press, 1957); 234.

24. John Lee Allman, "Uniforms and Equipment of the Black Hawk War and the Mormon War," *Western Illinois Regional Studies* 13, no. 1 (Spring 1990): 9.

25. *Ordnance Manual for the Use of the Officers of the United States Army* (Washington: G. and J. S. Gideon, 1841), 166.

26. *Ordnance Manual*, 179–180.

27. *Ordnance Manual*, 241.

28. Public Acts of the Second Congress, 1st Session, 271.

29. Sarah Welch Nossaman, "Pioneering at Bonaparte and Near Pella," *Annals of Iowa* 13, no. 6 (1922): 444.

30. Anonymous, "Phrenological Developments and Character of the Celebrated Indian Chief and Warrior, Black Hawk: With Cuts," *American Phrenological Journal and Miscellany* 1, no. 2 (November 1838): 53–54.

31. Willard Barrows, "History of Scott County, Iowa. Chapter I. General Remarks," *Annals of Iowa* 1 (1863): 50.

32. "Location and Fact of Black Hawk's Death and Burial," *Annals of Iowa* 18 (1933): 550.

33. Captain James H. Jordan, quoted in J. F. Snyder, "The Burial and Resurrection of Black Hawk," *Journal of the Illinois State Historical Society* 4, no. 1 (April 1911): 51.

34. On Jackson as the totemic figure most appropriate to primitive accumulation as the "heroic" phase of capitalism, see Michael Paul Rogin, "Liberal Society and the Indian Question," in *Fathers and Children: Andrew Jackson and the Subjugation of the American Indian* (New York: Alfred E. Knopf, 1975), 13.

35. Laura Mielke, "'Native to the question': William Apess, Black Hawk, and the Sentimental Context of Early Native American Autobiography," *American Indian Quarterly* 26, no. 2 (2003): 246–270.

36. Joseph Roach, *Cities of the Dead: Circum-Atlantic Performance* (New York: Columbia University Press, 1996), 2.

37. Gerald Vizenor, "Aesthetics of Survivance: Literary Theory and Practice," in *Survivance: Narratives of Native Presence*, ed. Gerald Vizenor (Lincoln: University of Nebraska Press, 2008), 1.

38. Arnold Krupat, "Patterson's Life; Black Hawk's Story; Native American Elegy," *American Literary History* 22, no. 3 (2010): 540.

39. Krupat, 540.

40. Jace Weaver, *That the People Might Live: Native American Literatures and Native American Community* (Oxford: Oxford University Press, 1997), xiii, cited in Krupat, "Patterson's Life," 543.

41. Black Hawk, 34.

42. Sarah Bezan, "Necro-Eco: The Ecology of Death in Jim Crace's Being Dead," *Mosaic: A Journal for the Interdisciplinary Study of Literature* 48, no. 2 (September 2015): 191.

43. Black Hawk, 34.

44. Chief Justice Robert Yazzie, "Life Comes From It: Navajo Justice," *In Context: A Quarterly of Humane Sustainable Culture: The Ecology of Justice* 38 (Spring 1994): 29. See also Robert H. Craig, "Institutionalized Relationality: A Native American Perspective on Law, Justice, and Community," *Annual of the Society of Christian Ethics* 19 (1999): 285–309; and Barbara A. Gray-Kanatiiosh and Pat Laderdale, "The Web of Justice: Restorative Justice Has Presented Only Part of the Story," *Wicazo sa Review* 21, no. 1 (Spring 2006): 29–41.

45. Susan A. Miller, "Native America Writes Back: The Origin of the Indigenous Paradigm in Historiography," *Native Historians Write Back: Decolonizing American Indian History*, ed. Susan A. Miller and James Riding In (Lubbock: Texas Tech University Press, 2011), 12.

46. Miller, 12.

47. "Black Hawk: Some Account of His Life, Death and Resurrection," *Annals of Iowa* 13, no. 1 (1921): 129.

48. Testimony of Willard Barrows, quoted in J. F. Snyder, "The Burial and Resurrection of Black Hawk," *Journal of the Illinois State Historical Society* 4, no. 1 (April 1911): 53.

49. "Black Hawk," 129.

50. Black Hawk, *Life of Black Hawk*, xxiii.

51. Throughout the narrative, Jackson is referred to as "Great Father," in what might be seen as a convention of settler figurations of "Indianness." Understood through the lens of kinship obligations as a component of the negotiation over the terms of sovereignty, however, one might read "Great Father" as an honorific that retains the trace of a respect of the forms of kinship. Makataimeshekiakiak's invocation of the Great Father, as such, might further be read as inverting the Oedipal structure of racialized self-and-national formation proposed by Michael Paul Rogin in his classic *Fathers and Children: Andrew Jackson and the Subjugation of the American Indian* (New York: Knopf, 1975).

2 / "Dressed in a strange fantasy": The Dialectics of Seeing and the Secret Passages of Desire

1. My thoughts on the relationship between the proliferation of type and domestic lead production were inspired by a blog posting by the typeface designer and academic Tobias Frere-Jones. Jones's post, "My Kind of Neighborhood," detailed the history and geography of a New York City type-foundry district in the nineteenth century, as the industry grew up in relationship to the proliferating culture of downtown newspapers; see https://frerejones.com/blog/my-kind-of-neighborhood. Much of the academic study of typeface has been conducted by other scholars and practitioners in design, such as Lorraine Ferguson and Douglass Scott, "A Time Line of American Typography," *Design Quarterly* 148 (1990): 23–54. While often considered outmoded, the work of Harold Innis, scholar of political economy and media, was important in starting to think about the relationships between mineral

extraction, material infrastructures, and cultures of print within capitalism. See Harold Innis, *A History of the Canadian Pacific Railway* (Toronto: University of Toronto Press, 1923); and Innis, *Empire and Communications* (Toronto: Clarendon Press, 1950).

2. For another perspective on the relationship between writing, media, and ecologies, see Randall Knoper, "Writing, American Literature, and 'Media Ecologies,'" *American Literary History* 23, no. 2 (2011): 362–379. Knoper does not engage the question of settler colonialism, and he is skeptical of the concept of a media ecology. Nonetheless, in drawing attention to the problem of ecology as a metaphor for media formations, he raises the question of how we might think relationships between writing, media infrastructures, and the geophysical metabolics that often travel under the euphemism of ecology.

3. See Philip Deloria, *Playing Indian* (New Haven, CT, and London: Yale University Press, 1998). See also Scott Lauria Morgensen, *Spaces Between Us: Queer Settler Colonialism and Indigenous Decolonization* (Minneapolis: University of Minnesota Press, 2011).

4. My sense of desire is broadly psychoanalytical, if heterodox. Desire, in my reading, is both a problem to be managed and an opportunity to break out of cycles of repetition, of attachments to loss, and to reach out into the world, but with a difference: to engage the world creatively, with pleasure, with interest. Desire is also ultimately unknowable. Desire does not pursue the object; the object incites desire.

5. "The North West," *Niles' Weekly Register*, August 25, 1832, 450.

6. "Western Indians," *Niles' Weekly Register*, May 12, 1832, 200.

7. "From the Army, &c.," *Niles' Weekly Register*, August 4, 1832.

8. "Affairs with the Indians," *Niles' Weekly Register*, September 1, 1832, 12.

9. "Black Hawk's Invasion," *Niles' Weekly Register*, September 1, 1832, 5.

10. "Description of the two distinguished prisoners (Black Hawk and the Prophet), at the time they were delivered to Jos. M. Street, by a gentleman who was present," *Niles' Weekly Register*, September 29, 1832, 79.

11. "The Indian War Over: A copy of a letter to the editor of the Globe, dating US Indian agency at Prairie du Chien, 3d September, 1832," *Niles' Weekly Register*, September 29, 1832, 78–79.

12. "The Indian War Over."

13. "The Indian War Over."

14. Tena L. Helton, "What the White 'Squaws' Want from Black Hawk: Gendering the Fan-Celebrity Relationship," *American Indian Quarterly* 34, no. 4 (Fall 2010): 498–520.

15. On contemporary views of Mississippian lead mining as well as historical perspective on the phenomenon of prices and international markets, see Henry Rowe Schoolcraft, *A View of the Lead Mines of Missouri* (New York: Charles Wiley and Co., 1819); and Joseph Schaefer, *The Wisconsin Lead Region* (Madison: State Historical Society of Wisconsin, 1932).

16. Lucy Hartley, *Physiognomy and the Meaning of Expression in Nineteenth-Century Culture* (Cambridge: Cambridge University Press, 2001), 22.

17. Western Shield, "Indians—Black Hawk, etc.," *Cincinnati Mirror, and Western Gazette of Literature, Science, and the Arts*, May 11, 1833, 131.

18. See Luke Gibbons, *Edmund Burke and Ireland: Aesthetics, Politics, and the Colonial Sublime* (Cambridge: Cambridge University Press, 2009).

19. "Gems of the Month," *New-England Magazine*, July 1833, 80.

20. Black Hawk, 74.

21. Frances Anne Butler [Fanny Kemble], *The Journals of Frances Anne Butler*, vol. 2 (Philadelphia: Carey, Less, and Blanchard, 1835), 157.

22. "Indians—Black Hawk, etc.," *Cincinnati Mirror, and Western Gazette of Literature, Science, and the Arts*, May 11, 1833, 131.

23. "Indians—Black Hawk, etc."

24. "Indians—Black Hawk, etc."

25. Thomas Moore, trans., *Odes of Anacreon*, Vol. 1 (London: J. Carpenter, 1804), 96–97.

26. Moore, 96–97.

27. Moore, 96–97.

28. "Original Biography: Muck-a-tay Mich-e-Kaw-Kaik, The Black Hawk," *New-York Mirror, a Weekly Gazette of Literature and the Fine Arts*, July 13, 1833, 9.

29. "Original Biography," 9.

30. "Original Biography," 9.

31. "Original Biography," 9.

32. "Original Biography," 9.

33. *Niles' Weekly Register*, "Miscellaneous," July 27, 1833, 356.

34. "Black Hawk," *Atkinson's Saturday Evening Post*, June 22, 1833, 3.

35. "Black Hawk," 3.

36. "Untitled," *Atkinson's Saturday Evening Post*, June 15, 1833, 3.

37. "Untitled," 3.

38. "Black Hawk," 3.

3 / Constantly at Their Weaving Work: Historiography and the Annihilation of the Body

1. The relationship between history and historiography and settler colonialism I develop in these pages owes its debt to historians and theorists of Haitian historiography, for whom historical representation was a distinctively political problem concerning the isolation of the island, its representation as a backward, dangerous, demonic place, its revolution exceptionally violent and evil, coextensive with efforts to shore up slavery in other parts of the Americas, and to punish Haiti for the audacity of its victory over France and the establishment of a black republic in the Caribbean. See Colin Dayan, *Haiti, History, and the Gods* (Berkeley: University of California Press, 1995); C. L. R. James, *Black Jacobins: Toussaint L'Ouverture and the San Domingo Revolution* (New York: Vintage, 1989); Michel-Rolph Trouillot, *Silencing the Past: Power and the Production of History* (Boston, MA: Beacon, 1995); Laurent DuBois, *Avengers of the New World: The Story of the Haitian Revolution* (Cambridge, MA: Belknap Press, 2005). I am also indebted to other scholars of history and historiography such as Walter Benjamin, Hayden White, and Karl Marx; but it is from scholars of the Caribbean that I draw my greatest inspiration, and to whom I owe the greatest debt.

2. The captivity narrative was a particularly fecund genre of noncanonical devotional literature among Western Christians, an ideological device for the promulgation of otherness as wickedness. First in Western Christianity and is encounter with Islam, whether on the North African coast of the Mediterranean or

Ottoman Turks after the conquest of Constantinople, captivity narratives consecrated the sufferings and salvation of the captive to the glory and grace of God, while demonstrating the perfidy of Muslims, their savagery, their disregard for all conventions and norms. The conventions of the genre were eventually put to use during the colonization of North America, where the figure of the "Indian savage" replaced that of the "Muslim fiend." The exemplary case is Mary Rowlandson's seventeenth-century "A Narrative of the Captivity and Restoration of Mrs. Mary Rowlandson." See Phillip Round, *By Nature and by Custom Cursed: Transatlantic Civil Discourse and New England Cultural Production 1620–1660* (Hanover, NH, and London: Tufts University Press, 1999). See also Paul Baepler, *White Slaves, African Masters: An Anthology of American Barbary Captivity Narratives* (Chicago: University of Chicago Press, 1999).

3. See Charles Rosenberg, *The Cholera Years: The United States in 1832, 1846, 1866* (Chicago: University of Chicago Press, 1962).

4. See Erin O'Conner, *Raw Material: Producing Pathology in Victorian Culture* (Durham, NC: Duke University Press, 2000). See also Owen Whooley, *Knowledge in the Time of Cholera: The Struggle Over American Medicine in the Nineteenth Century* (Chicago: University of Chicago Press, 2013).

5. William P. Edwards, *The Narrative of the Capture and Providential Escape of Misses Frances and Elmira Hall* (New York: William P. Edwards, 1832), 7–8, 17.

6. Richard M. Gottlieb, "The Reassembly of the Body from Parts," *Journal of the American Psychoanalytic Association* 55, no. 4 (December 2007): 1217–1251.

7. Edwards, *Narrative*, 7.

8. Edwards, 5, 11.

9. Edwards, 6.

10. Edwards, 6.

11. Edwards, 10.

12. Edwards, 6, 11–12.

13. Edwards, 14.

14. Edwards, 17–18.

15. Edwards, 5, 18.

16. Edwards, 9.

17. Edwards, 8.

18. John Allen Wakefield, *History of the War Between the United States and the Sac and Fox Nations of Indians and Parts of Other Disaffected Tribes of Indians* (Jacksonville, IL: Calvin Goudy, 1834), 107.

19. See Veena Das, "The Signature of the State: The Paradox of Illegibility," in *Anthropology in the Margins of the State* (Santa Fe, NM: School of American Research Press, 2004), 225–253.

20. Wakefield, *History*, 110.

21. Wakefield, 18.

22. Wakefield, 19.

23. On the state as the ideological guise of governmentality, see Timothy Mitchell, "Society, Economy, and the State Effect," in *State/Culture: State Formation After the Cultural Turn*, ed. George Steinmetz (Ithaca, NY: Cornell University Press, 1999), 76–97.

24. Wakefield, *History*, 18.

25. Wakefield, 18.

26. For an ostensibly Deleuzian approach to the relationship between affect and emotion, see Brian Massumi, *Parables for the Virtual* (Durham, NC, and London: Duke University Press, 2003).

27. See Alexandra T. Vazquez, *Listening in Detail: Performances of Cuban Music* (Durham, NC, and London: Duke University Press, 2013), 57–59.

28. Wakefield, *History*, 33–34.

29. Wakefield, 18.

30. See Sean P. Harvey, "'Must Not Their Languages Be Savage and Barbarous Like Them?': Philology, Indian Removal, and Race Science," *Journal of the Early Republic* 30, no. 4 (Winter 2010): 505–532.

31. Wakefield, *History*, 107–108.

32. Wakefield, 109.

33. Timothy Flint, *Indian Wars of the West* (Cincinnati, OH: EH Flint, 1833), 12.

34. Flint, 7.

35. Flint, 12.

36. Flint, 232.

37. Flint, 232.

38. Flint, 13.

39. Flint, 4.

40. See Shona Jackson's account of laborist theories of belonging in the greater Caribbean. Shona N. Jackson, *Creole Indigeneity: Between Myth and Nation in the Caribbean* (Minneapolis: University of Minnesota Press, 2012).

41. Flint, *Indian Wars of the West*, 7.

42. Flint, 8.

43. Flint, 8.

44. Flint, 240–241.

45. Flint, 241.

46. On the question of form and substance and stratification and territorialization, see Luciana Parisi, *Abstract Sex: Philosophy, Bio-Technology and the Mutations of Desire* (London and New York: Continuum, 2004), 19.

47. Elbert Smith, vi–vii.

4 / Things Sweet to Taste: Corn and the Thin Gruel of Racial Capitalism

1. Manu Karuka, *Empire's Tracks: Indigenous Nations, Chinese Workers, and the Transcontinental Railroad* (Berkeley: University of California Press, 2019), 8.

2. Arturo Warman, *Corn and Capitalism: How a Botanical Bastard Grew to Global Dominance*, Nancy L. Westrate, trans. (Chapel Hill and London: University of North Carolina Press, 2003), 180–181.

3. Jason W. Moore, *Capitalism in the Web of Life: Ecology and the Accumulation of Capital* (London: Verso, 2015), 242–249.

4. William Cronon, *Nature's Metropolis: Chicago and the Great West* (New York: W. W. Norton, 1991): 100–101.

5. Cronon, 475.

6. Jude Todd, "Corn Culture: A Story of Intelligent Design," *American Indian Quarterly* 32, no. 4 (Fall 2008): 478.

7. Gudmund Hatt, "The Corn Mother in America and in Indonesia," *Anthropos* 46, nos. 5–6 (September–December 1951): 854–858.

8. Black Hawk, *Life of Black Hawk* (New York: Dover, 1994), 37.

9. Black Hawk, 34–35.

10. Black Hawk, 35.

11. My thoughts on flame and fire, on homeliness and unhomeliness, are shaped by Jamieson Webster's reading of Gaston Bachelard's *The Psychoanalysis of Fire* (Boston, MA: Beacon, 1987) in her *Conversion Disorder: Listening to the Body in Psychoanalysis* (New York: Columbia University Press, 2018). I fear my reading of fire within the context of settler colonial and Indigenous societies does not do justice to their work, which attempts to draw fire away from long established and well-worn associations with sexuality. It may be more in tune with the reading of fire proposed by John Durham Peters in *The Marvelous Clouds* (Chicago: University of Chicago Press, 2015) for whom fire is our eldest medium, the forge whose capture ignites a new phase in human evolution, and who remained a constant—and necessary—companion of humanity well into the twentieth century; and for many people around the world, into the twenty-first: a truth that, in the face of climate catastrophe, we all may return.

12. Black Hawk, *Life of Black Hawk*, 37.

13. Black Hawk, 37–38.

14. Black Hawk, 38.

15. Black Hawk, 38.

16. Black Hawk, 41.

17. Black Hawk, 42.

18. Black Hawk, 42–43.

19. Black Hawk, 42–43.

20. Arturo Warman, *Corn and Capitalism*, 177.

21. Black Hawk, *Life of Black Hawk*, 49

22. Black Hawk, 50–51.

23. Black Hawk, 47.

24. Issac N. Kramer, *A Prairie Almanac: 1839 to 1919*, ed. Jean Strong (Bentonville, AR: Prairie Almanac Publisher, 1996), 12–13.

25. Kramer, 7.

26. Kramer, 7.

27. Kramer, 12–13.

28. Kramer, 13.

29. Kramer, 47.

30. Kramer, 39.

31. Kramer, 40.

32. Kramer, 47–48.

33. Kramer, 48. Questions respecting the sociolinguistic grammar of corn and its relationship to Indigenous and settler forms of expression are resonant with concerns raised by Matt Cohen in his works *The Networked Wilderness* and *Colonial Mediascapes*. For Cohen, the forms of language and means of communication employed by Native peoples extend well beyond the phonetic or the graphic to include distinctive arrangements of objects and spaces, as well as the more recognizable forms of wampum or other forms of object craft. The question of the multiple languages in which corn is implicated, the multiple languages it speaks, owes much to his inquiries into colonial media forms. See Matt Cohen, *The Networked Wilderness: Communicating in Early New England* (Minneapolis: University of

Minnesota Press, 2009); see also Matt Cohen and Jeffrey Glover, eds. *Colonial Mediascapes: Sensory Worlds of the Early America* (Lincoln: University of Nebraska Press, 2014).

34. Kramer, *Prairie Almanac*, 25–27.

35. John Durham Peters, *The Magnificent Clouds: Toward a Philosophy of Elemental Media* (Oakland: University of California Press, 2015).

36. Kramer, *Prairie Almanac*, 26.

37. These lines are taken from the postscript to Nossaman's narrative in the Annals of Iowa, composed by her daughter upon their publication in 1922. See Sarah Welch Nossaman, "Pioneering at Bonaparte and Near Pella," *Annals of Iowa* 13, no. 6 (1922): 451.

38. Nossaman, 447.

39. Nossaman, 441.

40. Nossaman, 441.

41. Nossaman, 450.

42. Nossaman, 450.

43. Nossaman, 450.

44. Nossaman, 450.

45. See Siri Hustvedt, *A Woman Looking at Men Looking at Women: Essays on Sex, Art, and the Mind* (New York: Simon and Schuster, 2016). Novelist and psychoanalyst, Hustvedt's writing offers an unlikely and penetrating set of insights on the relationship between creative work, ostensibly "intellectual" or academic activity, and the operations of the mind from a deeply felt sense of psychoanalysis as a diagnostic of the relational and the social. Her psychoanalysis is that of a clinician and an analysand; it is nimble and subtle in ways that many applications of psychoanalysis within literature and cultural studies are not. That is, there is nothing mechanical or reductive in it, nor does it fetishize complexity as a sign of rigor; rather, it treats the fetishization of complexity as a mode of reductiveness.

46. Oneita Fisher, "Life in a Log Home," *Annals of Iowa* 37, no. 7 (Winter 1965): 571–572

47. Fisher, 572.

48. Nossaman, 441.

49. Nossaman, 443.

50. Nossaman, 444.

5 / They Prove in Digestion Sour: Medicine, an Obstinacy of Organs, and the Appointments of the Body

1. Jason W. Moore, *Capitalism in the Web of Life: Ecology and the Accumulation of Capital* (London: Verso, 2015).

2. William Beaumont, *Experiments and Observations on the Gastric Juice and the Physiology of Digestion* (Plattsburg, NY: F. P. Allen, 1833), 10–12.

3. Beaumont, 6.

4. Beaumont, 10.

5. Beaumont, 11.

6. Beaumont, 12.

7. Beaumont, 21.

8. Beaumont, 21.

9. Beaumont, 3.

10. Beaumont, 7.

11. Beaumont, 19.

12. I borrow the concept of queer time and "elongation" and "twist" from Elizabeth Freeman, *Time Binds: Queer Temporalities, Queer Histories* (Durham, NC, and London: Duke University Press, 2010), x.

13. Beaumont, *Experiments*, 74.

14. Beaumont, 65.

15. Beaumont, 64.

16. Beaumont, 63.

17. Beaumont, 65.

18. Beaumont, 65.

19. Beaumont, 60.

20. Beaumont, 33.

21. Kendall Johnson, "Peace, Friendship, and Financial Panic: Reading the Mark of Black Hawk in 'Life of Ma-Ka-Tai-Me-She-Kia-Kiak," *American Literary History* 19, no. 4 (Winter 2007): 771–799.

22. William Joseph Snelling, quoted in Kendall Johnson, "Peace, Friendship, and Financial Panic: Reading the Mark of Black Hawk in the Life of Ma-Ka-Tai-Me-She-Kia-Kiak, *American Literary History* 19, no. 4 (Winter 2007): 773.

23. Laura L. Mielke, "'native to the question': William Appess, Black Hawk, and the Sentimental Contest of Early Native American Autobiography," *American Indian Quarterly* 26, no. 2 (Spring 2002): 246–270.

24. Frank Kelderman, "Rock Island Revisited: Black Hawk's Life, Keokuk's Oratory, and the Critique of US Indian Policy," *J19: The Journal of Nineteenth-Century Americanists* 6, no. 1 (Spring 2018): 67–92.

25. Black Hawk, *Life of Black Hawk*, ed. J. B. Patterson (New York: Dover Publications, 1994), 78.

26. Black Hawk, xix.

27. Black Hawk, xxi.

28. "Treaty with the Sauks and Foxes, 1832; September 21, 1832; Proclamation, February 13, 1833," *Indian Affairs: Laws and Treaties*, vol. 2, ed. Charles J. Kappler (Washington, DC: Government Printing Office, 1904), 349.

29. Black Hawk, *Life of Black Hawk*, 54.

30. Black Hawk, 55.

31. Black Hawk, xxiii.

32. Black Hawk, xxiii.

33. Black Hawk, 78.

34. Black Hawk, 43.

35. Black Hawk, 32.

36. Black Hawk, 68.

37. Black Hawk, 75.

38. Black Hawk, xxiii.

39. Black Hawk, 1.

40. Black Hawk, 1.

41. Black Hawk, 2.

42. Black Hawk, 3.

43. Black Hawk, 3.

44. Black Hawk, 3.
45. Black Hawk, 3.
46. Black Hawk, 3–4.
47. Black Hawk, 4.
48. Black Hawk, 6.
49. Black Hawk, 38–39.
50. Black Hawk, 31.
51. Black Hawk, 31.
52. Black Hawk, 28.
53. Black Hawk, 63.

BIBLIOGRAPHY

Allman, John Lee. "Uniforms and Equipment of the Black Hawk War and the Mormon War." *Western Illinois Regional Studies* 13, no. 1 (Spring 1990): 5–18.

Bachelard, Gaston. *The Psychoanalysis of Fire*. Translated by Alan C. M. Ross. Boston, MA: Beacon Press, 1987.

Baepler, Paul. *White Slaves, African Masters: An Anthology of American Barbary Captivity Narratives*. Chicago: University of Chicago Press, 1999.

Barker, Joanne. *Critically Sovereign: Indigenous Gender, Sexuality, and Feminist Studies*. Durham, NC, and London: Duke University Press, 2017.

Barker, Joanne, ed. *Sovereignty Matters: Locations of Contestation and Possibility in Native American Studies*. Lincoln: University of Nebraska Press, 2005.

Barrows, Willard. "History of Scott County, Iowa." *Annals of Iowa* 1 (1863).

Beaumont, William. *Experiments and Observations on the Gastric Juice and the Physiology of Digestion*. Plattsburg, NY: F. P. Allen, 1833.

Betasamosake Simpson, Leanne. *As We Have Ever Done: Indigenous Freedom through Radical Resistance*. Minneapolis: University of Minnesota Press, 2017.

Bezan, Sarah. "Necro-Eco: The Ecology of Death in Jim Crace's Being Dead." *Mosaic: A Journal for the Interdisciplinary Study of Literature* 48, no. 2 (September 2015): 191–207.

Black Hawk. *Life of Black Hawk*. Edited by J. B. Patterson. New York: Dover Publications, 1994.

Brander Rasmussen, Birgit. *Queequeg's Coffin: Indigenous Literacies and Early American Literature*. Durham, NC, and London: Duke University Press, 2012.

Brown, Tony C. "The Barrows of History." *Studies in Eighteenth-Century Culture* 37 (2008): 41–65.

Burt, Roger. "The Transformation of the Non-Ferrous Metals Industries in the Seventeenth and Eighteenth Centuries." *Economic History Review* 48, no. 1 (February 1995): 23–45.

Butler, Frances Anne [Fanny Kemble]. *The Journals of Frances Anne Butler.* Vol. 2. Philadelphia: Carey, Less, and Blanchard, 1835.

Cass, Lewis. *A Discourse Delivered at the First Meeting of the Historical Society of Michigan.* Detroit: G. L. Whitney, 1830.

Cohen, Deborah. *The Deadly Life of Logistics: Mapping Violence in Global Trade.* Minneapolis: University of Minnesota Press, 2014.

Cohen, Matt. *The Networked Wilderness: Communicating in Early New England.* Minneapolis: University of Minnesota Press, 2009.

Cohen, Matt, and Jeffrey Glover, eds. *Colonial Mediascapes.* Lincoln: University of Nebraska Press, 2014.

Law, Justice, and Community." *Annual of the Society of Christian Ethics* 19 (1999): 285–309.

Cronon, William. *Nature's Metropolis: Chicago and the Great West.* New York: W. W. Norton, 1991.

Das, Veena. "The Signature of the State: The Paradox of Illegibility." In *Anthropology in the Margins of the State*, 225–253. Santa Fe, NM: School of American Research Press, 2004.

Dayan, Joan [Colin]. *Haiti, History and the Gods.* Berkeley: University of California Press, 1995.

Deloria, Philip. *Playing Indian.* New Haven, CT, and London: Yale University Press, 1998.

Driel, Joppe van, and Lissa Roberts. "Circulating Salts: Chemical Governance and the Bifurcation of 'Nature' and 'Society.'" *Eighteenth-Century Studies* 49, no. 2 (Winter 2016): 233–263.

DuBois, Laurent. *Avengers of the New World: The Story of the Haitian Revolution.* Cambridge, MA: Belknap Press, 2005.

Edwards, William P. *The Narrative of the Capture and Providential Escape of Misses Frances and Elmira Hall.* New York: William P. Edwards, 1832.

El-Hibri, Hatim. *Visions of Beirut: The Urban Life of Media Infrastructure.* Durham, NC: Duke University Press 2021.

Estes, Nick. *Our History Is the Future.* New York: Verso, 2019.

Ferguson, Lorraine, and Douglass Scott. "A Time Line of American Typography." *Design Quarterly*, no. 148 (1990): 23–54.

Fisher, Oneita. "Life in a Log Home." *Annals of Iowa* 37, no. 7 (Winter 1965): 571–572.

Flint, Timothy. *Indian Wars of the West.* Cincinnati, OH: EH Flint, 1833.

Freeman, Elizabeth. *Time Binds: Queer Temporalities, Queer Histories.* Durham, NC, and London: Duke University Press, 2010.

Freud, Sigmund. *The Joke and Its Relation to the Unconscious.* Translated by Joyce Crick London: Penguin Classics, 2002.

Frickle Scott, and William R. Freudenburg. "Mining the Past: Historical
    Context and the Changing Implications of Natural Resource Extraction.
    Social Problems 43, no. 4 (November 1996): 444–466.
Ferguson, Lorraine, and Douglass Scott. "A Time Line of American
    Typography." *Design Quarterly* 148 (1990): 23–54.
Gibbons, Luke. *Edmund Burke and Ireland: Aesthetics, Politics, and the
    Colonial Sublime.* Cambridge: Cambridge University Press, 2009.
Givens Johnson, Patricia. *William Preston and the Allegheny Patriots.*
    Blacksburg, VA: Walpa Publishing, 1992.
Gomez-Barris, Macarena. *The Extractive Zone: Social Ecologies and Decolonial
    Perspectives.* Durham, NC, and London: Duke University Press, 2017.
Gordillo, Gaston R. *Rubble: The Afterlife of Destruction.* Durham, NC, and
    London: Duke University Press, 2014.
Gottlieb, Richard M. "The Reassembly of the Body from Parts." *Journal of the
    American Psychoanalytic Association* 55, no. 4 (December 2007): 1217–1251.
Gray-Kanatiiosh, Barbara A., and Pat Lauterdale. "The Web of Justice:
    Restorative Justice Has Presented Only Part of the Story." *Wičazo Ša
    Review* 21, no. 1 (Spring 2006): 29–41.
Greenberg, Joy H., and Gregory Greenberg. "Native American Narratives as
    Ecoethical Discourse in Land-Use Consultations." *Wičazo Ša Review* 28,
    no. 2 (Fall 2013): 30–59.
Greene, John C., and John G. Burke. "The Science of Minerals in the Age of
    Jefferson." *Transactions of the American Philosophical Society* 68, no. 4
    (1978): 1–113.
Hartley, Lucy. *Physiognomy and the Meaning of Expression in Nineteenth-
    Century Culture.* Cambridge: Cambridge University Press, 2001.
Harvey, Sean P. "'Must Not Their Languages Be Savage and Barbarous Like
    Them?': Philology, Indian Removal, and Race Science." *Journal of the Early
    Republic* 30, no. 4 (Winter 2010): 505–532.
Hatt, Gudmund. "The Corn Mother in America and in Indonesia." *Anthropos*
    46, nos. 5–6 (September–December 1951): 853–914.
Helton, Tena L. "What the White 'Squaws' Want from Black Hawk: Gendering
    the Fan-Celebrity Relationship." *American Indian Quarterly* 34, no. 4 (Fall
    2010): 498–520.
Heyl, Allen V., Allen F. Agnew, Erwin J. Lyons, and Charles H. Behre Jr., "The
    Geology of the Upper Mississippi Valley Zinc-Lead District." *Geological
    Survey Professional Paper* 309 (Washington: US Government Printing
    Office, 1959).
Hustvedt, Siri. *A Woman Looking at Men Looking at Women: Essays on Art,
    Sex, and the Mind.* New York: Simon and Schuster, 2016.
Inglis, Fred. *A Short History of Celebrity.* Princeton, NJ: Princeton University
    Press, 2010.
Innis, Harold. *Empire and Communications.* Oxford: Clarendon Press, 1950.
———. *A History of the Canadian Pacific Railway.* Toronto: University of
    Toronto Press, 1923.

Jackson, Shona N. *Creole Indigeneity: Between Myth and Nation in the Caribbean*. Minneapolis: University of Minnesota Press, 2012.

James, C. L. R. *Black Jacobins: Toussaint L'Ouverture and the San Domingo Revolution*. New York: Vintage, 1989.

Johnson, Kendall. "Peace, Friendship, and Financial Panic: Reading the Mark of Black Hawk in *Life of Ma-Ka-Tai-Me-She-Kia-Kiak*." *American Literary History* 19, no. 4 (Winter 2007); 771–799.

Karuka, Manu. *Empire's Tracks: Indigenous Nations, Chinese Workers, and the Transcontinental Railroad*. Berkeley: University of California Press, 2019.

Kelderman, Frank. "Rock Island Revisited: Black Hawk's Life, Keokuk's Oratory, and the Critique of US Indian Policy." *J19: The Journal of Nineteenth-Century Americanists* 6, no. 1 (Spring 2018): 67–92.

Khalili, Laleh. *Sinews of War and Trade: Shipping and Capitalism in the Arabian Peninsula*. London: Verso, 2020.

Knoper, Randall. "Writing, American Literature, and 'Media Ecologies.'" *American Literary History* 23, no. 2 (2011); 362–379.

Kramer, Issac N. *A Prairie Almanac: 1839 to 1919*. Edited by Jean Strong. Bentonville, AR: Prairie Almanac Publisher, 1996.

Krupat, Arnold. "Patterson's Life; Black Hawk's Story; Native American Elegy." *American Literary History* 22, no. 3 (2010): 527–552.

Lordon, Frederic. *Willing Slaves of Capital: Spinoza and Marx on Desire*. London and New York: Verso, 2014.

Lowenhaupt Tsing, Anna. *The Mushroom at the End of the World: On the Possibility of Life in Capitalist Ruins*. Princeton, NJ: Princeton University Press, 2015.

Luciano, Dana. "Geological Fantasies, Haunting Anachronisms: Eros, Time, and History in Harriet Prescott Spofford's 'The Amber Gods.'" *ESQ* 55 (2009): 269–303.

Massumi, Brian. *Parables for the Virtual: Movement, Affect, Sensation*. Durham, NC, and London: Duke University Press, 2002.

McGill, M. C. "The Diffusion of Ore-Heath Smelting Techniques from Yorkshire to the Upper Mississippi Lead Region." *British Mining* 43 (1991): 118–128.

Mielke, Laura L. "'native to the question': William Appess, Black Hawk, and the Sentimental Contest of Early Native American Autobiography." *American Indian Quarterly* 26, no. 2 (Spring 2002): 246–270.

Miller, Susan A. "Native America Writes Back: The Origin of the Indigenous Paradigm in Historiography." *Wičazo Ša Review* 23, no. 2 (Fall 2008): 9–28.

Miller, Susan A., and James Riding In, eds. *Native Historians Write Back: Decolonizing American Indian History*. Lubbock: Texas Tech University Press, 2011.

Mitchell, Timothy. "Society, Economy, and the State Effect." In *State/Culture: State Formation After the Cultural Turn*, edited by George Steinmetz, 76–97. Ithaca, NY: Cornell University Press, 1999.

Moore, Jason W. *Capitalism in the Web of Life: Ecology and the Accumulation of Capital*. London: Verso, 2015.

Moore, Thomas, trans. *Odes of Anacreon*. Vol. 1. London: J. Carpenter, 1804.

Morgensen, Scott Lauria. "Settler Homonationalism: Theorizing Settler Colonialism within Queer Modernities." *GLQ: A Journal of Lesbian and Gay Studies* 16, nos. 1–2 (2010): 15–131.

———. *Spaces Between Us: Queer Settler Colonialism and Indigenous Decolonization*. Minneapolis: University of Minnesota Press, 2011.

Nixon, Rob. *Slow Violence and the Environmentalism of the Poor*. Cambridge, MA: Harvard University Press, 2011.

Nossaman, Sarah Welch. "Pioneering at Bonaparte and Near Pella." *Annals of Iowa* 13, no. 6 (1922): 443–453.

O'Connor, Erin. *Raw Material: Producing Pathology in Victorian Culture*. Durham, NC, and London: Duke University Press, 2000.

Parisi, Luciana. *Abstract Sex: Philosophy, Bio-Technology and the Mutations of Desire*. London and New York: Continuum, 2004.

Peters, John Durham. "Infrastructuralism: Media as Traffic between Nature and Culture." In *Traffic: Media as Infrastructures and Cultural Practices*, edited by Marion Naser-Lather and Christoph Neubert. London: Brill, 2015.

———. *The Marvelous Clouds: Toward a Philosophy of Elemental Media*. Chicago: University of Chicago Press, 2015.

Povinelli, Elizabeth. *Economies of Abandonment: Social Belonging and Endurance in Late Liberalism*. Durham, NC, and London: Duke University Press, 2011.

———. *Empire of Love: Toward a Theory of Intimacy, Genealogy, and Carnality*. Durham, NC: Duke University Press, 2006.

Richardson, Tayna, and Gisa Weszkalnys. "Introduction: Resource Materialities." *Anthropological Quarterly* 87, 1 (2014): 5–30.

Rickard, T. A. *A History of American Mining*. New York: McGraw-Hill, 1932.

Roach, Joseph. *Cities of the Dead: Circum-Atlantic Performance*. New York: Columbia University Press, 1996.

Rogin, Michael Paul. *Fathers and Sons: Andrew Jackson and the Subjugation of the American Indian*. New York: Alfred A. Knopf, 1977.

Rosenberg, Charles. *The Cholera Years: The United States in 1832, 1849, and 1866*. Chicago: University of Chicago Press, 1987 [1967].

Round, Phillip. *By Nature and by Custom Cursed: Transatlantic Civil Discourse and New England Cultural Production 1620–1660* (Hanover, NH, and London: Tufts University Press, 1999).

———. "'The Posture That We Give the Dead': Freneau's 'Indian Burying Ground' in Ethnohistorical Context." *Arizona Quarterly* 50, no. 3 (Autumn 1994): 1–30.

Russell, Carl Parcher. *Guns on the Early Frontiers: A History of Firearms from Colonial Times through the Years of the Western Fur Trade*. Berkeley: University of California Press, 1957.

Schaefer, Joseph. *The Wisconsin Lead Region*. Madison: State Historical Society of Wisconsin, 1932.

Schoolcraft, Henry Rowe. *A View of the Lead Mines of Missouri*. New York: Charles Wiley and Co., 1819.

Smith, Elbert H. *History of Black Hawk*. Milwaukee: n.p., 1846.

———. *Ma-ka-tai-me-she-kia-kiak, or Black Hawk, and Scenes in the West: A National Poem in Six Cantos*. New York: Edward Kearny, 1848.

Snyder, J. F. "The Burial and Resurrection of Black Hawk." *Journal of the Illinois Historical Society* 4, no. 1 (April 1911): 47–56.

Swan, Robert J. "Prelude and Aftermath of the Doctors' Riot of 1788: A Religious Interpretation of White and Black Reactions to Grave Robbing." *New York History* 81, no. 4 (2000): 417–456.

Todd, Jude. "Corn Culture: A Story of Intelligent Design." *American Indian Quarterly* 32, no. 4 (Fall 2008): 471–484.

Trouillot, Michel-Rolph. *Silencing the Past: Power and the Production of History*. Boston, MA: Beacon Press, 1995.

Vazquez, Alexandra T. *Listening in Detail: Performances of Cuban Music*. Durham, NC, and London: Duke University Press, 2013.

Vizenor, Gerald, ed. *Survivance: Narratives of Native Presence*. Lincoln: University of Nebraska Press, 2008.

Wakefield, John Allen. *History of the War Between the United States and the Sac and Fox Nations of Indians and Parts of Other Disaffected Tribes of Indians*. Jacksonville, IL: Calvin Goudy, 1834.

Warman, Arturo. *Corn and Capitalism: How a Botanical Bastard Grew to Global Dominance*. Translated by Nancy L. Westrate. Chapel Hill and London: University of North Carolina Press, 2003.

Weber, Max. *The Protestant Ethic and the Spirit of Capitalism*. Mineola, NY: Dover Publications, 2003.

Webster, Jamieson. *Conversion Disorder: Listening to the Body in Psychoanalysis*. New York: Columbia University Press, 2018.

Whitney, J. D. *Report of a Geological Survey of the Upper Mississippi Lead Region: Made by the Authority of the Legislature of Wisconsin, Under a Contract with Professor James Hall, Principal of the Geological Commission of the State, 1859–1860*. Albany, NY: n.p., 1862.

Whooley, Owen. *Knowledge in the Time of Cholera: The Struggle Over American Medicine in the Nineteenth Century*. Chicago: University of Chicago Press, 2013.

Whittlesey, Charles. *Description of Ancient Works in Ohio*. Washington, DC: Smithsonian Institution, 1850.

Yazzie, Chief Justice Robert. "Life Comes from It: Navajo Justice Concepts." *New Mexico Law Review* 24 (Spring 1994): 175–190.

Index

Adam John Waterman is an independent scholar and writer. He lives in Beirut.

CPSIA information can be obtained
at www.ICGtesting.com
Printed in the USA
JSHW022309121221
21209JS00001B/13

9 780823 298778